D-DAY

THE GREATEST MILITARY OPERATION IN HISTORY

D-DAY

THE GREATEST MILITARY OPERATION IN HISTORY

Contributors:
Marc Desantis, Mike Haskew, Gavin Mortimer

Photographs for the Photo Gallery are credited as follows: Library of Congress, Prints and Photographs Division (145-147; 150, bottom), US Navy Photographs, National Archives (148), National Archives & Record Administration (149, 151, 153 top, 156, 157 top), Army Signal Corps Collection, National Archives (150, top), Library of Congress; Arche J. Lewis Collection (152), US Coast Guard Collection in the National Archives (153, bottom, 160), Library of Congress, Frank E. McKee Collection (154, top left), Library of Congress; Philip Edward Bonner Collection (154, top right and top middle), Courtesy of the U.S. Army Center of Military History (154, bottom; 155, bottom), National Archives (155, top), Public domain/ mediadrumworld.com (157, bottom and logo), Library of Congress; Dorothy Cutts Collection (158 top, both), Shutterstock.com, Everett Collection (158 bottom,159 bottom), Blackstone Studios (159, top).

For more information about the Future plc group, go to **http://www.futureplc.com**.

ISBN 978-1-4971-0468-6

Library of Congress Control Number: 2023952155

To learn more about the other great books from Fox Chapel Publishing, or to find a retailer near you,
call toll-free 800-457-9112 or visit us at ***www.FoxChapelPublishing.com***.

We are always looking for talented authors. To submit an idea, please send a brief inquiry to
acquisitions@foxchapelpublishing.com.

Printed in Canada
First printing

INTRODUCTION

In the early hours of June 6, 1944, the largest land, sea, and air operation in history got under way in northern France, as more than 150,000 Allied troops began the invasion of German-occupied Western Europe. Failure was not an option. Inside we tell the remarkable story of D-Day, from the months of meticulous planning and preparation that made it possible, to the invasion itself and the fierce fighting that followed as the Allies fought to liberate France. We celebrate some of the heroes of Operation Overlord, speak to D-Day veterans as they share their experiences, and discover the Allied leaders who conceived, shaped, and executed the ambitious plans. We look at the role the French Resistance played in the run-up to and during the invasions and how the German response may have helped the Allies gain a vital foothold, while also exploring the potentially devastating consequences for the world if the landings had failed.

D-DAY

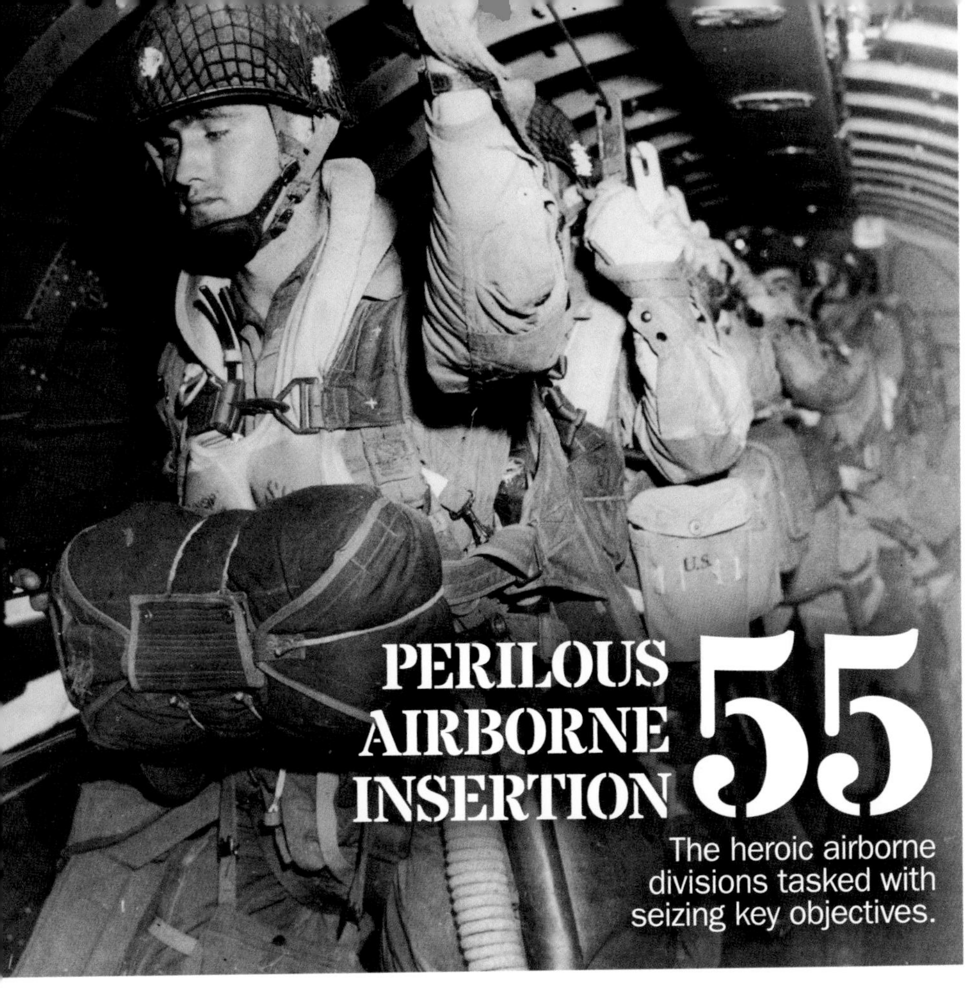

PERILOUS AIRBORNE INSERTION 55

The heroic airborne divisions tasked with seizing key objectives.

Beyond the Beaches

THE FRENCH RESISTANCE & D-DAY 84

Discover the many contributions made by the French Resistance before and during the Normandy assault.

SAS D-DAY MISSIONS 108

The daring special forces missions of Operation Overlord.

A D-DAY TIMELINE

ASSAULT ON FORTRESS EUROPE

After months of preparation, Allied forces assault Nazi defenses on the coast of French Normandy, establishing a foothold in Western Europe.

1940

OPERATION DYNAMO

JUNE 4, 1940 ■ THE FRENCH PORT CITY OF DUNKIRK

Operation Dynamo, the 10-day effort to evacuate soldiers of the French Army and the British Expeditionary Force from the continent of Europe at the port city of Dunkirk, concludes with the rescue of nearly 340,000 troops from annihilation or capture by victorious German forces following their invasion of France and the Low Countries on May 10. Dynamo involves scores of small civilian watercraft as well as military vessels and succeeds beyond expectations as planners expected to evacuate only about 30,000. The Battle of France ends in shattering defeat, and the Allies do not return to Western Europe until D-Day in 1944.

Above: British soldiers fire their rifles at low-flying German aircraft while awaiting evacuation from a Dunkirk beach.

1942

ROOSEVELT RECEIVES OPERATION ROUNDUP PLAN

APRIL 1, 1942 ■ WASHINGTON, DC

US Army Chief of Staff General George C. Marshall presents President Roosevelt with a blueprint for an invasion of Nazi-occupied Western Europe tentatively scheduled for 1943. British war planners have considered such an operation, codenamed Roundup, since 1941. However, success seems bleak until sufficient strength is amassed. Roundup is postponed at British urging in favor of peripheral efforts, including landings in North Africa and invasions of Sicily and Italy. The plan is eventually supplanted by Operation Overlord.

Right: A German soldier stands among the bodies of dead Canadian troops on the beach at Dieppe.

DISASTER AT DIEPPE

AUGUST 19, 1942 ■ FRENCH PORT OF DIEPPE ON THE ENGLISH CHANNEL

In response to pressure from Soviet Premier Joseph Stalin to mount offensive operations and soon open a second front in Europe, as well as to test the strength of German forces occupying defenses along the coast of France, the Allies mount Operation Jubilee, a heavy raid involving 6,000 troops, primarily Canadian, along with tanks and supporting air and naval forces. The effort is doomed from the start, and fails with more than 900 killed, 500 wounded, and 1,900 captured. However, Allied planners apply lessons learned at Dieppe in the refinement of Operation Overlord, the invasion of Normandy that takes place in 1944.

Canadian prisoners captured during the abortive Dieppe raid raise their hands as directed by a German soldier.

GENERAL DWIGHT EISENHOWER IS APPOINTED TO COMMAND OPERATION OVERLORD

December 6, 1943 ■ Cairo, Egypt

Below: Canadian Prime Minister William Mackenzie King confers with President Roosevelt and Prime Minister Churchill in Quebec.

1943

OVERLORD ADVANCES AT QUADRANT CONFERENCE

AUGUST 17–24, 1943 ■ QUEBEC CITY, CANADA

During the first Quebec (Quadrant) Conference, the Combined Chiefs of Staff present a tentative plan, codenamed Operation Overlord, for the invasion of Nazi-occupied France. President Franklin D. Roosevelt and Prime Minister Winston Churchill agree in principle to continue discussions and planning for the offensive that will eventually result in the liberation of Western Europe. A proposed date for the invasion of May 1, 1944, is selected, but the massive logistical marshaling of men and materiel in Britain must first be accomplished.

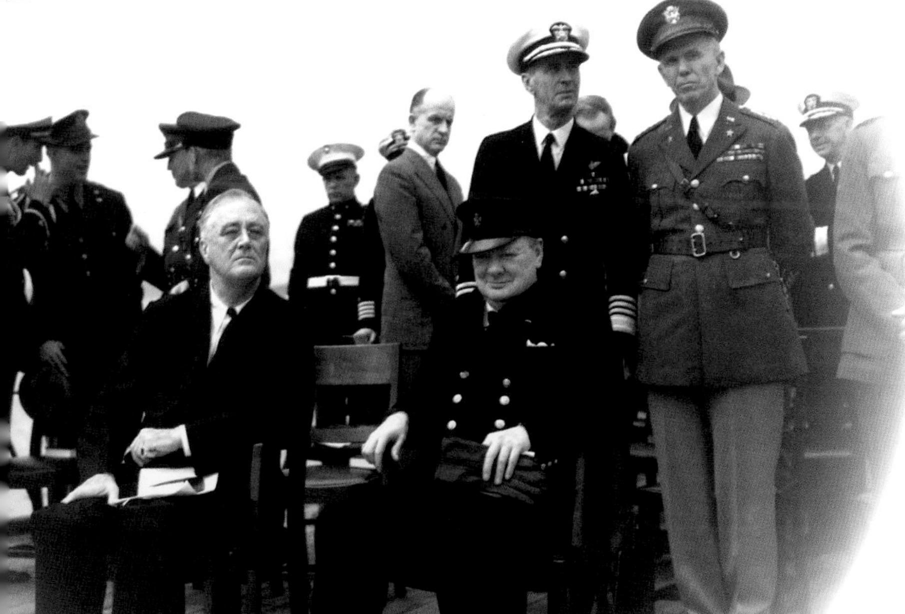

Left: General Marshall and others stand behind President Roosevelt and Prime Minister Winston Churchill during talks in August 1941.

EXERCISE TIGER

APRIL 28, 1944 ■ SLAPTON SANDS, DEVON

A large-scale rehearsal for the D-Day landings in Normandy, codenamed Exercise Tiger, ends in tragedy due to a series of errors and an attack by German torpedo boats off the English coast near Slapton Sands. Incorrect radio frequencies frustrate communications, while a British destroyer previously detailed to escort eight US Navy Landing Ship Tanks (LSTs) is mistakenly ordered to Plymouth for repairs. Two LSTs are torpedoed and sunk. Two others are heavily damaged, and more than 700 US Army and Navy personnel are killed. Many die due to improperly worn lifejackets and the lethally cold water, which causes hypothermia.

Top left: American soldiers engage in a training exercise at Slapton Sands prior to D-Day.

Left: This Sherman tank, raised from waters off Slapton Sands, stands as a memorial to Exercise Tiger.

Southwick House near Portsmouth served as headquarters for the Allied Expeditionary Force in 1944.

THE FINAL DECISION

JUNE 5, 1944 ■ SOUTHWICK HOUSE NEAR PORTSMOUTH

After foul weather has forced a 24-hour postponement of Operation Overlord, General Dwight Eisenhower, Allied supreme commander, convenes the seventh and final meeting of his most senior commanders at 4:15 a.m. to gauge support for launching the invasion during a window of somewhat favorable weather on June 6. Eisenhower listens to concerns and then considers the situation. Men are already aboard ships, and the next favorable tides and other atmospheric conditions are two weeks away. He announces, "Okay, we'll go!"

1944 — APRIL — June 5

D-DAY IS SCHEDULED FOR JUNE 5, 1944

May 17, 1944 ■ Southwick House near Portsmouth

BAD WEATHER FORCES EISENHOWER TO DELAY D-DAY

9:30 p.m., June 3, 1944 ■ Southwick House near Portsmouth

Allied Supreme Commander General Dwight D. Eisenhower poses with his subordinates charged with directing Op[illegible]ion Overlord

THE AIRBORNE ASSAULT GETS UNDERWAY

JUNE 5, 1944 ■ AIRFIELDS ACROSS BRITAIN

At approximately 11 p.m. on June 5, Allied aircraft begin taking off from airfields across Britain. Approximately 20,000 paratroopers and glider troops of the British 6th and American 82nd and 101st Airborne Divisions are to secure the flanks of the 50-mile (80-kilometer) invasion front. The 6th Airborne must seize or destroy bridges across the River Orne, the Orne Canal, and other waterways while controlling high ground between the Orne and the River Dives. The 101st is to seize key causeways, or exits, from Utah Beach, facilitating the advance of the US 4th Infantry Division. The 82nd is to capture the village of Sainte-Mère-Église and secure key bridges across the River Merderet.

British troops of the 6th Airborne Division blacken their faces prior to departure for Normandy.

EARLY AIRBORNE WARNINGS

JUNE 6, 1944 ■ COASTLINE OF FRENCH NORMANDY

Just after midnight, multiple sightings of transport planes, gliders, and Allied airborne troops on the ground begin to circulate among various German command posts. Sentries along the coast of Normandy radio alerts that they have seen low-flying Allied planes in the vicinity of the Cotentin Peninsula. Elite airborne troops of the 13th Company, 6th Parachute Regiment, serving as infantry, report enemy paratroopers near their positions. An officer of the 5th Battalion, 125th Mechanized Infantry Regiment spots British gliders and parachutes east of the River Orne.

BRITISH PARAS ASSAULT PEGASUS BRIDGE
12:21 a.m., June 6, 1944
■ Orne Canal, Normandy

MERVILLE BATTERY SILENCED
4:45 a.m., June 6, 1944
■ Sword Beach, Normandy

June 6

AMERICAN PARATROOPERS OCCUPY SAINTE-MÈRE-ÉGLISE
5 a.m., June 6, 1944
■ English Channel, off the coast of Normandy

The French city of Caen devastated by a sustained Allied bombing campaign before and after D-Day.

Allied bombers attack German coastal defenses in Normandy prior to the D-Day landings.

ALLIED BOMBING BEGINS

JUNE 6, 1944 ■ SKIES ABOVE NORMANDY

Over 100 bombers of Royal Air Force Bomber Command No. 1 Group and No. 100 Group raid German antiaircraft positions near the important communications center of Caen about eight miles (13 kilometers) behind the D-Day invasion beaches at about 12:30 a.m. Meanwhile, the first of nearly 1,200 bombers of the US 8th Air Force begin taking off from airfields in Britain to attack targets in Normandy to impede the Germans. Over 5,500 Allied bombers and fighters have been assigned to Operation Overlord, destroying enemy infrastructure while maintaining air superiority above the beaches.

American troops exit their landing craft under heavy German fire at Omaha Beach.

ARRIVAL OFF OMAHA BEACH

JUNE 6, 1944 ■ ENGLISH CHANNEL OFF NORMANDY COAST

Hours after embarking aboard transport vessels, soldiers of the US 1st and 29th Infantry Divisions arrive approximately 14 miles (23 kilometers) off Omaha Beach at around 3 a.m. on D-Day. When the order is given, the soldiers begin making their way down cargo nets into landing craft that bob intermittently with the swells of the restless English Channel. About the same time, troops of the US 4th Infantry Division arrive off Utah Beach and begin making similar preparations for the run-in to the landing beaches.

ALLIED NAVAL BOMBARDMENT BEGINS

5:30 a.m., June 6, 1944 ■ English Channel, off the coast of Normandy

MOVEMENT INLAND FROM OMAHA BEACH TAKES SHAPE

9 a.m., June 6, 1944 ■ Omaha Beach, Normandy

JUNE 6, 1944

AMERICAN RANGERS BEGIN ASSAULT ON POINTE DU HOC

7:11 a.m., June 6, 1944 ■ Cliffs of Pointe du Hoc between Utah and Omaha beaches

LANDING AT UTAH BEACH

JUNE 6, 1944 ■ UTAH BEACH, NORMANDY

Difficult currents push landing craft some distance from the intended landfall locations of the US 8th Infantry Regiment, 4th Division, coming ashore at Utah Beach about 6:30 a.m. Surprisingly little German resistance is encountered. Regimental commander Colonel James Van Fleet and assistant division commander Brigadier General Theodore Roosevelt Jr. decide to "start the war from here," rather than redirecting successive waves of troops and equipment to the original beach locations. The 8th Regiment begins offensive operations, eventually spearheading a six-mile (10-kilometer) drive inland. Only 197 men are killed, but some of the 4th Division's D-Day objectives are not accomplished due to the mistaken landing.

Right: German prisoners captured at Utah Beach sit inside a barbed-wire enclosure and await transport.

Below: American soldiers wade ashore at Utah Beach against surprisingly light German resistance on D-Day.

RELEASE THE PANZER RESERVES!

JUNE 6, 1944 ■ FIELD MARSHAL RUNDSTEDT'S HEADQUARTERS, SAINT-GERMAIN, FRANCE

Awake before 3 a.m., Field Marshal Gerd von Rundstedt, commander of German forces in the west, is convinced that reports of enemy airborne operations confirm an imminent amphibious landing. He requests approval from the high command for the release of armored reserves, but such orders require Hitler's personal approval. The Führer is asleep and not to be disturbed. At 10 a.m., Hitler denies Rundstedt's request. Finally, Hitler acquiesces at 2:30 p.m., but it is too late to push the invasion back into the sea.

Above: Field Marshals Gerd von Rundstedt and Erwin Rommel (left) discuss Atlantic Wall defenses prior to D-Day.

ORDEAL AND DECISION AT OMAHA BEACH

JUNE 6, 1944 ■ COMMAND SHIP USS AUGUSTA OFF OMAHA BEACH

Soldiers of the US 1st and 29th Infantry Divisions encounter the fiercest German resistance on D-Day at Omaha Beach. Early reports indicate that the first wave has foundered with heavy casualties and many soldiers pinned down on the beach by heavy enemy fire. For a time, General Omar Bradley, commander of US ground troops, considers a withdrawal from embattled Omaha and redirection of subsequent waves to other sectors. By midday, however, he is relieved with assurances that small groups of American soldiers have started moving up the bluffs, silencing German bunkers and machine gun nests at "Bloody Omaha," and that they have begun moving inland.

Right: American soldiers face heavy German resistance after landing on Omaha Beach.

4TH DIVISION LINKS UP WITH ELEMENTS OF 101ST AIRBORNE DIVISION

12 p.m., June 6, 1944 ■ Causeway exits from Utah Beach, Normandy

Pegasus Bridge across the Orne Canal is shown three days after its capture in a brilliant operation.

RELIEF AT PEGASUS BRIDGE

JUNE 6, 1944 ■ ORNE CANAL, NORMANDY

Following a precision insertion aboard gliders just after midnight, the 2nd Battalion, Oxfordshire, and Buckinghamshire Light Infantry (Ox and Bucks) swiftly seize the Benouville Bridge across the Orne Canal. Reinforced by the 7th Parachute Battalion at 3 a.m., they are finally relieved around 1 p.m. as Commandos arrive from Sword Beach. The span is later renamed Pegasus Bridge in their honor. Elsewhere, approximately 150 men of the 9th Parachute Battalion have lost half their number seizing the German battery at Merville, which threatened Sword Beach.

CANADIAN TROOPS FROM JUNO BEACH AND BRITISH FORCES FROM GOLD BEACH LINK UP

2:15 p.m., June 6, 1944 ■ Near village of Creully, Normandy

21ST PANZER DIVISION IS ORDERED TO END ITS COUNTERATTACK AND WITHDRAW

9 p.m., June 6, 1944 ■ Village of Lion-sur-Mer

Below: Field Marshal Erwin Rommel inspects the 21st Panzer Division in May 1944.

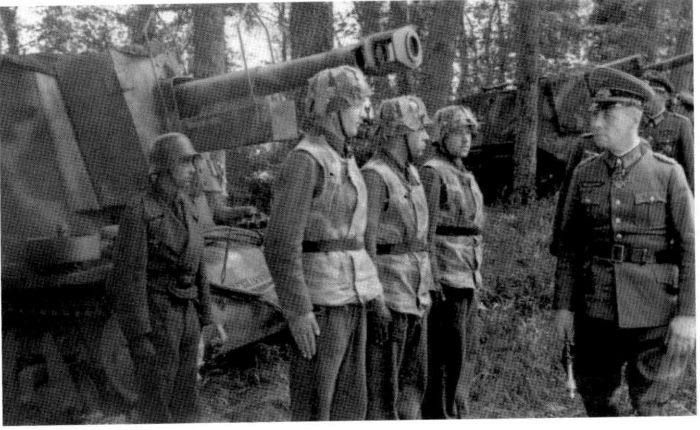

FRUSTRATED GERMAN COUNTERATTACK

JUNE 6, 1944 ■ NORMAN COUNTRYSIDE BETWEEN JUNO AND SWORD BEACHES

Late in the afternoon, elements of the 21st Panzer Division reach a 13km (8mi) gap separating Juno and Sword Beaches during the only major German counterattack on D-Day. That morning, 21st Panzer had been a short distance from the bridges across the River Orne and Orne Canal, positioned to possibly overrun British forces holding the spans. However, redirected to attack on the other side of the Orne, the division took hours to reorganize. When the attack is launched at about 4 p.m., 21st Panzer meets stiff opposition. Without reinforcements to exploit the advance to the coast, the Germans are obliged to withdraw. The Allied D-Day lodgment is secure.

PREPARING FOR D-DAY

Image source: National Archives and Records Administration, cataloged Identifier (NAID) 195516. Public Domain

18 THE ROAD TO D-DAY

Thoughts of a return to France started in 1940, but it would take four years of fighting and planning before the Allies were ready.

© Getty

Image source: IWM photograph collection TR 1347 Public Domain

25 WHY WAS NORMANDY CHOSEN FOR D-DAY?

For Hitler's Fortress Europe to crumble, a perfect location had to be chosen for the largest amphibious invasion in history.

28 RAMPART OF THE REICH

Hitler sought to defend his empire with the Atlantic Wall—the first line of defense for "Fortress Europe."

© Getty

36 ARCHITECTS OF VICTORY

Meet the Allied military leaders who conceived, shaped, and executed Operation Overlord.

Image source: U.S Federal Government Public Domain

Image source: U.S Federal Government Public Domain

Image source: UK Government Public Domain

32 THE D-DAY DECEPTION

Allied efforts to deceive the Germans were vital to the success of the Normandy invasion.

© Getty

THE ROAD TO D-DAY

Thoughts of a return to France started as soon as the last British soldiers were evacuated in 1940, but it would take four years of fighting and planning before the Allies were ready.

BY **DAVID SMITH**

American forces land on D-Day.

On June 4, 1940, the evacuation from Dunkirk was completed. The British Expeditionary Force had lost more than 66,000 men, but almost a quarter of a million had been snatched from the clutches of advancing German units. It did not mark the end of Britain's involvement on the Continent in the early months of the war—there were still British soldiers fighting alongside the remnants of the French Army, and 60,000 more were sent back to France after the evacuation from Dunkirk, forming a second British Expeditionary Force.

It was a futile gesture, as General Sir Alan Brooke found the French in a state of turmoil. Almost as soon as his men arrived, he ordered a stop to further reinforcements and headed back to the coast for evacuation, against the wishes of Winston Churchill. In Operation Aerial, 124,000 personnel were brought back to Britain. This time, the removal was to be more long-term, as the threat of a German invasion preoccupied the British, but there was still room for more optimistic thoughts. A return to the Continent was inevitable if the war was to end in victory, and planning started almost immediately.

Initial Planning

The losses sustained during the battle for France had been substantial. For almost every man lost, Britain had also lost a military vehicle of some description, with an incredible 64,000 still left in France. Almost 2,500 guns had been abandoned as well, while six destroyers had been sunk and more than 400 fighter planes downed by the enemy.

There was a realization that an invasion would require a huge amount of preparation. Germany would have to be weakened at the same time as Allied strength was built up. There could be no hope of an invasion before America entered the war, but even then it would take time for that nation's massive war-making capability to get up to speed.

In order for an invasion to succeed, sea lanes would need to be secure, bases would need to be set up, men and materiel amassed, and strategic targets in Germany bombed.

Churchill set up Combined Operations Headquarters (COHQ) after Dunkirk, initially giving it responsibility for launching raids on the coast of France and other enemy held territories (the first such raid was carried out by 120 Commandos on June 23, 1940). Under the command of Louis Mountbatten from October 1941, COHQ assumed the task of preparing for a return to France.

The Low Point

By the summer of 1942, hopes of an invasion seemed fanciful. The war was going badly, with German and Japanese forces apparently unstoppable. Russia seemed to be on the verge of collapse and the Russian leader, Joseph Stalin, was increasingly strident in his demands for the opening of a second front to ease the pressure on his beleaguered armies.

British and American planners still believed April or May 1943 was the earliest possible date for a full-scale invasion. The Arcadia strategy, agreed in December 1941 (two weeks after American

"IN ORDER FOR AN INVASION TO SUCCEED, SEA LANES WOULD NEED TO BE SECURE, BASES WOULD NEED TO BE SET UP, MEN AND MATERIEL AMASSED, AND STRATEGIC TARGETS IN GERMANY BOMBED."

entry into the war following Pearl Harbor), called for a sustained strategic bombing campaign, small-scale offensives, and the setting up of bases in preparation for an invasion of Europe, possibly on more than one front.

The scale of such an invasion had been laid out in Operation Roundup in early 1942. It was to be a major undertaking involving a total of 48 Allied divisions, but it was nowhere near ready. As a stop-gap measure, and in something of a panic over the situation on the Eastern Front, a smaller invasion was proposed, to be staged by the British before the end of 1942.

Operation Sledgehammer was to be an ad hoc invasion, with the British basically throwing anything they could spare across the Channel in an attempt to divert German attention from the crumbling Red Army. There was no chance of it achieving much and little enthusiasm for it, but the need to do something was becoming intolerable. Although Sledgehammer was eventually deemed a futile gesture, the need to act remained and would lead to one of the most costly failures of the entire war.

The Fallback Option

After the cancellation of Operation Sledgehammer, a different operation was turned to. A small-scale raid on the French port of Dieppe, codenamed Rutter, had been suggested by COHQ in April 1942. It might, the thinking went, be enough to satisfy Stalin and might just achieve something worthwhile.

Retrospectively, much would be made of the raid's role in the future planning of D-Day, but this was barely mentioned prior to the operation taking place. Mostly, it had a political imperative. It would show that the British took Stalin's concerns seriously, it would satisfy the craving of the public to carry the fight to the Germans, and it would also give employment to a neglected part of the army at the Allies' disposal. Canadian troops had been based and training in Britain for two and a half years but were yet to see action. Operation Rutter would boost morale among the Canadian troops, and among the populations of both Canada and Britain.

No records survive of any high strategic goals for the raid. There was a vague hope that it might somehow trigger a major air confrontation with the *Luftwaffe*, and it was anticipated the RAF would come out on top of such a clash, which might limit German air operations in the east. Still, practice of amphibious operations was badly needed. The British had not mounted a major amphibious assault since Gallipoli in 1917, while the Americans had to go back to their Civil War for their last experience. Both nations had doctrines in place, but it was untested. Mountbatten wrote that "this operation will be of great value as training for Operation Sledgehammer or any other major operation as far as the actual assault is concerned." It would turn out to be the only saving grace of the operation.

Disaster at Dieppe

Bad weather forced Rutter to be called off on July 4 (despite the patriotic overtones of the original chosen date, the Americans had nothing to do with the inception or planning of the raid) and there were thoughts that it should not be revived. Bernard Montgomery, responsible for the army side of the operation, declared his desire that it be shelved "for all time," but it was resurrected with a new codename, Jubilee, in August. There were distinct security risks involved with this, as the personnel involved had been briefed on their destination prior to the aborted launch of Rutter and had since been released on leave. Despite these concerns, the raid went ahead on August 19, 1942.

The Canadians bore most of the burden, providing 5,000 infantrymen for the assault. The Royal Navy provided 3,500 personnel, with 1,200 Commandos and 60 US Rangers completing the assaulting units. Four destroyers would shepherd the force to its target.

Dieppe had been chosen partly because it was considered essential to capture a port as part of any large-scale invasion—the amount of men and equipment needed to sustain a full-scale invasion of France would be immense. Other potential targets in Normandy, including Caen, Cherbourg, and St. Malo, had been discounted for various reasons.

There were some small successes involved with the raid, most notably when Commandos managed to knock out a German coastal gun position. Other than this, the landing was a disaster. Within 12 hours, more than 60 percent of the assaulting force had been killed, wounded, or captured.

German defenses had proved far more formidable than anticipated, communications between naval vessels and the shore were poor, and concrete tank barriers prevented Canadian armor from advancing into the town. All 27 of the tanks that made it to the beach were lost. Out of the 5,000 Canadians who took part in the operation, just over 2,000 returned to Britain. One destroyer and 33 landing craft were also lost. Perhaps most disappointing, the RAF did not achieve superiority over the *Luftwaffe* and actually lost more planes than the Germans. Despite this, morale among the returning Canadian troops was high as they had finally got involved in the war.

Lessons Learned

The raid also provided essential information on the mounting of amphibious assaults. Lessons were learned and distilled into a report soon after the operation ended. The key findings would shape planning for the eventual landings at Normandy. Surprise, it had been learned, could not be relied upon to give a decisive advantage. Continuous air support was essential, as was overwhelming fire support from naval vessels. Intensive training for the assault force was recommended, so that it could perform with "a coherence comparable to that of any other first line fighting formations."

The need for development of close-support naval vessels and specialized tanks for clearing beach defenses was also highlighted. As a result of the raid, Force J was formed, a naval assault force tasked with creating new doctrine. The result of their work, the "Force J Fighting Instructions," would be employed on D-Day.

"Dieppe occupies a place of its own in the story of the war," Churchill would comment, "and the grim casualty figures must not class it as a failure . . . Tactically it was a mine of experience . . .

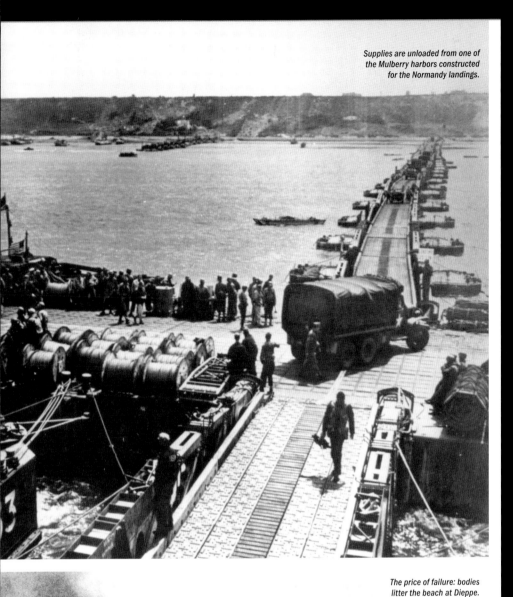

Supplies are unloaded from one of the Mulberry harbors constructed for the Normandy landings.

The price of failure: bodies litter the beach at Dieppe.

ENGINEERS IN THE FIRING LINE

Everyone's contribution would be important on D-Day, but the engineers would play a particularly critical role.

As well as planning on what might be considered the "macro scale" for D-Day, units had to plan on the micro scale too. Nowhere was this more true than for the engineers who would accompany the assault troops onto the beaches of Normandy.

The landing would have three phases: the assault phase, an initial dump phase (where ammunition and other supplies would be left on the beach for subsequent waves of troops), and a maintenance dump phase. The first two phases would take place on D-Day itself.

In the US 1st Army, allocated to Utah and Omaha beaches, Engineer Special Brigades were charged with supporting the assault infantry. One quarter of the men that landed on Omaha Beach on D-Day were engineers. In the first phase of the landing, special assault gapping teams would aim to clear gaps in the lines of obstacles protecting the beach. A total of 16 such teams accompanied the first wave of troops to the shore.

Engineer battalion beach groups were scheduled to follow eight minutes later, with ammunition and fuel to create dumps for the landing troops. They were also to improvise roads for armored vehicles and make sure exits off the beach were open.

The plan flew in the face of conventional thinking, which insisted that engineers could not work effectively under heavy fire, but it was an unavoidable gamble. Despite the many impediments to their work (including infantrymen sheltering behind beach obstacles and refusing to move), the American engineers cleared six routes off the beaches at Omaha, but they would suffer a casualty rate of a devastating 40 percent.

American combat engineers in England take a break while preparing for the D-Day invasion.

American troops land at Algiers as part of Operation Torch, ramping up the pressure on the Germans in North Africa.

THE REHEARSALS

The Allies were desperate to gain experience of amphibious landings, but those experiences were not always positive.

As well as the raid on Dieppe, various other smaller-scale operations (including a landing at Anzio in January 1944) provided valuable experience in the buildup to D-Day, and significant rehearsals for amphibious landings were staged. They would prove that even rehearsals could go badly wrong.

One such rehearsal took place in the Pacific, where the Americans were preparing for an amphibious assault on the Solomon Islands in 1942. The US Army's amphibious warfare doctrine had been laid down in a 1938 paper, but almost no training had been undertaken. Suitable beaches on Fiji were selected for practice landings and extractions on July 28 and 30. Problems included the fact that most of the landing craft used did not have front ramps, so heavily laden Marines had to clamber over the sides when approaching the beaches and several men nearly drowned. After a chaotic performance, the second day of landings was canceled, but several officers were not informed and landing craft set off again into the teeth of a live naval artillery barrage. It was a terrifying confirmation that amphibious landings required painstaking precision and cooperation.

Loading of landing craft at Anzio, one of many operations that provided invaluable, but often costly, experience for the Normandy landings.

Strategically the raid seemed to make the Germans more conscious of danger along the whole coast of occupied France."

It might have been cold comfort in the aftermath of the disastrous raid, but Churchill was not wrong. In fact, the Allies and the Germans learned contradictory lessons from the failure. While the Allies recognized that attacking a port head-on was too risky, the Germans believed they needed to boost their port defenses. Key elements were falling into place for the Normandy landings, but first, attention would be diverted to North Africa.

Operation Torch

The Allies were clearly not ready to contemplate a major invasion of France, and the May 1943 target was now unrealistic. The raid on Dieppe had also been little more than a token effort and a second front was still required. North Africa was chosen as an easier option, and Operation Torch finally commenced in North Africa in November 1942.

Preparations for a major invasion of Europe had not stopped, however. The precursor to the now-moribund Roundup, the massing of men and materiel in southern England, was still underway under the codename Bolero. In one of the seemingly endless streams of conferences, this one held at Casablanca in January 1943, several key points were agreed upon. First and foremost, the war against the U-boats in the Atlantic would be stepped up (it was essential before really large-scale shipments for the invasion could be risked). The scope of the strategic bombing campaign would be increased, and the buildup of forces in Britain would continue as quickly as possible.

The eventual success in North Africa led to the invasion of Sicily and then Italy, and with the Americans also preoccupied with their Japanese foe in the Pacific Theater, the date for a proposed invasion of France slipped. At the Trident Conference in Washington, DC, held in May 1943, the date was pushed back to the following May. The conference was also notable for the shift in balance in the relationship between the Americans

British soldiers evacuated from Dunkirk arrive back at Dover on May 31, 1940.

Image Source: IWM photograph collection H 1623 Public Domain

and the British. With America now fully engaged in the war and beginning to flex its industrial muscle, it was becoming the senior partner.

As such, the Americans vented their frustration over the delays in mounting the invasion of France and another interim operation was proposed: the medium-scale Roundhammer, which would utilize a mere three divisions in its initial assault phase. It was tentatively scheduled for May 1944.

D-Day Takes Shape

At the same time, lessons learned from Dieppe were being acted upon. The need for close-support naval vessels was solved by arming landing craft with a variety of weaponry, including five-inch rockets and 4.7-inch guns. Specialized armored vehicles (known as "funnies") were developed to deal with beach defenses (the "flail tank" for clearing mines is perhaps the most famous) and some tanks were converted for amphibious use. An emphasis was also placed on improving ship-to-shore communications.

At the same time, intelligence was being gathered on potential landing spots. After the beaches of Normandy were selected, aerial reconnaissance and even the purchase of tourist postcards helped the Allies piece together a picture of the defenses that would be awaiting them upon their invasion.

The command structure for the operation was also taking shape. Montgomery, with experience of working alongside the Americans in Italy (not with the greatest of harmony, it must be said) was put in charge of the Army Group that would handle the invasion. His first impression of the plans that had been drawn up was not favorable. Monty believed the scale of the initial invasion was far too small. Now codenamed Overlord, but based in part on the medium-size Roundhammer proposal, Monty believed it was seriously underpowered and immediately ramped up the scale of the initial assault. Five divisions would now storm the beaches, with three more airborne divisions protecting the flanks of the landing zones. D-Day was beginning to take a recognizable shape.

Stalin was also still free with his opinion, advocating a secondary, supporting invasion of southern France at the same time as Overlord. Codenamed Anvil, this operation did eventually take place but, being mounted significantly later than originally envisaged, it played no role in supporting the Normandy landings.

The Best Laid Plans

Planning for Overlord (and Operation Neptune, the initial phase of the invasion) continued, dealing with one immense problem after another. The decision, post-Dieppe, not to assault a major port, led to the adoption of two prefabricated "Mulberry" harbors, while the problem of fuel supply was apparently solved with the provision of the Pipeline Under the Ocean (PLUTO).

There was debate over which targets pre-invasion air strikes should concentrate on (bridges or rail yards) and how to ensure resupply for the hundreds of thousands of troops that would be put on shore if the initial assaults were successful.

With five beaches targeted, to be tackled by the British (Gold and Sword beaches), Canadians (Juno Beach), and Americans (Utah and Omaha beaches), the plan gradually took shape. It was the product of hard lessons and hard negotiating. There had been delays and compromises along the way and none of the elements would work flawlessly, opening the field for endless debate in the immediate aftermath and the decades that followed.

It was, however, little short of a miraculous undertaking, vast in ambition and unprecedented in scale. Churchill would later claim of D-Day (perhaps not entirely accurately but with his usual flair with words) that, "Everything proceeded according to plan. And what a plan!"

"THERE HAD BEEN DELAYS AND COMPROMISES ALONG THE WAY AND NONE OF THE ELEMENTS WOULD WORK FLAWLESSLY, OPENING THE FIELD FOR ENDLESS DEBATE."

The scale and the intensity of the scenes on Omaha were like nothing ever before seen in military history.

WHY WAS NORMANDY CHOSEN FOR D-DAY?

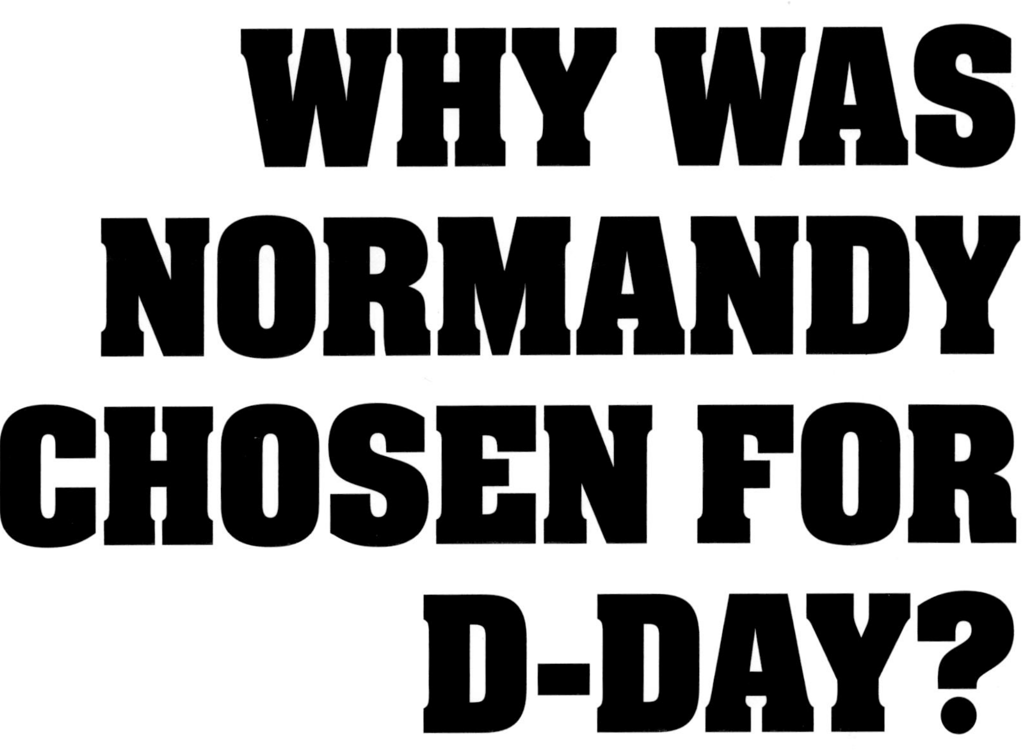

For Hitler's Fortress Europe to crumble, a perfect location had to be chosen for the largest amphibious invasion in history.

BY **JACK GRIFFITHS**

Western Europe had been under German occupation for four years when the decision was made to punch a hole in the Atlantic Wall. World War II was entering its final stages and the Allies believed that the time was right to grasp a foothold in France and begin the liberation of Western Europe from the grip of National Socialism.

The plan for D-Day was to land a task force on the French coast, where the Atlantic Wall—a system of defenses featuring machine guns, artillery, and fortifications that stretched from Norway to Spain—was at its weakest. The British high command was adamant that any invasion would not be a repeat of the failed 1942 attack on Dieppe, a miscalculation that had resulted in 3,000 Allied soldiers being cut down by German bullets in just eight hours.

The idea for D-Day, officially codenamed Operation Neptune, was initially conceived at the First Quebec Conference that took place in Canada in August 1943. Here, British Prime Minister Winston Churchill met with US President Franklin Delano Roosevelt, to agree on the future strategy of the war. The deliberation over what to do included a potential attack through the Mediterranean or the Balkans to target Fascist Italy, undoubtedly the Axis' junior member. They eventually settled on an attack on France's western seaboard, which would initiate Operation Overlord, the invasion of Western Europe. If successful, it could deliver a crippling blow and turn the tide of the war against Nazi Germany.

In the Atlantic, the Allies had finally gained the upper hand against the Kriegsmarine's U-boat wolf packs, allowing troops and supplies to be safely and freely shipped between the US and Britain. As a result, there was a realistic chance of an invasion of Western Europe to open up a second front against Hitler's armies. Soviet leader Stalin in particular was a huge advocate of the idea as an attack from the west would relieve the strain on the Soviet Union's Red Army on the Eastern Front. He had called for it ever since the Wehrmacht's blitzkriegs had first been unleashed on the USSR, in Operation Barbarossa in 1941.

Amphibious landings had previously been attempted by the USA in the Pacific Theater of the war against Imperial Japan. The Battle of Tarawa was a US victory, but with more than 3,000 casualties, it was a costly one. Invasions like this, and the ones at Crete, Attu, and Sicily, were fresh in the memory of the D-Day planners, making any seaborne attack a risky strategy. The Allied powers, however, believed that it was a gamble worth paying.

To prepare the armed forces for the mission ahead, bombing raids over Germany were scaled back so both the Royal Air Force and the United States Army Air Forces could assist with the landings. The leaders of both organizations were reluctant to do so because of the importance of eliminating key targets in the Ruhr—Nazi Germany's industrial heartland. However, they were swayed to turn their attention to shelling the submarine bases, infrastructure, and airfields of France. Their assistance would be invaluable in downing the *Luftwaffe* and leveling the Atlantic Wall.

The planning for the Normandy landings was meticulous. Frequent aerial reconnaissance runs were carried out by Spitfires, armed with cameras instead of guns. This was carried out over the French and Belgian coastlines to determine where the defenses were at their weakest. The aim was to photograph an area that would be suitable for a mass-amphibious assault. These images would establish which beachhead the initial attack would start from.

The photos taken by the reconnaissance aircraft were then transported to RAF Medmenham, Buckinghamshire, for analysis by stereoscopes, a type of 3D glasses. The photography was studied in depth, enabling planners to discover the exact locations and complexities of the German defenses. Inventive engineers created downsized replicas of the fortifications so tacticians could understand how to best bust through them. Divers in midget submarines also collected rocks from French beaches, enabling geologists to confirm whether the landscape could withstand tank tracks and the weight of other heavy vehicles. Infantry or armor getting stuck in the shingle would stunt any invasion and leave troops at the mercy of the German machine gun nests.

The obvious area for an invasion was Calais, due to the Dover Strait being the shortest part of the Channel. The Germans, however, weren't fools and had substantially fortified the area. After months of analysis, it was concluded the landings should be made on the beaches of Normandy, a much lighter-defended area. The Normandy beaches also had sand that could be traversed effectively by landing craft and amphibious vehicles, plus the area was sheltered from the strong Atlantic winds. In addition, the attack had the advantage of not being aimed at large ports, meaning the lethal street fighting that took place in Dieppe could be avoided. The assault would be primarily launched from the ports of Southampton, Portsmouth, Poole, and Portland. This offered another advantage over a Calais offensive, which would have required support from smaller docks such as Dover and Newhaven, which couldn't house as many vessels.

Above: The training had to be as detailed as possible to give the troops a fighting chance on the beaches.

It was initially planned that the landings would be made on three beaches, but this eventually grew to five over 60 miles (96.5 kilometers) of coastline. They were dubbed Sword, Juno, Gold, Omaha, and Utah. The first three would be assaulted by British and Canadian soldiers while US forces were to advance on the latter two. The landings would be orchestrated by Supreme Allied Commander Dwight Eisenhower, with support from fellow American General Omar Bradley and Britain's General Bernard Montgomery, who had previously led the Allies to victory in North Africa.

The attack would start with an artillery bombardment to soften up both the defenses and the defenders. This would be followed by aircraft bombing raids and then the infantry, followed by another attack from the air and then a final infantry blitz. The entire assault would be carried out by 23 divisions and it was essential that the first wave of soldiers believed in their ability to push forward as far as possible. This was to avoid overcrowding of the beaches as more landings would be made with reinforcements on a frequent basis. Eisenhower's strategy would only work if the troops had the mental steel and bravery to push on against the German gunfire.

In the months prior to D-Day, southern England became a restricted zone to prevent classified information being revealed to the enemy. High security meant that only the most senior of commanders knew the exact plans and logistics of Operation Neptune.

The 150,000 soldiers involved in D-Day, including British Commandos and US Marines,

> **"FREQUENT AERIAL RECONNAISSANCE RUNS WERE CARRIED OUT BY SPITFIRES, ARMED WITH CAMERAS INSTEAD OF GUNS."**

THE TRAGEDY OF SLAPTON SANDS

Live ammunition was used during Exercise Tiger to make the experience, and the danger, as authentic as possible.

The training sessions for D-Day were meant to be realistic, but not this realistic. Exercise Tiger was one of the largest of these rehearsals, but also the most catastrophic. The mock invasion took place on Slapton Sands, Devon, on April 28. It was the perfect location to practice, such were its similarities to the Normandy coastline.

Landing craft packed with US troops headed towards the beach in a simulated assault as the exercise began. However, it wasn't a secret that the training was taking place, and nine German E-boats had slipped into the bay undetected. As the small attack craft opened fire, the results were catastrophic. Many soldiers did not know how to use their life jackets and many drowned or froze to death in the water. An oversight in planning also meant that there were no Allied destroyers or battleships present, resulting in the landing craft being sitting ducks. This wasn't the end of the danger. On the beaches, the decision to include live ammunition had backfired and the naval shells that hit the shore actually killed some of the US servicemen.

Nearly 1,000 US soldiers died on that fateful day, but many consider the deaths to have not been in vain, due to the intense training contributing to the success of D-Day. The episode wasn't revealed to the public until decades after. A memorial now stands on the sands in honor of the lives that were lost.

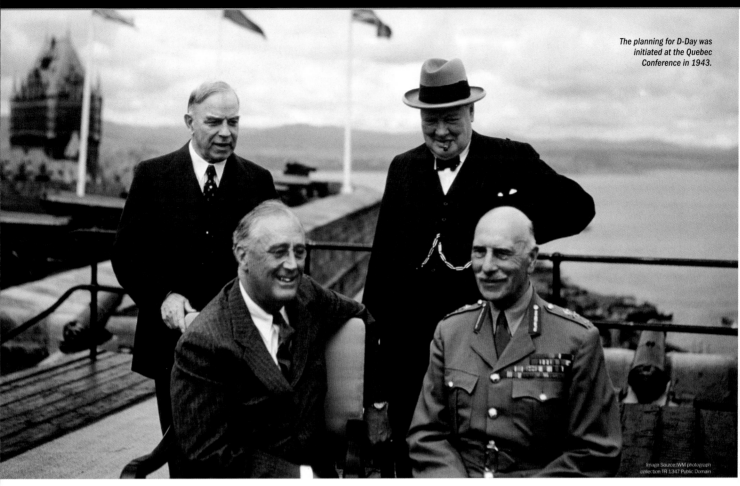

The planning for D-Day was initiated at the Quebec Conference in 1943.

Image Source: IWM photograph collection TR 1347 Public Domain

Below: D-Day was the largest amphibious invasion in military history.

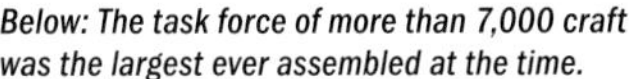

Below: The task force of more than 7,000 craft was the largest ever assembled at the time.

Below: D-Day wasn't the first attempt to invade Western Europe. Dieppe, in 1942, was an unmitigated disaster.

Image Source: IWM photograph collection B 5071 Public Domain

Image Source: Library and Archives Canada, Ref. PA-132651, Public Domain

Image Source: German Federal Archive, Public Domain

were drilled relentlessly to be ready. The exercises tested the soldiers' physical and technical capabilities as well as the mental impact and exhaustion that the landings would have on them. Beach combat wouldn't be the only type of warfare the infantry and paratroopers would be undertaking. Street-to-street fighting was practiced with the expectancy that Cherbourg and Le Havre would also be taken on the advance inland. Much of the training took place off the shores of Scotland to try and replicate the harsh coastal conditions and the mass deployment of troops.

As the distance to Normandy was much longer than to Calais, battleships and destroyers were required to escort the taskforce to make it across the sea safely. Rather than launching directly from the English coast, the vessels would be floating in the Channel on a Mulberry harbor—a portable artificial docking station made from 1,000,000 tons of concrete that gave craft and supply vehicles quick access to Normandy.

With the planning stage complete, D-Day was now reliant on the weather to go ahead. The initial date was set to be in May 1944, but this was delayed due to the lack of landing craft until June. It was calculated that June 5–7 would be the best date to launch the attack, with an appropriate tide and suitable weather conditions predicted, along with the benefit of light from a full moon. Closer analysis, however, revealed that on June 5 the water would be too choppy and the wind too strong for a landing, so it was delayed until the following morning.

In the early hours of June 5, 1944, unbeknownst to the Allies, many high-ranking Wehrmacht officers, including General Erwin Rommel, had left their posts on the night of the invasion, safe in the knowledge that no invasion was forthcoming. Rommel, in fact, was away celebrating his wife's birthday. This was a huge slice of luck as any German military response would now be delayed due to the hierarchy being nowhere near what would be a new front line in a matter of hours.

Back in London, Churchill remarked to his wife, Clementine, "Do you realize that by the time you wake up in the morning, 20,000 men may have been killed?" The D-Day die had been cast and H-Hour was about to begin.

RAMPART OF THE REICH

Hitler sought to defend his European empire from Allied attack with a massive series of fortifications. The Atlantic Wall was the first line of defense for "Fortress Europe."

BY **MARC DESANTIS**

By any measure, the Atlantic Wall was extraordinary. Stretching almost 1,700 miles (2,700 kilometers) from Spain in the south to the Netherlands in the north, the Wall's construction required enormous quantities of concrete—some 17 million cubic tons. It would also incorporate about 1.5 million tons of precious iron. A huge labor force worked to build the Wall, under the direction of Organization Todt, the Third Reich's construction agency. Adolf Hitler had made the defense of the West a priority, in late 1942, and had ordered that *Atlantikwall* be built as part of the effort to prevent the Western Allies from ever returning to the Continent. Indeed, Hitler's involvement had even seen him personally design the casemates and pillboxes.

The Führer wanted a coastal defensive belt of 15,000 strongpoints. Ports, assumed to be the likeliest initial targets of any invading force, would be guarded by giant naval artillery. The heaviest part of the German defenses that would be collectively termed the Atlantic Wall were to be found in the area running from the Scheldt River to the Seine River. This was the region where the

A German bunker at Longues-sur-Mer, Normandy, housing a 45-calliber naval gun.

Allies' main blow was expected, especially around the Pas-de-Calais area.

The reality of the Atlantic Wall, as of late 1943, however, failed to live up to Hitler's desires. Relatively little had been done by the time Field Marshal Erwin Rommel had been named commander of German Army Group B and put in charge of the defense of northwestern France and Belgium. The "Desert Fox" had tangled with both the British and the Americans in the North African desert earlier in the war, and he had fought with energy. Now he brought that same energy to the task of improving the fortifications he found.

The half-completed state of the Atlantic Wall left the hard-charging field marshal aghast. The German troops in the West had, up until then, had a soft war, utterly unlike the bloodbath the Germans in Russia had experienced. They had been content to enjoy the comforts of France, and had not worried themselves too much about the prospect of an invasion. As such, too little had been done to make the Atlantic Wall ready.

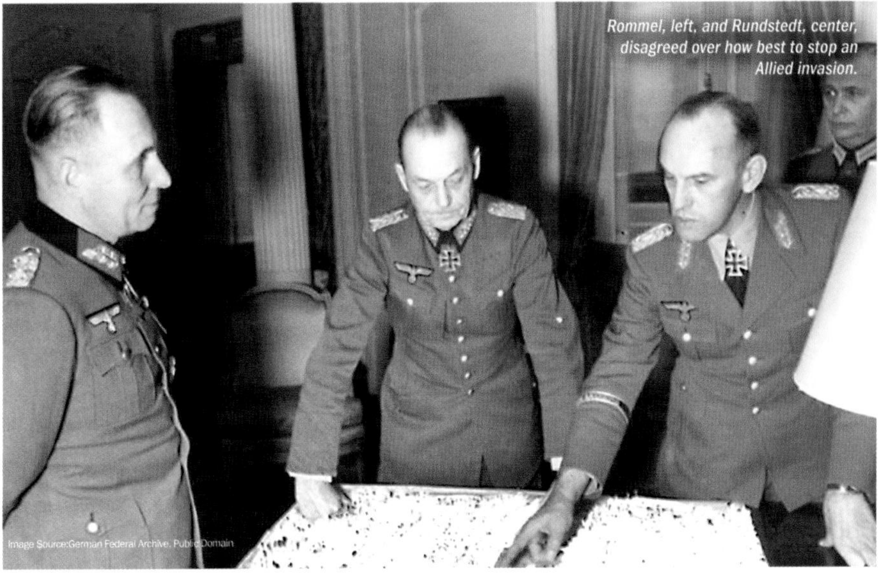
Rommel, left, and Rundstedt, center, disagreed over how best to stop an Allied invasion.

Image Source:German Federal Archive, Public Domain

German Strategy

By late 1943, when Rommel appeared and took command in northern France, that invasion was becoming ever more likely. A massive buildup of men and materiel in England had been continuing unabated, and eventually those soldiers would be hurled against Fortress Europe at some time in 1944. The need to improve the Atlantic Wall's defenses was obvious to Rommel, who found nowhere near the number of pillboxes, mines, beach obstacles, and bunkers he thought necessary. "The war will be won on the beaches," Rommel said. The decision would come very soon too, within the first 24 hours, he predicted. For both the Allies and Germans, these hours would constitute "the longest day."

Rommel had seen firsthand the devastating effect that Allied airpower could have on his army when he had fought in North Africa. For him, there could be no question of simply waiting for the Allies to come ashore. That would allow them to establish a lodgment in which the British and Americans, with their vast superiority in troops and supplies, could bring in overwhelming forces and achieve a breakout. Time would not be on the German side. Powerful counterattacks would have to be launched immediately, or all would be lost. Rommel therefore insisted that the panzers, Germany's armored formations, be brought close to the coast, thereby enabling him to strike back fast against any invaders.

There were, however, senior German officers who disagreed with Rommel's assessment. Chief among them was his superior, Field Marshal Gerd von Rundstedt, commander-in-chief of all German forces in the West. Like Rommel, Rundstedt was an experienced general, but he argued that meeting the Allies at the water's edge would leave German troops vulnerable to the massive bombardment of Allied warships that were sure to accompany the landing forces. The

"HITLER MADE THE DEFENSE OF THE WEST A PRIORITY AND WANTED A DEFENSIVE BELT OF 15,000 STRONGPOINTS. HIS INVOLVEMENT HAD EVEN SEEN HIM PERSONALLY DESIGN PILLBOXES."

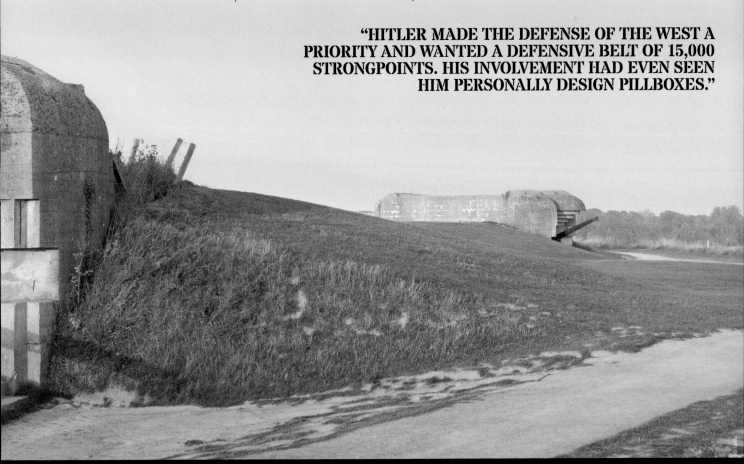

Right: Beach obstacles sited on the Atlantic Wall being inspected by Field Marshal Rommel in 1944.

Image source: German Federal Archive, Public Domain

panzers would be shattered by the shells of every Allied battleship, cruiser, and destroyer lying in the English Channel.

Hitler adopted a hybrid strategy that was satisfactory to neither party. He placed just three panzer divisions under Rommel's command, while the remaining four panzer divisions in France were to be kept well away from the coast, under the control of the German high command, without whose approval they would not move one mile towards a landing.

Mines, Mines, and More Mines

Strategic confusion was thereby baked into German defensive strategy from the outset. Rommel nevertheless applied himself to improving the Atlantic Wall to the greatest extent he could. In one feature, especially, the Wall was sorely lacking: mines. Since 1941, the German army in France had laid only 1.7 million of the deadly devices. While that might have seemed a terrifying number, Rommel did not hesitate to remind his subordinates that the British had deployed one million mines during one two-month stretch during the North African campaign. The Germans' low rate of laying mines had not been due to a lack of materials; on hand in France there was sufficient explosive compound to make some 11 million mines. The Germans in France, having had a relatively "easy" war, had simply lacked the motivation.

That motivation was now supplied in enormous quantity by Rommel. After lighting a fire under his men, mines were laid at a vastly increased rate. From a low of just 40,000 a month, mine laying soared to more than one million per month, bringing the total deployed to some four million by late May 1944, with another two million on their way from German factories. Rommel wanted 50 million mines all told, but he would never get close to that number before the Allies would at last arrive.

More than mines would be needed. Rommel also ordered the construction of obstacles in rear areas where airborne troops might land. Tall stakes with mines on the tops, dubbed "Rommel's asparagus," were intended to skewer parachute troops and break apart gliders. A half-million beach obstacles were also set down. These were intended to rip open enemy landing craft as they approached at high tide or topped with a mine to detonate when struck.

An illustration by Walter Molino of the huge German coastal fortifications.

© Getty

HITLER'S BUILDERS

The Organization Todt was the Third Reich's preeminent construction force and built Hitler's Atlantic Wall

Image source: German Federal Archive, Public Domain

A German soldier stands guard outside an Atlantic Wall fortification built by the Organization Todt.

The Third Reich's military efforts required huge amounts of construction, and this was beyond the capability of the Wehrmacht's own integral engineering units. Adolf Hitler turned to the Organization Todt to meet these needs. The OT was correspondingly enormous, with some 1.4 million workers tasked with constructing the bridges, roads, casemates, observation towers, bunkers, pillboxes, and myriad other structures for the German armed forces.

Organization Todt took its name from the Führer's principal architect and builder of the Autobahn, Fritz Todt. Todt had been assigned to construct the fortifications of the West Wall on the Franco-German border in 1938, and had completed the job, which involved building some 5,000 bunkers, very quickly.

Hitler would come to rely ever more heavily on Todt and his workers when war began in 1939. On the Atlantic coasts of France and Norway the Organization Todt built the hardened submarine pens for Hitler's U-boats. The OT also took up the task of bringing damaged factories in conquered territories back into operation, and assumed responsibility in the Balkans for mining the raw materials that fuelled the German war machine. For the Atlantic Wall, starting in the summer of 1942, the OT would pour millions of cubic tons of concrete to make Hitler's dream of a "Fortress Europe" a reality.

The wartime Organization Todt relied mainly on non-German workers to accomplish its orders. Some workers were conscripts, but many others were POWs and slave laborers. The majority of those building the Atlantic Wall were conscripts drawn from occupied France. This enabled the French Resistance to obtain information about the Wall, which was in turn passed on to the Allies.

A British soldier stands in front of a captured 380-mm German cannon at the Atlantic Wall.

Image source: IWM Photography collections B10467. Public Domain

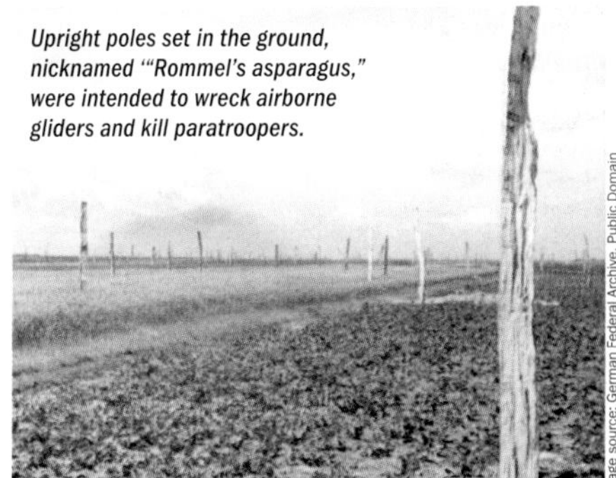
Upright poles set in the ground, nicknamed "Rommel's asparagus," were intended to wreck airborne gliders and kill paratroopers.

Image source: German Federal Archive. Public Domain

Problematically for Rommel, most of the mines were being laid in the area of northeastern France, particularly the Pas-de-Calais, because the German high command believed it offered the Allies the most direct route into Germany. Other areas, such as Normandy to the west, the site of the actual invasion, were not nearly as well protected.

Layers of Deadliness

In Normandy, where the Wall's fortifications would actually matter, the Germans had erected a layered defensive system. Inland, Rommel had deployed soldiers in the villages. Artillery backed up the soldiers, who were largely low-quality "garrison" troops, drawn largely from Eastern European non-Germanic peoples, deemed useful only for static defense in prepared positions. Interspersed between these strongpoints were flooded fields, to deter airborne landings, as well as Rommel's asparaguses.

Closer to the coast, Rommel had installed large numbers of artillery pieces in casemates up and down the Normandy coast. These guns were a hodgepodge of weapons drawn from all across Europe. Some were of German manufacture, such as the famed 88-mm gun, while many others were from stocks captured from Germany's enemies. The casemates were so thickly protected with reinforced concrete that they were virtually invulnerable to Allied naval guns or aerial bombardment. They were also constructed so that their openings faced to the sides, not to the front. This allowed their guns to deliver sweeping fire along the length of the beach while remaining protected from bombardment by the heavy guns of offshore ships. If they were going to be put out of action, the job would have to be done on the ground by assaulting infantry.

Those infantry would first have to get close. At Omaha Beach, where American troops would land, German infantry were preventing close assault, dug into trenches and armed with machine guns and rifles. The fields of fire of German machine guns overlapped, meaning there was no uncovered ground on which an invader might stay safe from attack. These German soldiers were also supported by heavier weapons, such as mortars and tank turrets, installed in circular concrete fortifications called Tobruks. Movement between these positions could be made via subterranean tunnels. Barbed wire, meanwhile, was strewn everywhere in prodigious quantities.

Field Marshal Rommel and officers tour the Atlantic Wall's battery at Salzwedel in 1943.

Image source: German Federal Archive. Public Domain

Simply getting onto and across the beach itself would be extremely dangerous. Rommel had many beach obstacles erected, such as big logs topped with mines. These were supplemented by welded steel rails that would tear open the flimsy hulls of approaching landing craft. Out to sea, Rommel had anchored naval mines to impede the approach of Allied shipping.

The Atlantic Wall Cracked

The Germans had made the Atlantic Wall into a formidable barrier. Nonetheless, it did not succeed in keeping the Allies from establishing a beachhead in northern France, as Rundstedt had feared. Against a less numerous or determined enemy, with fewer resources, the Atlantic Wall might have sufficed in stopping them at the beach as Rommel had wished. The Wall, however, could not cope with the hurricane of fire and steel that the Allies were prepared to throw at it during Operation Overlord.

The sheer length of the coastline that had to be defended, and the willingness of the Allies to land their troops on a less-protected stretch of Normandy coastline, allowed them to avoid the heaviest German defenses around Pas-de-Calais. At none of the D-Day landing sites did the Atlantic Wall hold up the invading Allies for even a day. What's more, once the Wall had been breached in just one place, as it was in Normandy, the remaining fortifications along the coast were rendered utterly irrelevant to the ensuing battle for the lodgment area.

THE D-DAY DECEPTION

Allied efforts to deceive the Germans as to the time and place of the invasion of northern Europe, codenamed Operation Fortitude, were comprehensive and contributed heavily to the success of the Normandy invasion.

BY **MARC DESANTIS**

Adolf Hitler's armies had overrun much of Western Europe by the summer of 1940. After the evacuation of British troops from Dunkirk, the continent was a dark empire groaning under Nazi oppression. If Europe was to be freed, the Western Allies, led by Britain and the United States, would have to land large armies of their own on the continent and evict the Germans.

This would not be easy. The German army had four years in which to dig in, and the coastal defenses of the Atlantic Wall made the choice of a landing site for an invasion force problematic. The Allies could try to seize a seaport, which would ease the burden of transporting men and supplies across the English Channel, but this was expected by the Germans, meaning that the coastal ports were heavily defended by both troops and artillery.

A landing site well away from a port, where the beach was less guarded, was an alternative, though the Germans, and especially Hitler himself, thought it less likely that the Allies would attempt such a plan.

The Allied operation to retake Europe in 1944 was codenamed Overlord, and it had to succeed. If the invasion failed for any reason, there would be no second chance. The Allies would have shown their hand; organizing a second invasion attempt would be out of the question. A victorious Hitler would then be able to transfer many of his divisions to the Eastern Front, and mastery of Europe would in turn be ultimately decided by the battle between the Führer and Soviet leader Joseph Stalin.

Operation Fortitude

It was therefore crucial that the Germans did not know the precise time and place of the landings. These vital details would be obscured through a far-reaching deception plan, Operation Bodyguard, which encompassed multiple webs of misinformation. The buildup of men, equipment, and supplies in Britain during 1943 and early

As part of Operation Fortitude, Lieutenant General George S. Patton was named the commander of the fictitious First United States Army Group (FUSAG).

1944 could never be hidden from the Germans, and so it was no secret at all that an invasion was in the works. The aim of Bodyguard was instead to confuse the Germans as much as possible. Doing so would keep Nazi troops rooted in place, well away from the chosen Normandy landing sites that were to be assaulted during Operation Neptune, itself a component of Overlord. The less troops the Germans had in Normandy, the more likely it would be that the Allies would be able to breach Hitler's vaunted Atlantic Wall.

One major component of Bodyguard was Operation Fortitude, which was divided into two parts: Fortitude North and Fortitude South. The ultimate aim of both was to convince the Germans that the Allies would not be striking at northern France when and where they did, and thus safeguard the Neptune landings.

Allied deception efforts were cast to reinforce preexisting German prejudices. German generals believed that the main Allied landing would come in the Pas-de-Calais area because this offered the shortest crossing point between England and France. The Nazis also strongly believed that the Allies would need to seize a port to conduct a successful invasion. Allied efforts were crafted to confirm German notions.

The goal of Fortitude South was to make the fictional Pas-de-Calais invasion more believable. Allied deceivers turned to the US Army's Lieutenant General George S. Patton to lend credibility to a strike there. Patton was one of the most aggressive commanders that the Allies had and the Germans, who judged him the best Allied general, were certain that he would be playing a big part in any invasion. Patton's appointment in early 1944 as the commander of the First United States Army Group, or FUSAG, thus made complete sense to the Germans.

FUSAG was in fact a totally fictitious organization, though many of its component units were genuine. As part of Operation Quicksilver, itself a subplan of Fortitude South, the purpose of FUSAG was to show the Germans that there was a major Allied formation readying itself to invade France.

The phantom army that was FUSAG, supposed to number around one million soldiers, was supported by more than just the naming of Patton as its overall commander. Phony wireless traffic, messages of the kind that would be generated by troops engaged in training and other pre-invasion activities, were generated on a daily basis. These signals were of course intercepted, as the Allies had intended, by the Germans.

To enhance the deception, empty FUSAG tents sprouted up all over southeastern England. Fake ammunition dumps, airfields, hospitals, and fuel depots appeared. Dummy tanks and trucks made out of rubber were inflated, and dummy airplanes of wood and canvas were parked beside airstrips. Pretend landing craft to move these fake soldiers over the Channel were deployed in English rivers and creeks. German aerial reconnaissance planes had no way of telling whether these were all fakes. To German intelligence, FUSAG was not only real, but growing rapidly in size.

Fortitude North's goal was to convince the Germans that an Allied attack on Norway was also in the cards. Norway had been conquered by Germany in the spring of 1940, and Hitler had since garrisoned it with a large number of troops. Keeping those occupation forces, which numbered around 380,000 men, in Norway meant they would not be available to help defend France against Neptune.

"FORTITUDE NORTH'S GOAL WAS TO CONVINCE THE GERMANS THAT AN ALLIED ATTACK ON NORWAY WAS ALSO IN THE CARDS."

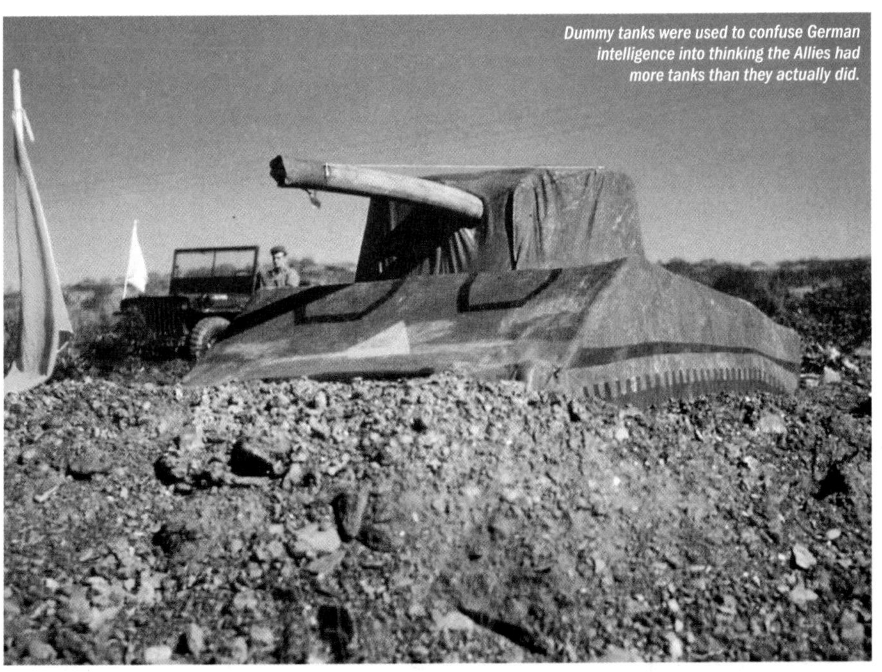

Dummy tanks were used to confuse German intelligence into thinking the Allies had more tanks than they actually did.

Codenamed "Brutus," Captain Roman Garby-Czerniawski of the Polish Army sent messages to the Abwehr to fool the Germans about Operation Quicksilver.

The Yugoslavian Duško Popov, codenamed "Tricycle," sent the Germans an imaginary order of battle for FUSAG.

Fake landing crafts were located in harbors in southeastern England in the run-up to D-Day.

To convince Hitler that Norway was under threat, Fortitude North saw the creation of the fictional British Fourth Army. To make it appear that the Fourth Army was real, Allied radio operators engaged in fake wireless traffic that they knew the Germans would intercept and decode. The Fourth Army had its own commanding officer, Sir Andrew Thorne, and was headquartered at Edinburgh Castle. The wireless signals were of the kind that a real army would produce, with the additional elements of messages about skiing and cold-weather operations, as would be expected from troops readying themselves to invade Norway. Fake subordinate formations included the 303rd Anti-aircraft Regiment, the 55th Field Dressing Station, and the VII Corps Postal Unit. The total size of the Fourth Army was pegged at 250,000 men, including an airborne division. This formation was also said to possess 250 tanks and had an attached tactical air force.

Not every aspect of Fortitude North was faked, however. British Commando raids against German forces in Norway and an increase in Allied aerial reconnaissance in Norwegian skies all painted a plausible picture that an invasion was under preparation. So effective were Allied efforts that a German fighter plane actually strafed Edinburgh Castle just three days after Allied wireless traffic had identified it as Fourth Army headquarters. The overall effect of Fortitude North was palpable. German troops that might otherwise have been withdrawn by Hitler for service in France remained in Norway, thereby easing the Allied burden on D-Day.

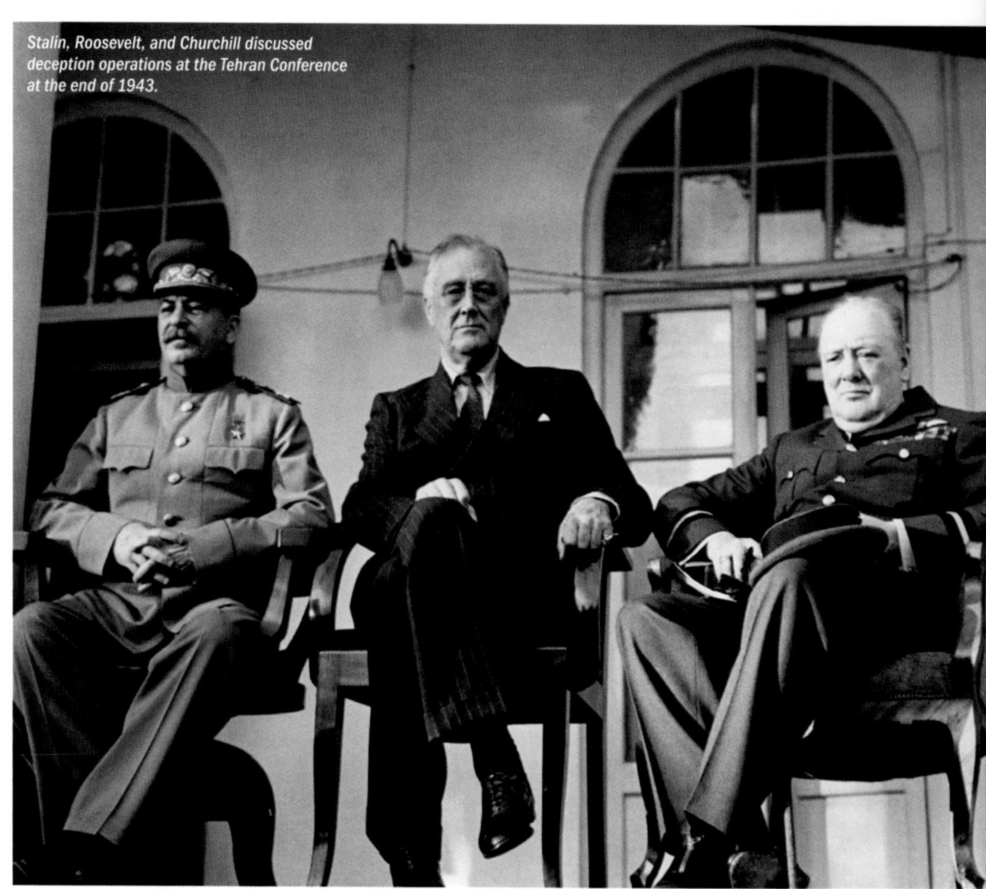

Stalin, Roosevelt, and Churchill discussed deception operations at the Tehran Conference at the end of 1943.

D-DAY'S BODYGUARD

Protecting D-Day in a web of deceit, Fortitude was but one part of Operation Bodyguard, the overall deception effort to protect the Normandy invasion.

At the Tehran and Cairo conferences of the Allied powers in November and December 1943, the multitude of deception operations concerning the upcoming invasion of Europe was given the codename Operation Bodyguard. The name was chosen on the basis of a remark made by British Prime Minister Winston Churchill, when he said, "In wartime, truth is so precious that she should always be attended by a bodyguard of lies."

Operation Fortitude was just one of the 36 subplans that comprised Operation Bodyguard. The Bodyguard strategy, which the various operations subsumed within it sought to enact, had several goals, but all were geared towards fooling Adolf Hitler as to the exact timing and location of the D-Day landings.

Among these goals was the aim of convincing the Nazis that the Allies would not have enough troops in Britain to carry out an invasion until July 1944 at the earliest, well after the actual planned date of D-Day. The false reason given for this delay was the need to support the bombing campaign against Germany with long-range bombers sent from America, which in turn was holding back the transport across the Atlantic of the troops required to take part in such an ambitious amphibious invasion.

A related aim was to persuade Hitler that, while the required delay was real, the Allies still had sufficient forces to make a landing of some kind if the Germans dared to weaken their defenses anywhere. This was done to keep Nazi occupation forces spread out and stuck in sectors that the Allies had no interest in attacking, such as Norway.

One Bodyguard subplan, Operation Zeppelin, dealt with the supposed threat of a major Allied attack in the Balkans in the spring of 1944. This was a bogus operation, but the goal was, again, to prevent the Germans from withdrawing troops from that sector and sending them to northern France for use against the D-Day assault forces of Operation Neptune.

A similar Bodyguard subplan, Operation Ironside, worked to pin down the German First Army in the region of Bordeaux, on France's western coast, about 300 miles (480 kilometers) south of Normandy. Operation Vendetta, meanwhile, acted to hold the German 19th Army in the south of France, where it was guarding the Riviera against an Allied attack.

In addition to the remarkable cleverness of their Bodyguard efforts, the Allies had one extraordinary intelligence advantage in the form of Ultra, the top secret codebreaking operation headquartered in Bletchley Park, England. German units in the field relied on the Enigma machine to transmit messages via wireless, and these signals were being intercepted by the Allies and then

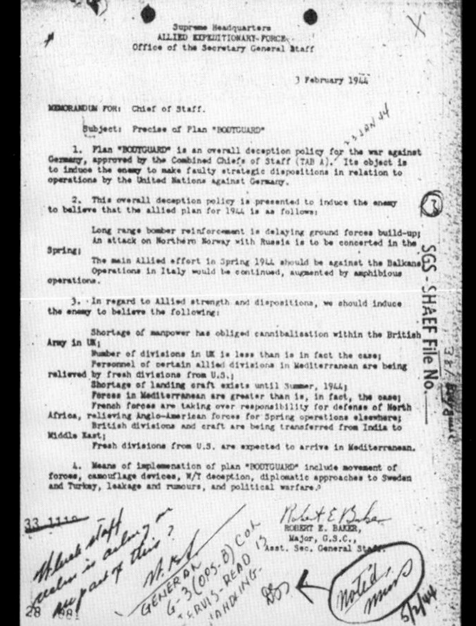

Supreme Headquarters
ALLIED EXPEDITIONARY FORCE
Office of the Secretary General Staff

3 February 1944

MEMORANDUM FOR: Chief of Staff.

Subject: Precise of Plan "BODYGUARD"

1. Plan "BODYGUARD" is an overall deception policy for the war against Germany, approved by the Combined Chiefs of Staff (TAB A). Its object is to induce the enemy to make faulty strategic dispositions in relation to operations by the United Nations against Germany.

2. This overall deception policy is presented to induce the enemy to believe that the allied plan for 1944 is as follows:

Long range bomber reinforcement is delaying ground forces build-up;
An attack on Northern Norway with Russia is to be concerted in the Spring;
The main Allied effort in Spring 1944 should be against the Balkans;
Operations in Italy would be continued, augmented by amphibious operations.

3. In regard to Allied strength and dispositions, we should induce the enemy to believe the following:

Shortage of manpower has obliged cannibalisation within the British Army in UK;
Number of divisions in UK is less than is in fact the case;
Personnel of certain allied divisions in Mediterranean are being relieved by fresh divisions from U.S.;
Shortage of landing craft exists until Summer, 1944;
Forces in Mediterranean are greater than is, in fact, the case;
French forces are taking over responsibility for defense of North Africa, relieving Anglo-American forces for Spring operations elsewhere;
British divisions and craft are being transferred from India to Middle East;
Fresh divisions from U.S. are expected to arrive in Mediterranean.

4. Means of implementation of plan "BODYGUARD" include movement of forces, camouflage devices, W/T deception, diplomatic approaches to Sweden and Turkey, leakage and rumours, and political warfare.

ROBERT E. BAKER,
Major, G.S.C.,
Asst. Sec. General Staff.

SGS - SHAEF File No.

A memorandum dated February 3, 1944, outlining Operation Bodyguard, made for Supreme Headquarters Allied Expeditionary Force (SHAEF).

deciphered by Ultra. One of the greatest benefits of Ultra in relation to the D-Day deception was that it granted Allied planners a peek into German thinking, and allowed them to confirm that their deception efforts were being believed.

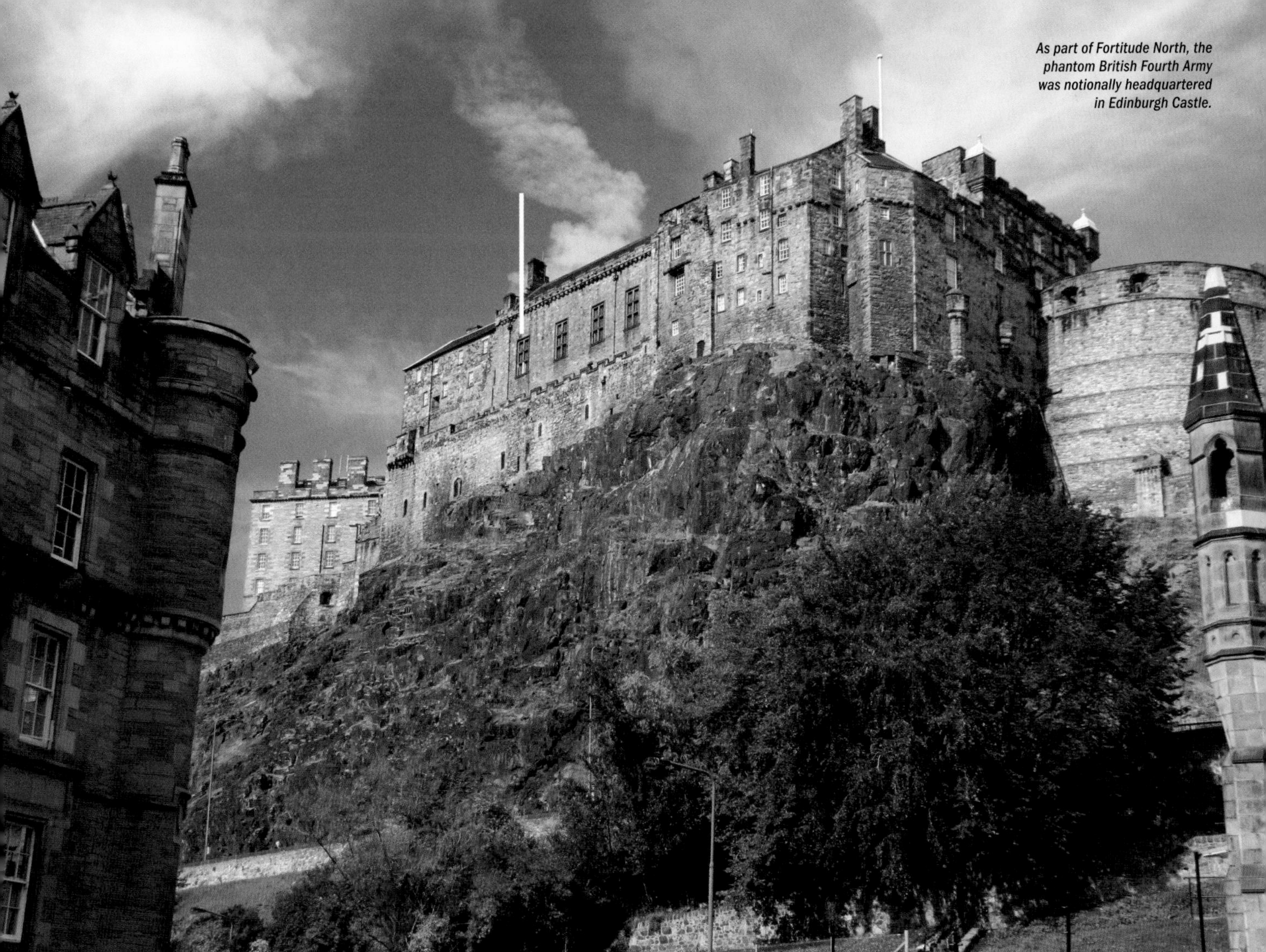

As part of Fortitude North, the phantom British Fourth Army was notionally headquartered in Edinburgh Castle.

Double-Crossing the Führer

To further the Fortitude deceptions, both North and South, Allied-controlled double agents reported precisely what the Allies wanted German intelligence to hear. This included messages that an invasion force was actually being assembled for use against Norway, for example. All of the German agents that had been sent to Britain either before or during the war had been quickly picked up by British authorities and many had been brought within the Double-Cross System run by British intelligence.

The turned agents fed German intelligence only the stories their British handlers produced them to transmit to Germany via wireless—and so the Nazis were learning that there was a major buildup of British, Canadian, and American troops in southeastern England, just across from Pas-de-Calais. These half-truths and lies were all designed to mislead the Germans as to the real time and place of D-Day.

Not all of the Double-Cross agents were committed Nazis who had been unlucky enough to get caught. One sterling agent was the Spaniard Juan Pujol García, codenamed "Garbo." Garbo detested both Nazism and communism. After first being rejected by British intelligence, he had begun his own private intelligence war against Hitler by becoming an agent for the Abwehr, German military intelligence. From his perch in Lisbon, Garbo plied false intelligence to the Abwehr, which all the while thought he was sending his messages from Britain. The Abwehr trusted him utterly, but by early 1942, Garbo had at last been brought within the British fold and taken to England. From there, Garbo funnelled erroneous information to Germany about the upcoming invasion.

"TO FURTHER THE FORTITUDE DECEPTIONS . . . DOUBLE AGENTS REPORTED PRECISELY WHAT THE ALLIES WANTED GERMAN INTELLIGENCE TO HEAR."

Another Double-Cross luminary was codenamed "Brutus." His real name was Roman Czerniawski, a captain in the Polish Army who had escaped to France after the fall of Poland, but had then been captured by the Gestapo in 1941. Czerniawski accepted an Abwehr offer to spy inside England in exchange for a promise not to execute 100 captured members of the Interallié, an underground organization he had established in France. After a staged escape to Britain, Czerniawski soon went to work for the Double-Cross operation. As Brutus, he sent phony intelligence to Germany concerning Operation Quicksilver, supplying details about FUSAG and its planned Pas-de-Calais landing.

A third Double-Cross standout was the Yugoslavian Duško Popov, codenamed "Tricycle." Popov began to work for German intelligence, but was actually working for British intelligence the whole time. With regard to D-Day, Tricycle supported Quicksilver by supplying the Germans with an entirely fictitious order of battle for FUSAG, which acted to lock the German 15th Army in place in Pas-de-Calais.

In Retrospect

Allied deception efforts were effective in persuading Hitler and much of the German high command that the main invasion would strike Pas-de-Calais. While much hard fighting was necessary to make Operation Neptune a success, Operation Fortitude was a critical element that kept the bulk of German fighting forces away from Normandy.

ARCHITECTS OF VICTORY: LEADING OVERLORD

A core group of Allied military leaders conceived, shaped, and executed Operation Overlord, the campaign that began the liberation of Western Europe from Nazi oppression.

BY MIKE HASKEW

The preparations for an Allied return to the continent of Europe via the English Channel, by landing in force on the coast of France, began soon after the ignominious defeat during the Battle of France and evacuation at Dunkirk during the dark spring of 1940.

Four years later, the Allies did, in fact, return, assaulting Hitler's Fortress Europe across a 50-mile (80-kilometer) front on the beaches of Normandy. Thousands of troops, aircraft, and ships took part in Operation Overlord, while the planning and buildup of supplies and materiel, plus execution of the landings, were all fraught with risk.

Maintaining security for D-Day was a constant challenge. Allocating scarce resources without crippling operations in other theaters, plus coordinating offensive efforts on land, sea, and air, were monumental tasks.

Despite differing perspectives and concerns over various aspects of command and control, these commanders and many others rose to the occasion, leading the combined arms of the Allied military to victory in Western Europe. The preparation and execution of Overlord required incredible organization and dexterity—along with good fortune. In less than a year, however, Hitler's dream of world domination was shattered, and Nazi Germany was vanquished.

War Theatre #12 (France) - OPERATIONS
Orig 4x5 neg and print rec'd 3 Aug 46 from Hdqs., XIX Tactical Air Command, Office of Photo Officer, APO #141, % Postmaster, N.Y., N.Y.
(over)
MISSION M-51-1
61303 A C
61303 AC

General Miles Dempsey led the British landings at Gold, Juno, and Sword beaches on D-Day.

General Omar Bradley faced a critical command decision at Omaha Beach on D-Day.

UNITED STATES

GENERAL DWIGHT EISENHOWER

The affable Eisenhower managed an often-prickly Allied partnership.

Dwight Eisenhower's rise to high command was nothing short of meteoric. In early 1941, he was a lowly colonel. Then, however, he caught the attention of US Army Chief of Staff General George C. Marshall and rapidly advanced, passing over more senior officers, and achieving general rank. Chosen to command Allied forces during the Operation Torch landings in North Africa in November 1942, he was subsequently named to lead SHAEF (Supreme Headquarters Allied Expeditionary Force) in December 1943 as plans for the invasion of Normandy, slated for the following spring, took shape.

Eisenhower, cordial and diplomatic, proved himself a capable administrator and master of coalition warfare, managing the demands of war as well as the towering egos of subordinates and petty infighting that is common among allies in wartime. All major decisions concerning the execution of Operation Overlord rested with Eisenhower, and he handled the tremendous responsibility as few could have done. After bad weather forced a postponement, he alone gave the order to proceed with D-Day, even penning a short statement for the press should the landings fail. He said succinctly, "If any blame or fault attaches to the attempt, it is mine alone." During the planning and execution of Operation Overlord and the campaign in Western Europe, Eisenhower was the man of the hour, shouldering resolutely the mantle of supreme command. •

Trafford Leigh-Mallory advocated the Transportation Plan, bombing enemy logistics centers, prior to D-Day.

GREAT BRITAIN

AIR MARSHAL TRAFFORD LEIGH-MALLORY

Trafford Leigh-Mallory brought central command to Allied air assets.

Unity of command was essential to the planning and success of Operation Overlord, and a vital aspect of that unity rested with air operations before, during, and after the Normandy invasion. While Air Chief Marshal Arthur Tedder, Deputy Overlord Supreme Commander; Air Chief Marshal Arthur Harris, leader of Royal Air Force Bomber Command; and General Carl Spaatz, commander of US Strategic Air Forces in Europe, each held their own priorities, Leigh-Mallory was experienced in combined arms operations, particularly those involving army ground troops, and had previously led RAF Fighter Command.

His appointment as commander-in-chief of the Allied Expeditionary Air Force for Overlord was confirmed in August 1943, and his prioritization of the Transportation Plan, a bombing offensive targeting the German-controlled railroads and transportation infrastructure, proved invaluable in the establishment and expansion of the Normandy beachhead, although it invited criticism due to collateral damage and inevitable French civilian casualties.

As the Normandy campaign concluded in late 1944, Leigh-Mallory was appointed to command Allied air forces in Southeast Asia. He was killed in a plane crash en route to his new post.

★ ★ ★

GREAT BRITAIN

AIR CHIEF MARSHAL ARTHUR TEDDER

As Deputy Supreme Allied Commander for Overlord, Tedder worked well with allies.

Following great success commanding air operations in the Middle East, Air Chief Marshal Arthur Tedder was appointed Deputy Supreme Allied Commander for Operation Overlord. Tedder had first met Eisenhower after the Operation Torch landings in late 1942, and they cooperated closely. Indeed, some of Tedder's countrymen, including Winston Churchill, considered him too close to the Americans.

His experience in preparing major air operations contributed significantly to the success of Overlord, particularly his advocacy of tactical air power and heavy bombing raids against the German transportation system, which crippled Nazi efforts to reinforce beleaguered units in Normandy. Tedder regularly intervened in air operations, ostensibly under the command of Air Marshal Trafford Leigh-Mallory, and criticized several strategic decisions made by General Bernard Montgomery, commander of Allied ground forces. Eisenhower praised his deputy, writing in his diary, "Certainly in all matters of energetic operation, fitting into an allied team, and knowledge of his job, he is tops. Moreover, he is a leader type."

Prior to Operation Overlord, Tedder won praise for his command in the Middle East.

Image source: WMCollection Photo No. TR 1457

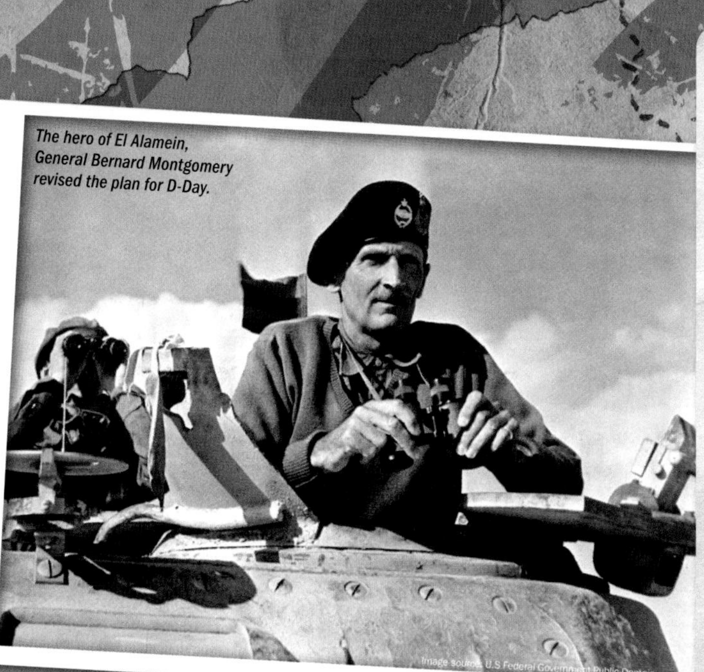

The hero of El Alamein, General Bernard Montgomery revised the plan for D-Day.

Image source: U.S Federal Government Public Domain

★ ★ ★

GREAT BRITAIN

GENERAL BERNARD LAW MONTGOMERY

Montgomery directed Allied ground forces during the critical D-Day deployment.

General Bernard Montgomery was a veteran of combat command and a hero among the Allied nations when chosen to lead the ground forces for Operation Overlord in early 1944, after transferring from the Mediterranean. Montgomery's first contribution to Overlord was a recommendation to expand the invasion front and increase the troops committed from three divisions to five infantry divisions and three airborne divisions, enough to ensure a successful lodgment.

Montgomery had developed a reputation as a superb organizer and planner, although critics complained that he was overly cautious, perhaps due to his experience in World War I when seriously wounded at the First Battle of Ypres. Having seen the carnage of the Western Front in 1914, he strove to minimize casualties later in his career. Montgomery had commanded a division during the Battle of France in 1940, led the Eighth Army to victory at El Alamein, one of the turning points of World War II, in North Africa in 1942, and also commanded British forces in Sicily and Italy.

Often abrasive, Montgomery regularly clashed with other senior officers, both American and British, while commanding Allied ground forces and 21st Army Group. Nevertheless, he emerged from the war as the most famous British army commander since the Duke of Wellington. Prime Minister Winston Churchill described him as "indomitable in retreat, invincible in advance, insufferable in victory."

"HAVING SEEN THE CARNAGE OF THE WESTERN FRONT IN 1914, [MONTGOMERY] STROVE TO MINIMIZE CASUALTIES LATER IN HIS CAREER."

GREAT BRITAIN

ADMIRAL BERTRAM RAMSAY

Ramsay led the largest seaborne combat operation in history on D-Day.

When the British Expeditionary Force and French troops had their backs to the English Channel in 1940, Admiral Bertram Ramsay executed Operation Dynamo, the sealift rescue of nearly 340,000 troops from the port of Dunkirk to Britain, enabling the Allies to live and fight the Nazis another day. Ramsay was 60 in 1944 when chosen as commander-in-chief of the Allied Naval Expeditionary Force for Operation Overlord (the landing phase itself was codenamed Operation Neptune)—he had retired from the Navy in 1938, but was summoned back to active service with the outbreak of World War II.

He went on to command naval forces during the Operation Torch landings in North Africa in November 1942, and Operation Husky in Sicily, in July 1943. The experience made Ramsay the logical choice for Overlord. His responsibilities for D-Day and beyond included clearing mines for thousands of ships crowding the English Channel; providing security against German aircraft, U-boats, and surface vessels; the pre-invasion bombardment of targets on the Normandy coast; and the landing of 150,000 combat troops.

Image source: WMCollection Photo No: A 23440

Background images: Map: Rocio Espin. Flags and texture: Getty

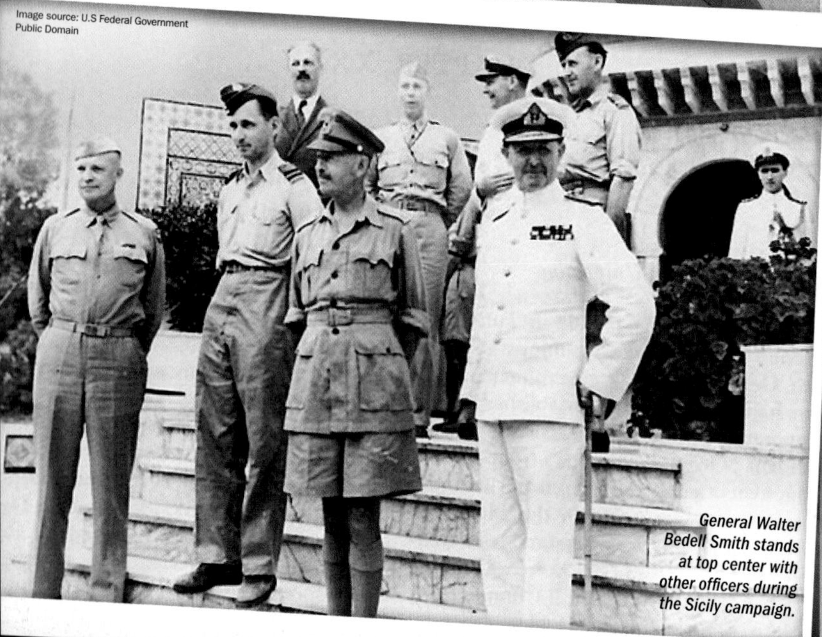
Image source: U.S Federal Government Public Domain

General Walter Bedell Smith stands at top center with other officers during the Sicily campaign.

UNITED STATES

GENERAL WALTER BEDELL SMITH

Chief of Staff Walter Bedell Smith represented Eisenhower capably.

General Walter Bedell Smith performed a vital role in the command structure of SHAEF as chief of staff to General Dwight Eisenhower, supreme commander of Operation Overlord. Eisenhower called Smith "the greatest general manager of the war," and administrative duties fell to Smith that otherwise would have occupied much of the supreme commander's time.

Smith was a young officer when Chief of Staff General George C. Marshall recognized his talent. He rose to the post of secretary of the Combined Chiefs of Staff in February 1942, and when Eisenhower was appointed to command in the European Theater of Operations in June, he requested Smith as his chief of staff. Smith had already demonstrated an ability to work cooperatively with his British allies, but nevertheless was sometimes seen as Eisenhower's "hatchet man," delivering orders in a forthright, brusque manner.

Prior to moving to SHAEF with Eisenhower, Smith had negotiated with Italy to conclude that nation's armistice with the Allies, and his skills were essential to the success of the D-Day invasion. He served Eisenhower at SHAEF from 1944 through to the end of the war.

"EASY-GOING BRADLEY WAS POPULAR . . . AND EARNED THE NICKNAME OF THE 'GI'S GENERAL' . . . ON D-DAY, [HIS] TROOPS AT [OMAHA BEACH] FACED THE STIFFEST GERMAN RESISTANCE."

UNITED STATES

GENERAL OMAR BRADLEY

Bradley led First Army during Overlord and later 12th Army Group.

A classmate of SHAEF Supreme Commander Dwight Eisenhower at the US Military Academy (class of 1915), Bradley commanded the US First Army during Operation Overlord and then assumed command of the 12th Army Group in August 1944. The easy-going Bradley was popular with the troops and earned the nickname of the "GI's General." He was, however, capable of making difficult decisions, and replaced another West Point classmate, General Roscoe Woodruff, at division level prior to D-Day due to Woodruff's lack of amphibious experience.

Bradley led the 82nd Infantry Division during its transition as the first operational airborne division in the US Army and gained prominence in North Africa while serving as deputy commander of II Corps under General George S. Patton, Jr. He succeeded Patton, leading II Corps in Tunisia and Sicily before reassignment to Britain in preparation for Overlord.

On D-Day, Bradley's troops faced the stiffest German resistance as elements of the 1st and 29th Infantry Divisions landed under fire at Omaha Beach and sustained heavy casualties. Aboard the heavy cruiser USS Augusta, Bradley considered evacuating those troops onshore and redirecting subsequent waves to other landing zones. His decision to refrain, however, was vindicated later that morning when a satisfactory foothold was gained, although the troops were unable to achieve all of their assigned D-Day objectives.

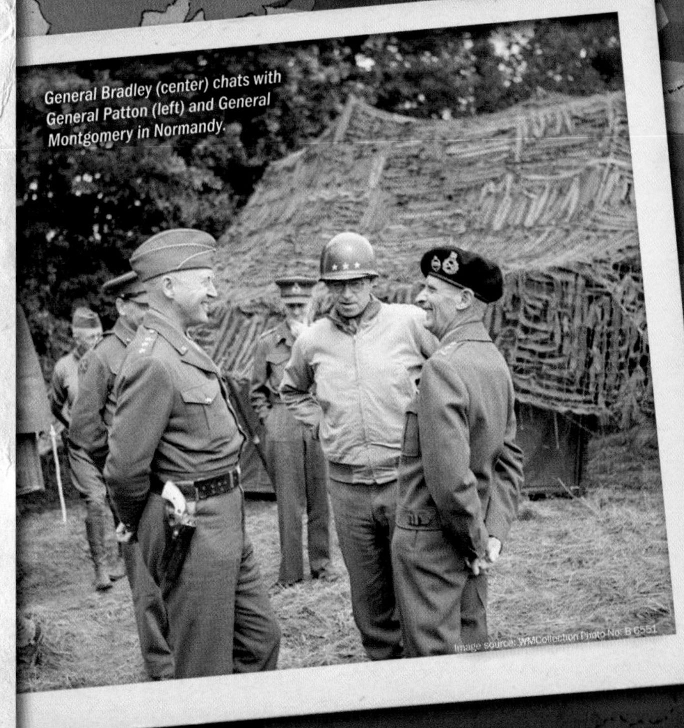
General Bradley (center) chats with General Patton (left) and General Montgomery in Normandy.

Image source: IWMCollection Photo No. B 6551

★ ★ ★

GREAT BRITAIN

GROUP CAPTAIN JAMES M STAGG

Accurately predicting the weather, Group Captain Stagg advised SHAEF Supreme Commander Dwight Eisenhower.

RAF Group Captain James Martin Stagg, Operation Overlord chief meteorologist, advised Supreme Commander Dwight Eisenhower that unfavorable weather would disrupt naval and landing operations plus ground Allied aircraft if Overlord proceeded, as scheduled, on June 5, 1944. Eisenhower postponed the Normandy invasion by 24 hours, relying on Stagg's prediction that a narrow window of decent weather would permit Overlord to proceed on June 6. Eisenhower polled his lieutenants during a meeting at Southwick House early on June 5, and then ordered Overlord to proceed.

Stagg's forecast proved accurate and the Allied liberation of Nazi-occupied Western Europe was unleashed. Otherwise, the next period of favorable atmospheric conditions was two weeks away. Ships packed with soldiers would have been recalled, and the security of the invasion might have been compromised. Stagg was only commissioned in 1943, having previously led the British Polar Year Expedition to the Canadian Arctic in 1932, plus served in the British Meteorological Office and been superintendent of Kew Observatory.

Image source: UK Governement Public Domain

SHAEF Meteorologist Group Captain James M. Stagg provided weather information prior to D-Day.

★ ★ ★

GREAT BRITAIN

GENERAL MILES DEMPSEY

General Dempsey commanded the British 2nd Army on D-Day.

A friend of General Bernard Montgomery, commander of Allied ground forces during Operation Overlord, General Miles Dempsey was a trusted field officer who led the British 2nd Army during the Normandy invasion and the campaign that followed, through to the end of World War II. Dempsey was a veteran of World War I, seriously injured during a mustard gas attack that subsequently required the removal of a lung. Between the wars, he served with occupation troops in Germany and in the Middle East.

Dempsey led the 13th Infantry Brigade during the Battle of France in 1940 and, at the age of 42, was among the youngest brigadiers in the British Army. When the 13th Brigade was evacuated from Dunkirk, only 500 of its original 3,000 men were present. Dempsey was praised for his leadership and promoted to command XIII Corps in North Africa, Sicily, and Italy. Throughout these campaigns, Dempsey displayed a sharp understanding of combined arms, prompting Montgomery to select him to command 2nd Army during Overlord. His competent command and cooperation with the Americans hastened the Allied victory in Western Europe.

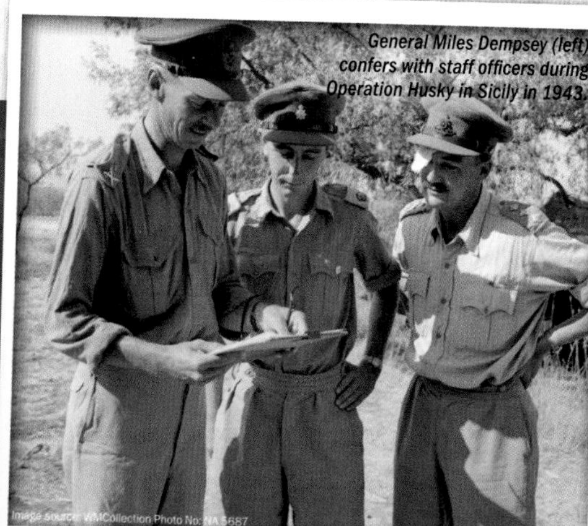

General Miles Dempsey (left) confers with staff officers during Operation Husky in Sicily in 1943.

Image source: IWMCollection Photo No: NA 5687

Image source: UK Federal Government Public Domain

General Frederick E. Morgan served as COSSAC and conceived the original Operation Overlord plan.

★ ★ ★

GREAT BRITAIN

GENERAL FREDERICK E. MORGAN

General Morgan laid the foundations for the 1944 Normandy invasion.

A name often omitted from the major figures of Operation Overlord is that of General Frederick E. Morgan. A veteran of World War I and the Battle of France, he was selected in March 1943 as chief of staff to supreme Allied commander (COSSAC) for the invasion of Europe, although no supreme commander had yet been designated.

When Eisenhower was appointed to lead the invasion, Morgan remained deputy chief of staff to General Walter Bedell Smith. By that time, the COSSAC staff had grown to more than 900 personnel responsible for planning Operation Overlord, a direct assault on Western Europe, Operation Rankin, a plan to deal with a total Nazi collapse, and Operation Cockade, a complex deception to keep the Germans off-balance regarding the location of the invasion.

Morgan and his staff chose Normandy as the invasion site due to its proximity to bases in Britain, and it being within the range of Allied aircraft. The original Overlord plan, encompassing three divisions and three landing beaches, was modified and expanded significantly, but Morgan had placed the cornerstone for operational victory.

THE ALLIED INVASION

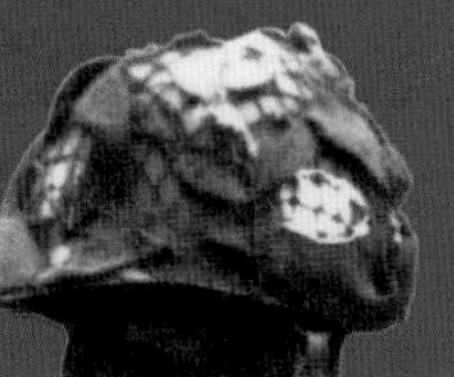

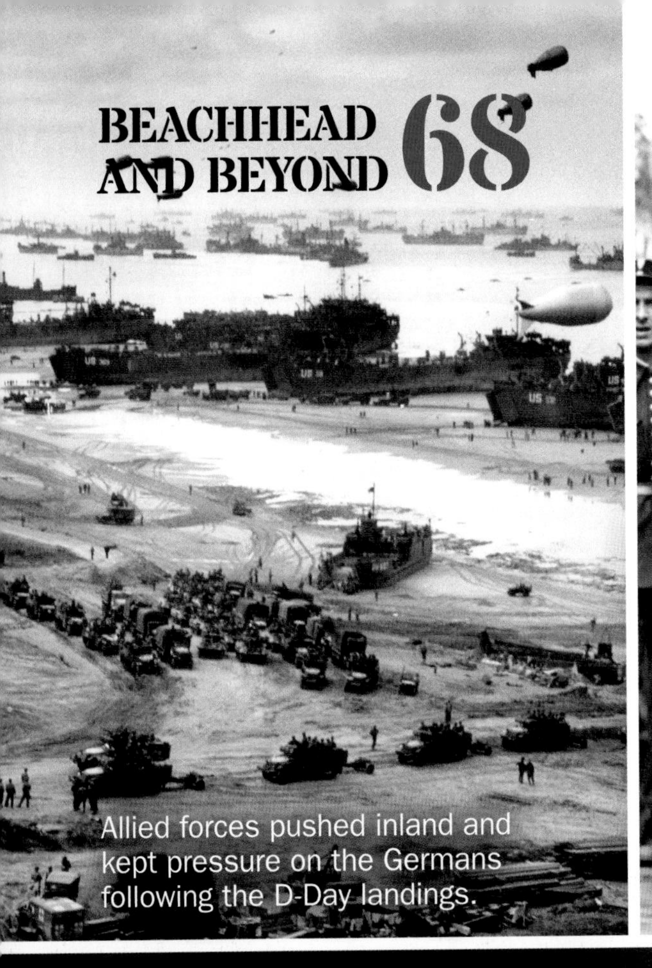

BEACHHEAD AND BEYOND 68

Allied forces pushed inland and kept pressure on the Germans following the D-Day landings.

84 THE FRENCH RESISTANCE & D-DAY

Sabotage, espionage, intelligence gathering, and small-scale combat were among the many contributions made by the French Resistance

HITTING THE BEACHES 59

On the morning of June 6, 1944, Allied troops came ashore in Normandy.

ANATOMY OF AN LCVP 66

The Higgins boat was the small landing craft that changed the war.

GERMAN RESPONSE 90

Poor leadership fatally hampered the German retaliation to D-Day.

THE WORLD HOLDS ITS BREATH

BY CHARLIE GINGER

Their parachutes mushrooming into the morning air, Allied paratroopers land in the fields of Normandy ready to take the fight to the Wehrmacht.

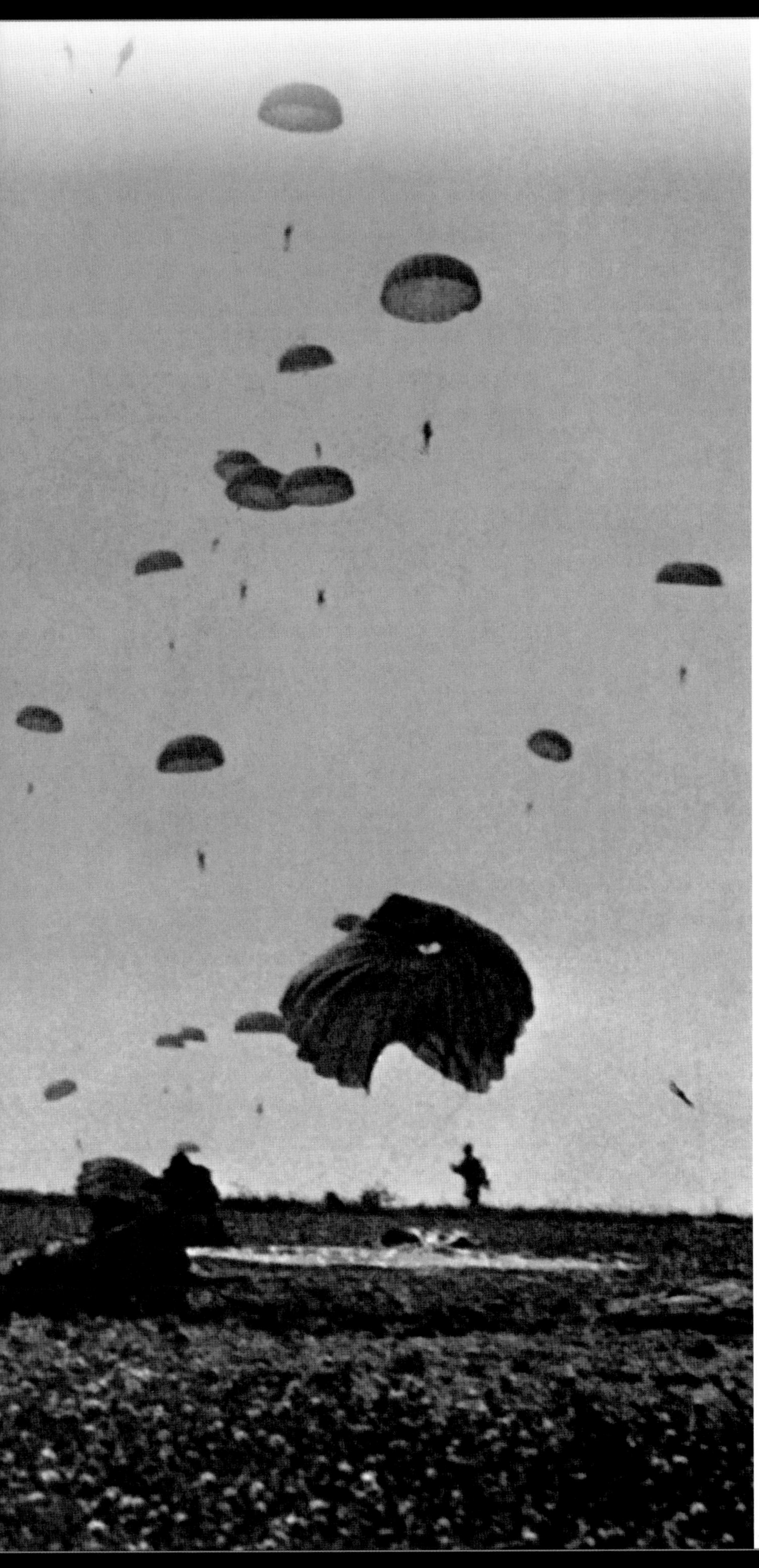

In the early hours of June 6, 1944, an Allied invasion of Europe began that would change the course of the war, heralding the beginning of the end for Nazi Germany.

One of the most monumental undertakings in military history—let alone World War II—Operation Overlord, for all its scale, was in fact a slave to Mother Nature. Following a series of delays due to adverse weather conditions, the go-ahead was finally given for Operation Overlord to commence in the first week of June 1944. As midnight approached on the night of June 5, airfields across Southern England erupted in an explosion of noise as three airborne divisions (the British 6th and US 82nd and 101st) took to the skies in 1,200 aircraft and made for France. D-Day was underway.

Overlord was to be an assault aided by aerial and naval support. At around midnight on June 5, an airborne armada of over 2,000 American, Canadian, and British planes began bombing hundreds of targets along the German coast, aiming their payloads at targets including pillboxes and radar installations. They benefitted greatly from the Allies' aerial dominance, as the bulk of the *Luftwaffe* had been summoned back to Germany to defend the Third Reich against relentless bombing sprees. It was hoped that this nighttime blitz would soften up the ground for the paratroopers tasked with landing in France. These brave men were due to parachute in during the early hours (prior to the seaborne assault, code-named Operation Neptune), with the aim of capturing strategically vital bridges and causeways along the River Orne and to the north of the town of Carentan.

The ground was heavily flooded in places—a deliberate effort by the Germans to inhibit such an invasion—and many Allied paratroopers drowned beneath the weight of their own equipment. However, if the bridges could be seized then the inevitable German counterattacks would be stymied. That would buy some time for the troops landing on the beaches to secure a foothold, and would enable the paratroopers to move inland and secure nearby towns and villages.

Landing in pitch blackness, the first troops to touch down in Normandy hailed from D Company of the 2nd Battalion, Oxfordshire and Buckinghamshire Light Infantry. Sporting blackened faces and an array of rifles and sub-machine guns, these paratroopers had been transported across the Channel in six Horsa gliders with the intent of snatching bridges on the River Orne and the Caen Canal. They would experience a mixed reception.

A HEARSE ABOVE THE CLOUDS

Despite not having weapons or engines, gliders played a vital role in the successful Allied invasion of northern France.

Eight American paratroopers lie dead next to the wreckage of a glider that either fell victim to German flak fire or smashed into the ground as its pilots attempted to land.

Known as "flying coffins" by the men who boarded them, gliders were used throughout WWII when stealth was required. Coming in a range of shapes and sizes, well-known models included the American Waco GC-4A and the British Horsa, the latter of which was capable of transporting small vehicles or up to 25 troops. Over 3,600 Horsas were manufactured during the war, each one had a 88-foot (27-meter) wingspan, weighing over 8,000 pounds (3,600 kilograms) when empty and piloted by a crew of two.

Almost 400 British gliders saw action on D-Day, including both the Horsa and the heavier Hamilcar, which was built to deliver a tank of up to 40 troops. Due to the lack of parachutes on board, glider pilots faced a foreboding task: land safely or die trying—there was no plan B.

Once the towing lines attached to the motorized planes guiding them were released, the courageous men at the helm of the gliders that slipped through the night sky on June 6 had to guide their planes down onto enemy territory. Over 100 of them were either killed or seriously injured by enemy flak guns or when their gliders (made from wood and fabric) broke apart upon landing.

Despite their faults, gliders enabled Allied troops to silently infiltrate hostile territory. Those that landed unscathed could sabotage or secure key objectives in the race to establish a firm holding in Normandy before the Nazis' panzer divisions could be unleashed. Without these flimsy winged wonders, the Germans would have had far more warning of the imminent invasion, time they would no doubt have used to destroy the bridges the Allies planned to seize.

Allied bombers head for home after a bombing raid in support of the D-Day invasions.

Touching down, or in some cases thumping down so hard that the glider splintered on impact, those tasked with racing across the canal met ferocious machine gun fire before successfully claiming the bridge. Their comrades dashing to do the same on the River Orne moved so swiftly that they took their target before any defenders could land a shot. The codewords that would notify their superiors of their triumph—"ham" and "jam"—were beamed into the night just an hour and a half after the first planes had taken off from RAF Tarrant Rushton in Dorset.

The sight of paratroopers descending en masse across Normandy sent many German troops into a state of utter confusion. Some were convinced this was merely a diversion to draw their gaze away from a main Allied thrust at Pas-de-Calais, while others were certain they were already facing a full-scale assault. This wave of panic was compounded by Operation Titanic, a crafty SAS maneuver that saw the Allies drop hundreds of dummy paratroopers onto Normandy that were primed to explode. The invasion force of detonating dupes managed to persuade the Wehrmacht to relocate forces in several locations before realising they had been tricked. Unfortunately for them, the Allies' ploys were far from over.

A Marauder bomber behind German lines.

Operation Bodyguard—a vast effort to trick the Germans at every opportunity—included a series of smaller operations to try and turn German radar technology against itself. The aim was to make radar operators believe that enormous Allied fleets were sailing for destinations further along the French coast.

Desperate to conceal their intentions, the Allies had worked tirelessly for months creating a variety of dummy armies, tanks, and bases that would keep the enemy guessing. A number of deceptive operations took place on June 5 and 6, one of which was Operation Taxable.

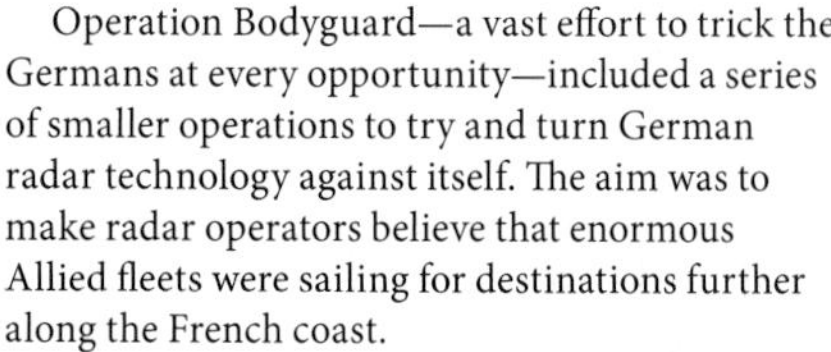

Involving 18 boats, and Lancaster bombers from 617 Air Squadron, Operation Taxable saw the small boats making for Cap-d'Antifer (east of the real landing sites) while the Bombers dispersed tin foil strips (known as "chaff") in the sky above them. These efforts combined to create the mirage of a sizable fleet on German radar. Even so, this deception failed to provoke the Germans into either an attack or any significant troop redeployments. The only lasting impact of the mission was the deployment of mines that the boats laid before heading home.

A similar campaign, code-named Operation Glimmer, was conducted by 218 Squadron. Six Short Stirling planes worked in unison with a seaborne unit known as Special Task Force B to drop chaff, launch radar-reflecting balloons, and operate radar-jamming equipment while en route towards Pas-de-Calais. This gave the impression that the Allies were taking the fastest route from England to France, and the ruse triggered a German response in the form of reconnaissance planes taking to the skies to examine the apparent "threat," and German radio operators alerting headquarters to an invasion fleet.

Although neither operation seemed to completely convince the stretched German forces stationed in Normandy, they did contribute to a growing air of puzzlement that bought crucial

USS Arkansas fires on German positions during the opening phase of D-Day.

Battleship USS Nevada during the naval bombardment of the beaches of Normandy.

time in numerous positions. In such a dangerous theater, every sliver of extra time could prove to be the difference between success and failure, life and death. In fact, the confusion spread by the Allies' precise planning resulted in the German 15th Army remaining in Calais. Their deadly panzer divisions—which could have helped achieve Hitler's aim of driving the invaders into the sea—were also kept out of the fray until it was too late.

As these deception operations played out with varying levels of success, the battle on land grew in intensity. Aside from several vital bridges, a monstrous German gun battery at Merville also had to be conquered. If it were left in enemy hands, it would unleash hell on both the Allied fleet and landing boats. Only a quarter of the 6th Division charged with taking out this emplacement had been dropped in the correct locations, but the assault went ahead regardless. A brave band of men under the leadership of Colonel Terence Otway overcame a lack of heavy weaponry (it hadn't been dropped on time) to overwhelm the guns and destroy them as 6 a.m. loomed.

The airborne divisions dotted throughout Normandy began to shoot their way inland, having managed to fend off several German counterattacks and hold their ground, often helped by reinforcements. Meanwhile, the 4,000 ships of the Allied fleet primed their guns for an almighty barrage. The fleet had transported the landing troops across the English Channel, a journey D-Day planners had feared would be scuppered by German U-boats. Having safely reached the coast of France, its contingent of gunships—including 68 destroyers and leviathans such as USS Arkansas, Nevada, and Warspite—prepared to bombard the Germans' coastal defenses prior to the advance of Allied landing boats.

With the morning fog lifting, the Germans were met with the sight of the imposing gunships now setting their turrets on them. A shuddering roar signaled the beginning of a barrage that saw an astonishing 600 guns fire around 2,000 tons worth of shells at German positions, both along and behind the beaches on which Allied troops were due to be deployed.

According to one member of the pressed infantry ranks who bore witness to this ear-splitting attack, "you could feel the ground shaking." One radio operator is said to have exclaimed that the ships were "firing jeeps." It would therefore be easy to assume (and many crouching in the landing boats and stalking the decks of gunships must have done so) that a bombardment on this scale would leave nothing but rubble in its wake. However, to the misfortune of the men about to storm the beaches targeted by the fleet, the Allied shells had made little physical impact.

Famed for its engineering prowess, the German army had erected a series of almost impenetrable concrete pillboxes along the coast of France following the nation's surrender in 1940. Their ingenious construction now paid dividends as direct hits thumped into their exterior walls to no avail, save for carving out a few dents. Deafened but by no means defeated, these imposing fortresses would soon be raining fire down on the sands below.

Eventually the naval barrage subsided and the loaded landing crafts started their engines. Nothing more could now be done from air or sea—it was time for Operation Neptune. Wave upon wave of LCVP boats began their steady journey towards the churned up sands of Normandy, each boat brimming with nervous soldiers about to charge into a hail of bullets and a place in history.

"THE SIGHT OF PARATROOPERS DESCENDING EN MASSE ACROSS NORMANDY SENT MANY GERMAN TROOPS INTO A STATE OF UTTER CONFUSION."

B-26 MA

Only 17 percent of B-26s were lost in battle, the lowest ratio of any Allied plane during the war.

MARTIN B-26G MARAUDER

ROLE: **HIGH-PERFORMANCE TWIN-ENGINE MEDIUM BOMBER**
NATIONS SERVED: **USA, UK, SOUTH AFRICA, FRANCE**
LENGTH: **58.3 FT (17.7 M)**
WINGSPAN: **71 FT (21 M)**
MAXIMUM SPEED: **285 MPH (458 KM/H)**
MAXIMUM ALTITUDE: **19,800 FT (6,035 M)**
RANGE: **1,100 MILES (1,770 KILOMETERS)**
CREW: **6/7 MEN**
ENGINES: **2 x 1,930HP PRATT AND WHITNEY R-2800-43**
ARMAMENT: **11 x .50-CALIBER BROWNING MACHINE GUNS**
BOMB LOAD: **4,000 LB (1,814 KILOGRAMS)**

"After some modifications and extra pilot training, the B-26 began to realize its potential as a bomber that could turn the tide of the war."

RAUDER

BY JACK GRIFFITHS

B-26 bomber nicknamed "A Kay Pea's Dream," which was later hit by flak during a raid over France.

Image source: U.S Federal Governement Archive. Public Domain

Nicknamed the "Flying Torpedo," this US Army Air Force war bird played a vital role during Operation Overlord.

Coming in almost 20 variants, the B-26 was the workhorse of the United States Army Air Force (USAAF) bombing operations of World War II. First introduced in 1941, 201 Marauders were ordered straight off the drawing board with no time to build and test a prototype.

Part of President Roosevelt's 50,000 aircraft for US defense program, it went on to serve in both the Pacific and European Theaters of the war, and was responsible for striking a variety of targets in the run-up to D-Day.

An innovative cantilever shoulder wing monoplane design, the aircraft began unimpressively as it recorded a number of training accidents with 15 crashing in 30 days, earning it the nicknames "Widow Maker" and "Martin Murderer."

The design put cruise efficiency ahead of handling at low speeds, so many crews initially stayed well away from the aircraft. However, after some modifications and extra pilot training, the B-26 began to realize its potential as a bomber that could turn the tide of the war.

Used for tactical air support, 5,157 B-26s were constructed, with the RAF also purchasing 522. It was most effective in the European Theater, operating in medium-altitude attacks in Normandy and the invasion of Italy. B-26s also saw service in the Battle of Midway in the Pacific Theater. As the war ended, the role of the Marauder was fast diminishing. The majority were retired from service by 1947, and only a handful remain in existence today as relics of the mass World War II bombing operations.

From the B model onwards, the B-26 became the first aircraft of the war to use powered weapons pods.

In early models, the gunner had to lie prone, but in later B-26s, the crew could sit in an upright position.

In addition to the larger guns, .30-inch machine guns were installed on the front and rear transparent nose cones.

ARMAMENT

The B-26 boasted some serious weaponry. 11 .50-inch machine guns provided an immense amount of firepower with four guns on the fuselage sides, one in the nose, two in the dorsal and tail area, and two in ventral positions. These turrets were the first of their kind and rotated on large ball bearings. Experienced gunners could turn 360 degrees and create a diagonal swathe of fire to shoot Axis fighters out of the sky.

As well as the main armament, some B-26s included several smaller .30-inch machine guns, which were dotted around the fuselage. These guns acted in a defensive capacity and would protect the aircraft from enemy fighters and anti-aircraft positions when on bombing runs. The rear gun was invaluable as it helped take down Messerschmitts, Zeros, and any other Axis planes on the bomber's tail. However, the B-26's main feature was its bombs. It had two bomb bays, one in the fore and one in the aft. Up to 4,000 pounds (1,814 kilograms) could be carried for devastating strike sorties.

PROPULSION

To carry the weighty payload, the B-26 used two four-bladed propellers. It was the first Allied aircraft built in World War II to use four blades in its propulsion system and could generate up to 1,930 horsepower. The Pratt and Whitney R-2800-43 wasn't limited to the Marauder, and was also used on other US aircraft such as the F4U Corsair, F6F Hellcat, and P47 Thunderbolt fighters. The 18-cylinder engine was incredibly versatile and was used in planes in the Korean War as well as World War II.

The undercarriage of the B-26 was unique in its design. Using a tricycle shape, it incorporated a nose wheel rather than the traditional tail wheel. It had a landing speed of 130 miles per hour (209 kilometers per hour), unusually high for a plane of the era, and remained an effective, if unorthodox, control system for a medium bomber. The design of the B-26 was altered in development and it originally featured a twin tail, but this was dropped in favor of a single fin to give the tail gunner a better view of oncoming targets.

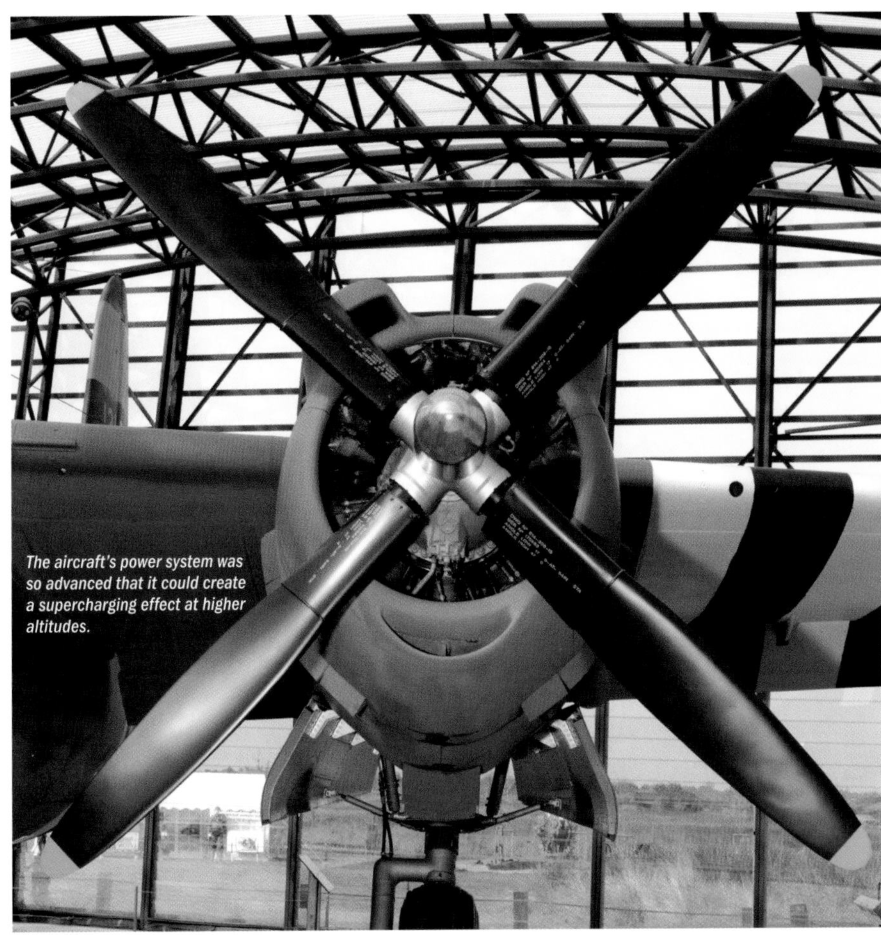

The aircraft's power system was so advanced that it could create a supercharging effect at higher altitudes.

The bombs painted under the cockpit indicate how many missions the plane had flown.

THE B-26 OF THE UTAH BEACH MUSEUM

Having been at the museum since 2011, the Marauder is a popular exhibition and one of only six left in existence

The Marauder on display at the Utah Beach Museum in Normandy arrived in France on May 20, 1945. It was put into service too late to fly in any combat missions and it resided in the French base at Mont-de-Marsan, just south of Bordeaux. After the war, it was painted in French Army colors and given to Air France, who used the aircraft to train future mechanics. It was later donated to the French Air and Space Museum in 1967 and locked away in storage for 25 years. However, in 1993, it resurfaced as technicians tasked with refurbishing the plane found that numerous pieces of original equipment were missing. A restoration team managed to locate the missing parts as the B-26 neared its original condition. In 2011, the plane was moved to the Utah Beach Museum and repainted in the colors of the 386th Bomb Group, who served with distinction on D-Day. For more information on the museum and its work, please visit: www.utah-beach.com

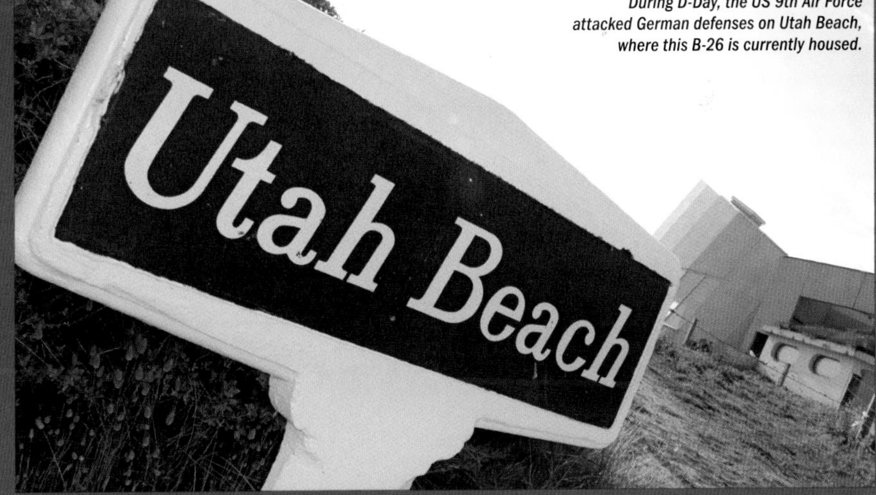

During D-Day, the US 9th Air Force attacked German defenses on Utah Beach, where this B-26 is currently housed.

"THE REAR GUN WAS INVALUABLE AS IT HELPED TAKE DOWN MESSERSCHMITTS, ZEROS, AND ANY OTHER AXIS PLANES ON THE BOMBER'S TAIL."

Above: Based on practicality rather than comfort, the cockpit wasn't big on crew luxuries.

COCKPIT

The armor-plated cockpit of the B-26 was operated by a pilot and a co-pilot. A center console stood at the front, which included the throttle as well as propeller and mixture controls. The controls for the landing gear and flaps were at the back of the console. Notoriously tricky to handle for many pilots, many had no experience of twin-engine aircraft prior to the B-26. The weight of the Marauder also made the stalling speed and landing speeds higher than the majority of other planes in the US Military. The early issues with the B-26 were down to its rushed production, as it was overloaded with equipment and put into low-level attack missions, something it was completely ill-equipped to undertake.

The crew of a Marauder comprised a pilot, co-pilot, bombardier, radio operator, navigator, dorsal gunner, and tail gunner.

BOMBERS OF THE USAAF

The other aircraft that the USA used to bomb Germany and Japan into submission.

B-25 MITCHELL

The Mitchell was once the most heavily armed plane in the world. It participated in the 1942 Tokyo Raid, the first Allied attack to strike the Japanese home islands.

B-24 LIBERATOR

The most produced US aircraft of the war, an astonishing 18,400 were made. The Liberator served all over the world utilizing its range of more than 2,000 miles.

DOUGLAS A-26 INVADER

Also sometimes called a B-26 but not to be confused with the Marauder, the A-26 was a versatile and long-serving aircraft. It served in the Korean and Vietnam wars.

B-17 FLYING FORTRESS

As the name suggests, the B-17 was a giant of the sky. Many were based in the UK and deployed to Germany to take part in relentless daylight bombing raids.

Image source: U.S Library of Congress's Prints and Photographs division ID fsac.1a35397. Public Domain

a

a,b,c Image source: U.S Federal Governement Archive. Public Domain

b

c

Image source: U.S Federal Governement Archive. Public Domain

The design was put forward by Peyton M. Magruder of the Glenn L. Martin Company, but was a work in progress for the first few years of its life.

CONSTRUCTION

It may have been rushed off the production line, but the B-26 was a sophisticated war machine. Entering, and subsequently winning, a competition for a new US medium bomber in 1939, one of the major differences between it and its predecessors was the use of plastic. Before the Marauder, military aircraft were made mostly out of metal, but the B-26 changed this by using cheap and readily available plastic. It also used butted seams rather than lapped seams in its covering, making the fuselage more streamlined, earning it the "torpedo" nickname.

The Marauder carried so much equipment that it couldn't sustain much flak before getting in trouble. This made it ineffective at low-level attack missions, meaning it was soon changed to a medium-level bomber to make it more durable in combat. The original models also suffered from problems with the landing gear, but these were corrected by a heat-treatment process that improved the hydraulic system.

"BEFORE THE MARAUDER, MILITARY AIRCRAFT WERE MADE MOSTLY OUT OF METAL, BUT THE B-26 CHANGED THIS BY USING CHEAP AND READILY AVAILABLE PLASTIC."

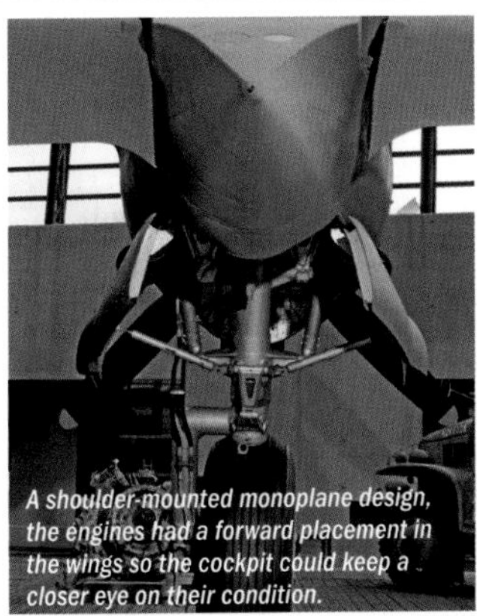

A shoulder-mounted monoplane design, the engines had a forward placement in the wings so the cockpit could keep a closer eye on their condition.

A small wing area helped give the B-26 a formidable top speed of 285 mph (458 km/h).

THE AMERIKA BOMBER PROJECT

During the latter stages of the war, a long-range bomber was sought after by the Axis powers. With the added resources and manpower from the USA bolstering Britain and the USSR, attacks on the American mainland could stunt Allied wartime production significantly. The "Amerika Bomber" and "Project Z" programs were put forward by Nazi Germany and Imperial Japan respectively. The Germans prototyped the Messerschmitt Me 264 for strikes on New York from continental Europe in December 1942. Heavily armored and fitted with a turbocharged engine, it would have been very similar to the USAAF B-29 Superfortress. The proposal could have feasibly worked, but constant Allied bombing and a lack of raw materials in the Third Reich dashed hopes of a transatlantic attack. As for Project Z, the Japanese simply did not have the engine power to make a realistic effort at attacking the USA. The Ha-44 engine was the most powerful available at the time, but it would have suffered cooling problems trying to lift a bomber capable of sustained attacks on American soil.

Only three ME 264s were built before the German project was abandoned.

Moments before leaping into the dark skies above Normandy on D-Day, American paratroopers make final preparations aboard their transport.

PERILOUS AIRBORNE INSERTION

Three Allied airborne divisions, inserted by parachute and glider, were tasked with seizing key objectives and holding until relieved in the predawn hours of D-Day.

BY MIKE HASKEW

From airfields across Britain, hundreds of transport planes stretched into the skies and turned for the coast of France in the predawn hours of June 6, 1944. They carried nearly 20,000 airborne troops, the vanguard of the Allied invasion of Nazi-occupied Western Europe. While Operation Overlord was fraught with risk on land, sea, and air, its airborne element was perhaps the most perilous of all. Prior to D-Day, Air Marshal Trafford Leigh-Mallory, commanding Overlord air operations, was so concerned that he recommended in writing to Supreme Commander Dwight Eisenhower that the airborne element be scrapped. He warned that half the planes and 70 percent of the gliders could be lost with intolerable casualties.

Nevertheless, Eisenhower decided the airborne phase of Overlord was worth it. The insertion of paratroopers and glider troops in the enemy rear would disrupt the German response to the landings on the five Normandy beaches. The airborne forces would seize key objectives, facilitate the movement of ground forces inland, silence enemy gun emplacements, and capture or blow up bridges.

Eisenhower was keenly aware that earlier airborne operations during the 1943 Sicily invasion had been costly due to friendly fire and weather conditions resulting in losses of aircraft and scattering of men across great distances. Still, the three Overlord airborne divisions, the American 82nd and 101st and British 6th, had trained for just such a moment as the tip of the Allied spear.

During the narrow window of favorable weather allowing the invasion to proceed, high winds were sure to buffet the planes. German flak would be heavy. The enemy had flooded lowlands, anticipating airborne soldiers coming to earth laden with gear and drowning. Fields were laced with obstacles to tear wings off gliders. To compound the worries, though, elements of the 82nd had fought in Sicily, the 6th and 101st had never fired a shot in anger. Their combat baptism would occur in Normandy.

Immediate objectives of the D-Day airborne insertion were ambitious. The 6th Airborne, commanded by General Richard N. Gale, was to support British and Canadian landings at Gold, Juno, and Sword beaches, anchor the invasion's left flank, and control 24 square miles (62 square kilometers) of territory. Among other objectives, the paras and glider men were to capture bridges across the River Orne and Caen Canal, holding them until a linkup with ground troops was established, silence a battery of 100-mm guns threatening Sword Beach at Merville, and destroy five bridges across the River Dives to prevent German counterattacks.

The American divisions were to secure the invasion's right flank, supporting inland progress from Utah and Omaha beaches. The 82nd, under General Matthew Ridgway, was to parachute astride the River Merderet, capture the coastal town of Sainte-Mère-Église, secure the area between the village and the English Channel, establish a defensive line with crossings of the Merderet, and link up with the 101st. General Maxwell Taylor's 101st was to support the US 4th Infantry Division's drive from Utah Beach, seizing four exits from narrow causeways that rose above a flooded, marshy area behind Utah, stretching into the valley of the River Douve and the Merderet. The 101st was also ordered to destroy a battery of 122-mm guns that menaced Utah Beach at Saint-Martin-de-Varreville, capture the La Barquette lock on the River Douve, blow up

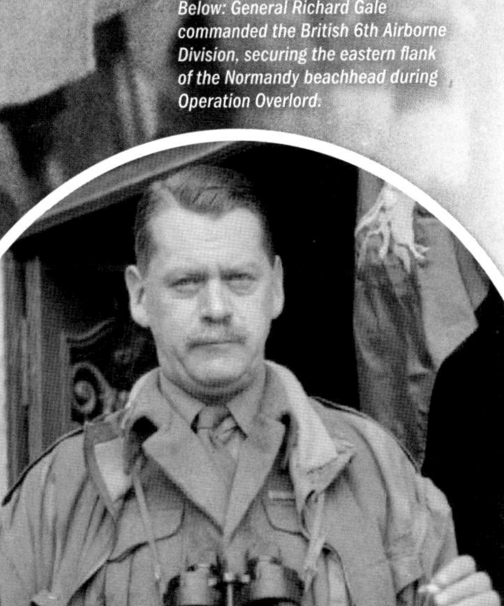

Below: General Richard Gale commanded the British 6th Airborne Division, securing the eastern flank of the Normandy beachhead during Operation Overlord.

EISENHOWER VISITS THE 101ST

Troops in good spirits as the supreme commander of the Allied expeditionary force comes to visit prior to their insertion.

General Dwight Eisenhower talks with paratroopers of the US 101st Airborne Division just before their departure for Normandy.

On the eve of their deployment to France, paratroopers of the 502nd PIR, 101st Airborne Division, received a distinguished visitor at Greenham Common airfield. General Dwight Eisenhower, supreme commander Allied expeditionary force, had come to wish them well. With the burden of command weighing heavily on his shoulders, Eisenhower grinned and greeted the men, moving easily and with confidence among them. He asked one of them, whose face was blackened with camouflage, where he was from.

"Michigan!" the trooper chimed. "Oh yes! Michigan," the general grinned. "Great fishing there—been there several times and like it!"

Eisenhower worried mightily about the paratroopers, and the rest of the invasion host as well. Years later, in his memoir *Crusade in Europe*, he wrote of the airborne encounter: "I found the men in fine fettle, many of them joshingly admonishing me that I had no cause for worry, since the 101st was on the job, and everything would be taken care of in fine shape. I stayed with them until the last of them were in the air, somewhere about midnight. After a two-hour trip back to my own camp, I had only a short time to wait until the first news should come in."

A photographer documented Eisenhower's visit, producing several memorable images of the D-Day epic. Interestingly, the supreme commander had intended to visit a unit of the 82nd Airborne Division, but Generals Matthew Ridgway and James Gavin asked him to stay away, fearing his appearance would be a distraction.

Left: British paras of the 6th Airborne Division synchronize their watches prior to jumping into Normandy on D-Day.

bridges around Carentan and Saint-Côme-du-Mont, establish a defensive perimeter, and ultimately link up with the 4th Division.

High winds and German anti-aircraft fire assailed the aircraft pressing toward drop and landing zones in darkness on June 6, 1944. Some gliders snapped towlines, plunging into the sea. Transport planes were blown off course, and inexperienced pilots confronted with flak took evasive action, scattering paratroopers across miles of Norman countryside. About 40 percent of the 6th Airborne actually came down in its assigned areas. In many cases, the Americans were widely dispersed. Two entire sticks of paratroopers from Company A, 502nd Parachute Infantry Regiment (PIR), 101st were dropped into the Channel and drowned. General Don F. Pratt, assistant 101st commander, was killed when his glider crashed. General James M. Gavin, commanding the 508th PIR, came down in an apple orchard and was lost for over an hour.

Groping in darkness, men of the 101st "click-clacked" dime-store cricket toys for recognition. The 82nd opted for the call of "Flash" and response of "Thunder" as the 6th used "Ham" and "Jam." To the west, American units sometimes became intermingled. Officers collected clutches of troopers and set off. The Germans were taken by surprise. Reports of airborne insertions filtered through command posts. Around 2 a.m., a transport flew low over Saint-Floxel, disgorging 101st troopers on top of the headquarters of the German 709th Infantry Division, where they quickly engaged in a firefight with sentries.

Amid the unfolding chaos, a remarkable feat of airmanship occurred at the bridge over the Orne and the Bénouville Bridge across the Caen Canal. Just after midnight, Sergeant Jim Wallwork brought his glider to a stop 150 feet (46 meters) from the canal bridge. Other gliders executed similar accurate landings. Immediately, Lieutenant Den Brotheridge led 30 men of 1st Platoon, 2nd Oxfordshire, and Buckinghamshire Light Infantry in the rush to capture the span. Brotheridge was shot in the neck and later died, the first Allied casualty to enemy fire on D-Day. The bridge over the Orne was also taken, and within hours reinforcements from Lieutenant Colonel Richard Pine-Coffin's 7th Parachute

Vehicles cross Pegasus Bridge after its capture by British airborne troops in the predawn hours of D-Day.

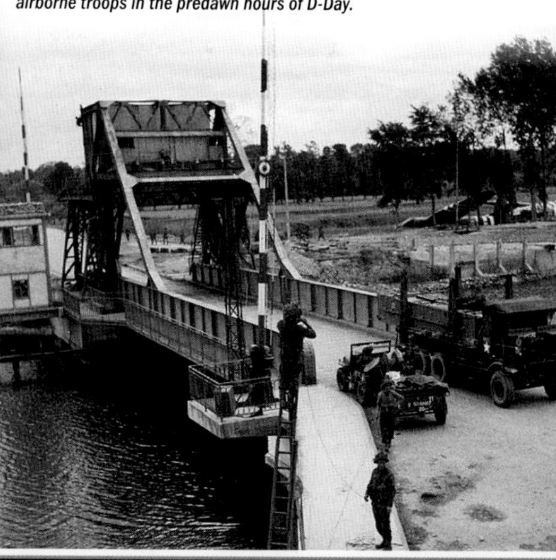

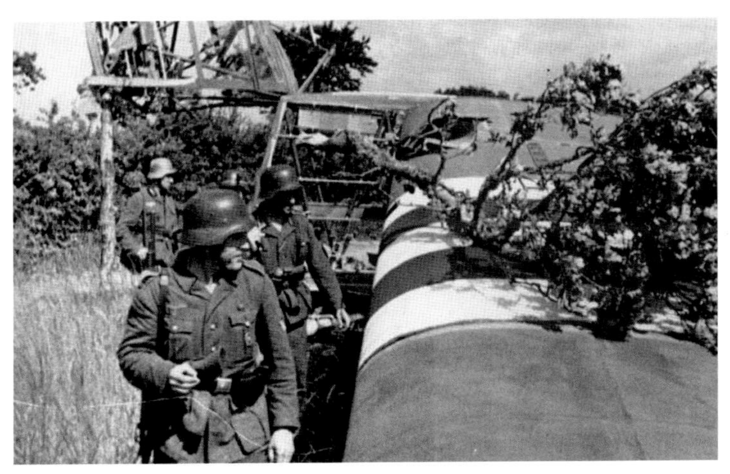

Above: German soldiers inspect the wreckage of a Waco glider after it has delivered its human cargo on D-Day, June 6, 1944.

Above: Paras of the 6th Airborne Division listen during a briefing for Operation Tonga, the British phase of the D-Day airborne insertion.

Battalion arrived. The lightly armed paras withstood numerous German counterattacks until relieved after 1 p.m. by Lord Lovat's 1st Special Service Brigade advancing from Sword Beach. After D-Day, the Bénouville Bridge was renamed Pegasus Bridge, referencing the British airborne emblem and the heroism of Brotheridge's command.

When Lieutenant Colonel Terence Otway, commanding the 9th Battalion, 3rd Brigade, the Parachute Regiment, was informed that silencing the Merville Battery was his unit's D-Day mission, brigade commander Brigadier James "Speedy" Hill called it a "Grade-A stinker of a job." A garrison of 160 German soldiers defended the concrete casemates. Two sides were flanked by 10-foot-deep anti-tank ditches, and long spirals of barbed wire encircled the entire battery. At least 15 machine gun and small-arms positions confronted any would-be attackers.

Otway's command was badly scattered. Assembling only 150 of his 600-man battalion, he led the force into action. About 4:15 a.m., he growled, "Everybody in! We're going to take this bloody battery!" Surprise and audacity compensated for lack of numbers. Within 20 minutes, the Merville Battery was in British hands. The price was high; half the men in the assault lay dead. Elsewhere, the bridges across the Dives were destroyed as planned.

"SURPRISE AND AUDACITY COMPENSATED FOR LACK OF NUMBERS. WITHIN 20 MINUTES, THE MERVILLE BATTERY WAS IN BRITISH HANDS. THE PRICE WAS HIGH; HALF THE MEN IN THE ASSAULT LAY DEAD."

After D-Day, the 6th Airborne remained at the front for 82 days, long beyond its intended duration, sustaining 542 killed and nearly 2,400 wounded and missing in Normandy.

Elements of the 82nd Airborne ran into stiff resistance attempting to establish crossings of the Merderet at La Fière and elsewhere. Lieutenant Colonel Edward "Cannonball" Krause led 108 men of the 505th PIR, about one-quarter of its strength, in the swift capture of Sainte-Mère-Église. The main road from Carentan to the port of Cherbourg was cut, but one platoon was set upon by Germans outnumbering them five to one. The Americans fended off attacks for eight hours, only 16 of their 42 men emerging unscathed. By midnight, the 82nd had a toehold across the Dives at Chef-du-Pont and a tenuous link with the 4th Division while holding Sainte-Mère-Église against fierce German counterattacks.

Lieutenant Colonel Robert G. Cole, commander of the 502nd PIR, 101st, discovered that the Soviet-made guns he was to destroy had been removed. Advancing to Causeway 3, his ad hoc force of 101st and 82nd men found the exit undefended. They linked up with the advancing 4th Infantry Division at 1 p.m. At about noon, 40 paratroopers under Lieutenant Colonel Julian Ewell took the Causeway 1 exit, losing 18 men in a brawl with 70 Germans of the 91st Airlanding Division. Airborne troops reached the Causeway 2 exit after elements of the 4th Infantry Division had already crossed.

When Lieutenant Colonel Patrick Cassidy, 1st Battalion, 502nd PIR, determined that causeway exits 3 and 4 were secure, he turned toward a cluster of buildings, ordering Sergeant Harrison Summers to lead a squad in clearing them. With others reluctant to follow, Summers dashed forward alone, killing 36 Germans. Other paratroopers completed the rout. About 150 troopers of the 501st and 506th PIR seized the La Barquette lock and fought off heavy counterattacks.

Perhaps the most famous American airborne action on D-Day occurred when Lieutenant Richard Winters led a dozen men of Company E, 2nd Battalion, 506th PIR, in silencing a battery of four German 105-mm guns firing toward Utah Beach from the farmstead of Brécourt Manor. The assault is remembered as a textbook example of small unit action, recounted in detail in Stephen Ambrose's book *Band of Brothers*. The American airborne divisions suffered nearly 2,500 killed, wounded, and missing on D-Day. Like their British counterparts, they spent weeks in the line prior to withdrawal to Britain.

The airborne contribution to the success of Operation Overlord was significant. Most objectives slated for D-Day were achieved, and the flanks of the invasion beaches were secured. Despite stiff resistance, casualties were far below pre-invasion estimates. The calculated risk had paid off.

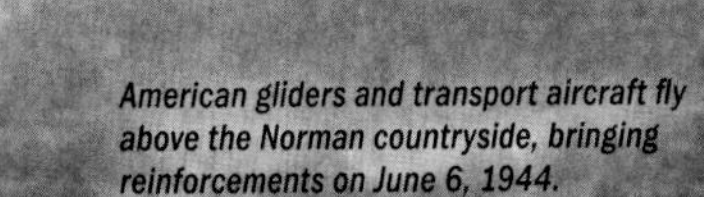

American gliders and transport aircraft fly above the Norman countryside, bringing reinforcements on June 6, 1944.

American troops of the 1st Infantry Division enter the water under fire at Omaha Beach on D-Day.

HITTING THE BEACHES

On the morning of June 6, 1944, Allied troops came ashore in Normandy, battling German resistance to initiate the ground campaign of Operation Overlord.

BY MIKE HASKEW

The skies were overcast and the English Channel waters were rough. Although weather conditions were less than ideal, an Allied armada, poised for hours with troops packed aboard transports, turned for its rendezvous points off the coast of Normandy.

The Allies had not attempted to secure a permanent lodgment in northwest Europe since their disastrous defeat four years earlier. However, on June 6, 1944, the might of Operation Overlord, the carefully planned and orchestrated invasion of Normandy, was underway. It was time to test Hitler's boast that the fortifications he had erected from Scandinavia to the Spanish frontier—the vaunted Atlantic Wall—were impregnable, manned by thousands of soldiers plus studded with artillery, machine-gun emplacements, and concrete bunkers. Many of these were designated "Widerstandsnests" (WN), or "resistance nests." Although some defenses were incomplete, the Germans had sown countless landmines and erected beach obstacles that were either topped with mines or designed to rip open landing craft hulls.

Just after daylight, more than 150,000 British, American, Canadian, and French soldiers were going to discover whether Hitler's assertion was justified. Bombers delivered payloads and warships pounded targets on shore, while aircraft carrying airborne and glider troops droned overhead.

World War II was in its sixth year, and the outcome of the conflict hinged largely on the success or failure of this single day, D-Day. Planning and preparation had been underway for months. Along with the three airborne divisions deploying on June 6, five infantry divisions would hit German-held beaches along 50 miles (80 kilometers) of French coastline in Normandy. Their objectives were ambitious, and the risks were incalculable. Success meant the Third Reich's days were numbered, but failure meant an uncertain future, potentially the ruin of Allied hopes for ultimate victory.

The first waves of Allied troops of the American First Army, under General Omar Bradley, and the British Second Army, under General Miles Dempsey, were slated to come ashore beginning at 6:30 a.m. on beaches codenamed (from east to west) Sword, Juno, Gold, Omaha, and Utah. Aboard a transport headed for Juno Beach, the Canadian Broadcasting Company (CBC) reported that a breakfast of scrambled eggs, bacon, coffee, bread, and jam was served at about 3:30 a.m. Across the invasion fleet of nearly 7,000 ships, similar activities were underway. The soldiers, heavily laden with equipment, would shortly climb down cargo nets into landing craft, circling as forces were marshaled, and then head towards the beaches, where smoke was rising amid the din of battle.

Overlord's amphibious operations began on the American beaches, Utah, and Omaha. The western-most, Utah, three miles (five kilometers) long and divided into three sectors—Tare Green, Uncle Red, and Victor—had been a late addition to the offensive because of its proximity to the deepwater port of Cherbourg, possession of which could facilitate future operations. The first Allied soldiers to come ashore were men of the US 8th Infantry Regiment, 4th Division, commanded by Colonel James Van Fleet, set to land near the village of Les Dunes de Varreville. When three of four Navy patrol boats guiding the first wave struck mines and sank, the 20 landing craft approaching Utah drifted 5,900 feet (1,800 meters) east of their intended landing zone, coming ashore in lightly defended Victor sector. When Van Fleet realized the error, he conferred with Brigadier General Theodore Roosevelt, Jr., assistant division commander, and the two decided to "start the war from here!"

Elements of three German divisions, the 91st Airlanding, 243rd and 709th, defended Utah Beach, but the misdirection worked in the Americans' favor. The 4th Division was tasked with capturing four narrow causeways that bridged a flooded, marshy area just off the beach, linking up with airborne troops that were to secure the causeway exits inland, taking control of coastal roads near the towns of Carentan and Sainte-Mère-Église, and preparing for a concerted attack on Cherbourg.

Resistance was sporadic as the Americans encountered some small-arms fire from beachfront houses, but moved rapidly inland after neutralizing German strongpoints WN7 near La Madeleine, WN5 at La Grande Dune, WN4 about 2,000 feet (640 meters) off the beach, and after a brief fight, WN3 at Beau Guillot. They captured three of the four causeways by late morning and made contact with paratroopers of the 101st Airborne Division around Pouppeville at noon. By the end of June 6, about 23,000 troops of the 4th Division were ashore. They had pushed inland 3.7 miles (six kilometers) and were only a mile from Sainte-Mère-Église, where elements of the 82nd Airborne Division awaited relief. The assault at Utah Beach was a resounding success. Casualties were few, with less than 300 troops being killed or wounded.

"IT WAS TIME TO TEST HITLER'S BOAST THAT . . . THE ATLANTIC WALL . . . [WAS] IMPREGNABLE."

Elsewhere, though, the Americans found the going extremely rough. Omaha Beach was the longest stretch of Normandy coastline assaulted on D-Day. Much of its six miles (10 kilometers) was heavily defended by three battalions of the crack German 352nd Infantry Division. A sea wall about 10 feet (three meters) high covered a third of the invasion area while towering cliffs provided strong defensive positions. Omaha Beach extended from the mouth of the River Vire on its western edge to Port-en-Bessin in the east, and five exits led from the shoreline into the towns of Saint-Laurent-sur-Mer, Colleville-sur-Mer, and Vierville-sur-Mer. The assault troops were to capture the coastal towns; push across the Bayeux-Isigny road; advance south and west towards the village of Isigny and Pointe du Hoc, where Rangers had been tasked with eliminating a German gun position; then finally make contact eastward with the British 50th Division advancing from Gold Beach.

The assault at Omaha Beach was assigned to the 1st Infantry Division and the attached 116th Regiment, 29th Infantry Division. The Americans divided Omaha into three zones with corresponding subsectors from east to west, including Fox (Green and Red sectors), Easy (Green and Red sectors), Dog (Green, White, and Red sectors) and Charlie. The 16th Regiment, 1st Division, was assigned Easy Red and Fox Green, while the 116th Regiment was to hit Dog Green, White, and Red. Awaiting them were heavily mined beaches with thickly strewn obstacles and 13 heavily defended strongpoints. Typical of these was WN62, which caused much of the misery experienced by the Americans. Housing two 75-mm cannons, a 50-mm mortar, and a 50-mm cannon in concrete casemates with numerous machine guns and rifle positions adding to its firepower, WN62 overlooked Easy Red and Fox Green.

The first wave at Omaha clawed towards the beach at 6:30 a.m., immediately running into problems. Accurate enemy fire and strong surf caused some landing craft to disgorge their troops quite a distance from the shore. Soldiers entered the sea with the water over their heads, some drowning under the weight of their packs. Others were shot down as soon as the ramps of their landing craft lowered. Compounding the problems at Omaha, many DD (Duplex Drive) Sherman tanks, which were meant to provide much-needed fire support, foundered when they were released as far as three miles (five kilometers) offshore. Only two of the 29 DD Shermans of the 741st Tank Battalion managed to reach Omaha Beach. Others were swamped, sinking to the bottom of the Channel. The 743rd Tank Battalion later landed directly on the beach. In contrast, 27 Shermans made it ashore to support the landings at Utah.

At the Dog beaches, the 116th Regiment ran into interlocking fire from German machine gun nests, and mortar and artillery rounds blasted craters among them. Bullets rippled through the surf, and soldiers took shelter behind obstacles. One landing craft took a direct hit from a German mortar round and simply disappeared. Another was lost, along with all 32 men on board. Company A came ashore at Dog Green and quickly suffered horrendous casualties, losing about 65 percent of its strength in just ten minutes. Twenty-two of its dead hailed from the town of Bedford, Virginia, population 3,200, and they are now forever remembered as the "Bedford Boys." The 16th Regiment also ran into heavy German resistance as some troops came ashore in the wrong locations.

At 7 a.m., the second wave headed towards Omaha, but the situation was desperate. Virtually no movement off the beach had been accomplished. The US War Department report stated, "The enemy fire, which had decimated the first waves, was not neutralized when the larger

"COMPANY A CAME ASHORE AT DOG GREEN AND QUICKLY SUFFERED HORRENDOUS CASUALTIES, LOSING ABOUT 65 PERCENT OF ITS STRENGTH IN JUST TEN MINUTES."

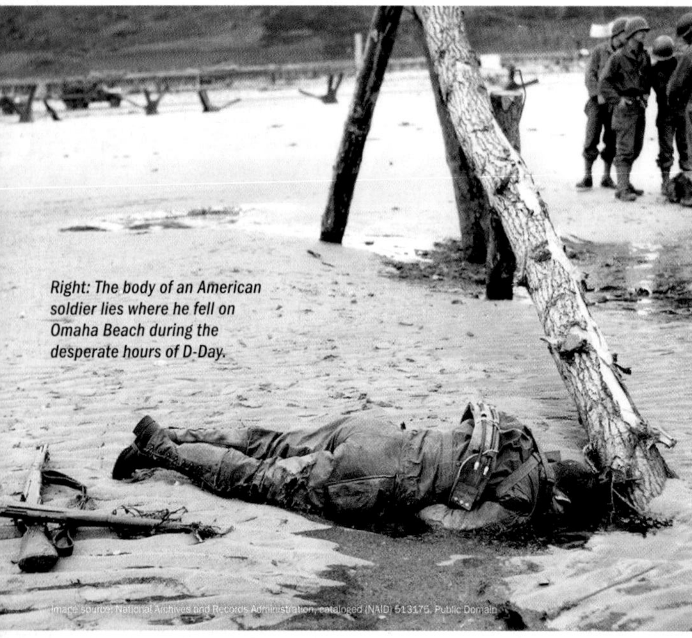

Right: The body of an American soldier lies where he fell on Omaha Beach during the desperate hours of D-Day.

Image source: National Archives and Records Administration, cataloged (NAID) 513175. Public Domain

Below: Soldiers of the US 4th Infantry Division wade ashore at Utah Beach, a relatively quiet area as D-Day progressed.

Image source: U.S. federal government. Public domain.

British troops of No. 4 Commando advance house-to-house in Ouistreham with the support of a DD Sherman tank.

Image source: IWM collections, photograph MH 2012, Public Domain

Soldiers of the British 50th Division rush ashore, at Gold Beach, in the center of the Allied landing area in Normandy.

Image source: IWM collections, photograph B 5246. Public Domain

landings commenced." The situation deteriorated to the point that General Bradley, aboard the cruiser USS Augusta, considered withdrawing the troops from Omaha and diverting further landings to other sectors. Around 8 a.m., however, General Norman Cota, assistant commander of the 29th Division, led an advance off Dog Green between strongpoints WN68 and WN70. Elsewhere, non-commissioned and junior officers got small groups to move forwards, penetrating less heavily defended areas and taking German fortifications from the rear.

By D-Day's end, the Americans had suffered about 2,500 killed, wounded, and missing at Omaha Beach, by far the largest loss on June 6, 1944, but 34,000 American troops had made it ashore. Their shaky lodgment was only 4,500–6,000 feet (1,370–1,829 meters) at its deepest, near Colleville, and toeholds had been established around Vierville and St. Laurent, far from the assigned D-Day objective of a five-mile (eight-kilometer) beachhead. Some German troops held out among the beach defenses, and a dangerous gap existed between the Americans on Omaha and the British at Gold Beach. The Omaha landings further failed to approach the town of Isigny, where efforts to link up with the 4th Division off Utah Beach were to proceed the following day.

"The long line of beach lay ahead and immediately behind hung a thick pall of smoke as far as the eye could see," remembered wireless operator I.G. Holley of Company B, 1st Battalion, Royal Hampshire Regiment, as his landing craft approached Gold Beach on D-Day. "Down goes the ramp, out goes the captain with me close behind. We were in the sea to the tops of our thighs. Floundering ashore, we were in the thick of it . . . The beach was filled with half-bent running figures . . . A near one blasts sand all over me and my radio goes dead . . . A sweet rancid smell is everywhere, never forgotten by those who smell it—burnt explosives, torn flesh, and ruptured earth."

The five-mile (eight-kilometer) length of Gold Beach was in the center of Allied D-Day operations. To the west was the port of Arromanches, the village of Longues-sur-Mer, and beyond Port-en-Bessin at Omaha Beach. To the east were the towns of Le Hamel and La Rivière. Gold Beach was divided into four sectors—How, Item, Jig, and King. Twenty-nine companies of the German 716th Division manned most defenses at Gold, while elements of the 352nd Division were present. The defenders had fortified houses along the beachfront and constructed concrete strongpoints, including a battery of 155-mm guns at Longues-sur-Mer. Altogether, 500 machine guns, 90 heavy guns, and 50 mortars were assembled to contest any landing.

The British 50th Division, including the East Yorkshire, Devonshire, Dorset, and Hampshire Regiments, along with No. 47 Royal Commando, was tasked with cutting the road between the cities of Bayeux and Caen, capturing Arromanches, destroying the Longues-sur-Mer battery, and linking up with the Americans off Omaha Beach to the west, plus the Canadians advancing from Juno Beach to the east.

Less than an hour before sunrise, the pre-invasion naval bombardment of Gold Beach

RANGERS AT POINTE DU HOC

A handful of US Army Rangers scaled cliffs and assaulted German gun emplacements that threatened Utah and Omaha beaches.

Image source: National Archives USA. Public domain

German prisoners are marched away as Rangers relax at Pointe du Hoc after displaying an American flag to discourage friendly fire.

Four miles (six kilometers) west of Omaha Beach loomed the 100-foot (30-meter) high cliffs of Pointe du Hoc. Allied reconnaissance had determined that the Germans had placed a formidable battery of six 155-mm howitzers there, capable of bombarding both Omaha and Utah beaches. To deal with the threat that countless air raids had apparently failed to eliminate, 225 men of the 2nd Battalion, US Army Rangers, were ordered to scale the cliffs and silence the guns on the morning of D-Day.

Under the command of Lieutenant Colonel James Rudder, the Rangers trained extensively for perhaps the most hazardous mission of any Allied ground troops on June 6, 1944. Although the mission appeared suicidal, the Rangers borrowed scaling ladders from the London Fire Brigade and employed grappling hooks attached to long ropes that were fired from rocket launchers, intending to climb hand over hand to the summit of Pointe du Hoc.

At about 7 a.m., after a delay of about 40 minutes, the Rangers landed under fire at the base of the cliffs. They soon discovered that several of their waterlogged ropes, now significantly heavier, could not reach the required height. Undaunted, they pressed on, driving the German defenders from the crest only to discover the guns had been removed. Five of them were found hours later, in an orchard, and destroyed by dropping thermite grenades down their barrels.

Maintaining their position at Pointe du Hoc until relieved on June 8, the Rangers fought off numerous counterattacks. By then, only 90 were left uninjured.

got underway. Combined with earlier air attacks, the naval guns were highly effective. The light cruiser HMS Ajax duelled the Longues-sur-Mer battery just after dawn, silencing the guns with six-inch rounds directly through two of its four casemates.

Efforts to clear beach obstacles were stymied as strong winds pushed the tides into the area earlier than expected. Twenty landing craft carrying tanks were damaged during their runs to shore. The first British troops hit the beach at about 7:15 a.m., and the 1st Battalion, Royal Hampshire Regiment, took casualties immediately. Near Le Hamel, a German 88-mm gun fired from the cliffs, but British troops assaulted the position with the support of a tank equipped with a spigot mortar. In Item sector, four of the 14 landing craft carrying No. 47 Commando were sunk, but the troops managed to strike west toward Port-en-Bessin. At La Rivière, the 5th Battalion, East Yorkshire Regiment, and 6th Battalion, Green Howards, made steady progress under fire from German 88s.

By early afternoon, both Le Hamel and La Rivière were taken. The Commandos captured high ground near Port-en-Bessin by evening, and contact with Canadian forces from Juno Beach was established. About 25,000 British troops were ashore with only 400 casualties. As night fell, the penetration at Gold Beach was six miles (10 km) deep. Although the Bayeux-Caen road was not cut and no linkup had been made with the Americans, the effort at Gold had produced outstanding results.

East of Gold Beach, the Canadian 3rd Infantry Division was to assault Juno Beach, a length of six miles (10 km) from Saint-Aubin in the east to La Rivière in the west. The center of Juno was the small village of Courseulles-sur-Mer. The focus of the Canadian landings included two sectors, Mike to the west and Nan to the east. The North Shore Regiment, the Queen's Own Rifles, and the Regina Rifles landed in Nan sector, while the Royal Winnipeg Rifles assaulted Mike. Companies of No. 48 Royal Marine Commando and the Canadian Scottish Regiment held the flanks. The Canadians were tasked with cutting the Bayeux-Caen road, taking the Carpiquet airfield west of Caen, and linking up with the British troops at Gold and Sword beaches.

The first Canadian troops landed about 7:55 a.m., slightly behind schedule after contending with difficult tides that left beach obstacles submerged, destroying or damaging about 30 percent of the landing craft. The German defenders of the 716th Division fortified houses and buildings close to the shoreline. As the Canadians waded ahead, German fire, zeroed in on the water's edge, intensified. Aside from Omaha, the Canadians at Juno encountered the fiercest enemy resistance on D-Day. For more than two hours, the fighting raged along the beach.

"In the Nan sector, the North Shore Regiment lands under heavy German fire," the CBC reported. "At 8:30 a.m., the Queen's Own Rifles land at Nan sector, held up by high seas. The soldiers have to run 600 feet (183 meters) from the shore to a sea wall under fire from hidden German artillery. Only a few men of the first company survive."

German fire wreaked havoc among the troops coming ashore, and Company B, Royal Winnipeg Rifles, was reduced to one officer and 25 men in their dash for the sea wall. Some units suffered 50 percent casualties, but by midmorning the Canadians had taken Saint-Aubin and the village of Bernières. Supported by tanks, they fought house-to-house in Courseulles. One troop of the 1st Hussars reached and briefly cut the Bayeux-Caen road, the only Allied unit to attain its final objective on D-Day. As night fell, the Canadians had landed more than 21,000 troops and suffered 1,200 casualties while achieving the deepest penetration of June 6, advancing nine miles (15 kilometers). Contact with the British 50th Division off Gold Beach was established, but the Carpiquet airport remained in enemy hands and a dangerous 1.8-mile (three-kilometer) gap existed between Juno and Sword beaches.

"BY MIDMORNING THE CANADIANS HAD TAKEN . . . THE VILLAGE OF BERNIÈRES. SUPPORTED BY TANKS, THEY FOUGHT HOUSE-TO-HOUSE IN COURSEULLES."

Within 45 minutes of landing across the five miles (eight kilometers) of Sword, the easternmost invasion beach, the British 3rd Division was pushing inland. Surprisingly, the Germans had constructed light defences along the most direct route to Caen, a communications and transportation center about nine miles (15 kilometers) from Sword Beach, but resistance from the German 736th and 125th Regiments, 716th Division, and elements of the 21st Panzer Division stiffened as the day wore on.

Sword Beach—divided into Oboe, Peter, Queen, and Roger sectors—stretched from the town of Lion-sur-Mer in the east to the city of Ouistreham at the mouth of the River Orne in the west. The objectives of the 3rd Division and the supporting 27th Armored Brigade included capturing Caen and converging on Carpiquet airfield, linking

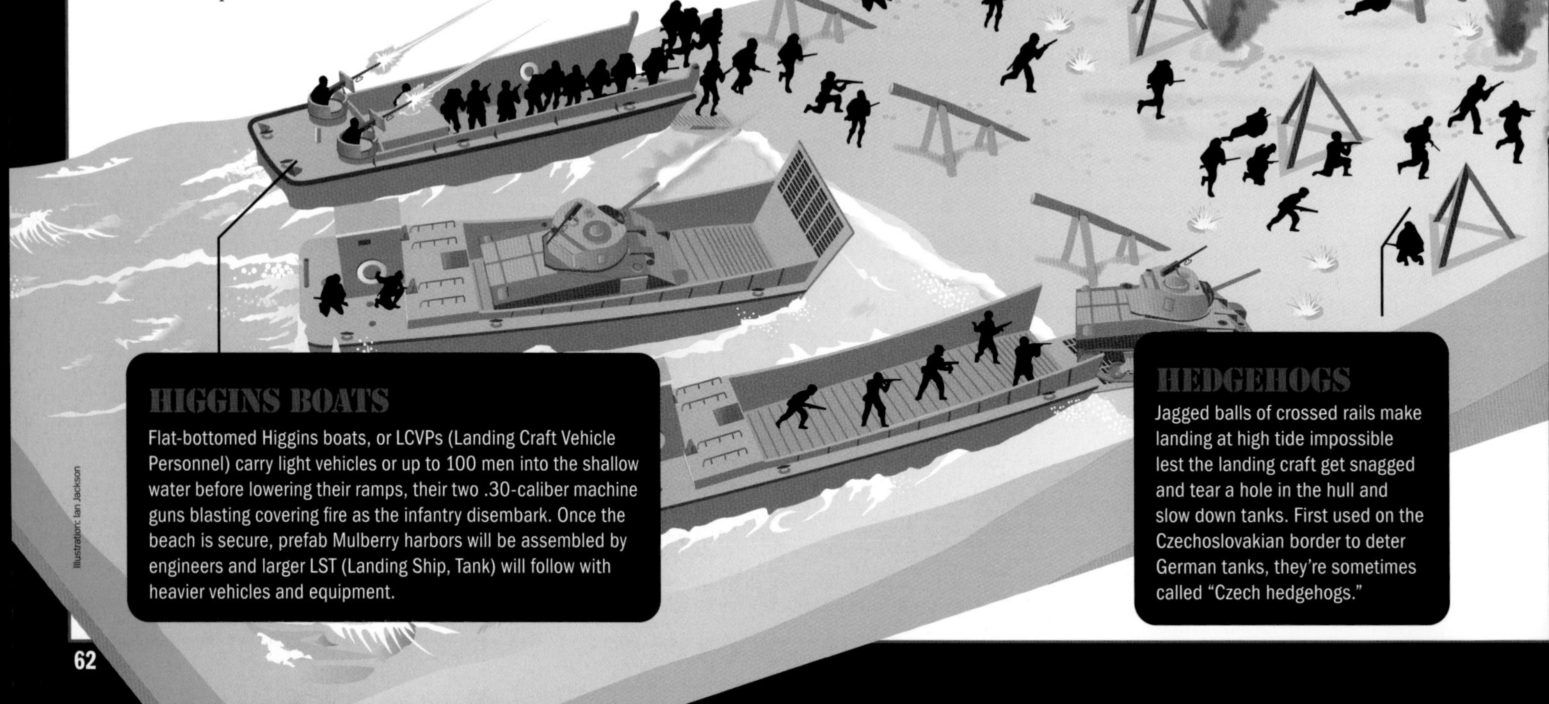

TELLER MINES

Mounted on stakes and angled seawards towards the invaders, anti-vehicle Teller mines can be triggered in high tide by landing craft. Contains an anti-tampering device that can trigger the 11 pounds (five kilograms) of TNT interfered with—enough to take the track off a tank.

HIGGINS BOATS

Flat-bottomed Higgins boats, or LCVPs (Landing Craft Vehicle Personnel) carry light vehicles or up to 100 men into the shallow water before lowering their ramps, their two .30-caliber machine guns blasting covering fire as the infantry disembark. Once the beach is secure, prefab Mulberry harbors will be assembled by engineers and larger LST (Landing Ship, Tank) will follow with heavier vehicles and equipment.

HEDGEHOGS

Jagged balls of crossed rails make landing at high tide impossible lest the landing craft get snagged and tear a hole in the hull and slow down tanks. First used on the Czechoslovakian border to deter German tanks, they're sometimes called "Czech hedgehogs."

Illustration: Ian Jackson

up with the Canadians from Juno Beach in the process. The 1st Special Service Brigade, including Commando units under Simon Fraser, Lord Lovat, was to advance 3.1 miles (five kilometers) to the bridges across the Orne and the Caen Canal, where troops of the British 6th Airborne had seized the spans and awaited relief.

Landing at 7:25 a.m., the British moved rapidly inland. By afternoon, the King's Shropshire Light Infantry and Staffordshire Yeomanry had advanced towards Caen and attempted to link up with the Canadians. While Lord Lovat's Commandos reached the critical bridges by 1:30 p.m., the push inland met the only German armored counterattack of the day. Elements of the 21st Panzer Division advanced late in the day through the gap between Sword and Juno, its 192nd Panzergrenadier Regiment reaching the Channel coast. However, no reinforcements were available to exploit the gain, and the Germans were forced to retire.

At the end of the day, 29,000 troops were ashore at Sword Beach with only 630 casualties. Still, Caen—a D-Day objective—was out of reach and the junction with the Canadians had not occurred.

Although numerous D-Day objectives were not achieved on June 6, and the beachhead in several areas, particularly at Omaha, was vulnerable to counterattack, much had been accomplished. Casualties were surprisingly light, with about 4,900 killed, wounded, or missing, and the Germans had been taken comprehensively by surprise. The Allies had returned to northwest Europe in force, but much difficult fighting lay ahead in Normandy. Without doubt, though, the success of D-Day heralded the beginning of the end for Hitler's Third Reich.

ARTILLERY CASEMENT

Safely encased in thick concrete, German artillery positions shell Allied ships approaching the beach. Taking them out prior to landing is a crucial part of the early bombardment from sea or air, as not even light tanks have the firepower to dent their shells. Infantry have to take out casements the hard way, getting under the guns to lob grenades into the closely packed rooms, or by storming the connecting trenches.

LAND MINES

Land mines can be buried beneath the sand to strike the unsuspecting, with infantry mines triggered by a web of tripwires. S-mines, or "Bouncing Betties," propel themselves 23-47 inches (60-120 centimeters) upward on a small explosive charge before the main charge explodes.

MACHINE GUN NEST

Connected to the bunkers and pillboxes by trenches, machine gun nests guard the trails off the beach, pinning down the attackers from their superior position with suppressing fire from the infamous MG42. Though vulnerable to bombardment by Allied ships and planes, only changing the ammo belt will afford the Allied infantry vital seconds with which to launch an attack.

American troops successfully advance over the sea wall on Utah Beach.

BARBED WIRE

Used in vast quantities along seawalls to deny the attackers cover, coils of vicious barbed wire can slow the Allies down as they carefully cut it or flatten it to cross—simple things made more difficult by the hail of machine gun fire. Loose coils of wire are more difficult to cross as they snare on the unwary.

SEAWALL

The 10 foot (three meter) concrete seawall is as much protection against coastal erosion and unseasonably high tides as it is Allied assault, but it can make exiting the beach difficult for infantry and impossible for vehicles. It does, however, provide the attackers with rare shelter from the German guns.

THE LANDINGS

The deployment of Allied troops on June 6, D-Day.

Speciality Key

 COMBAT ENGINEERS

 COVERT INTELLIGENCE GATHERING

 AMPHIBIOUS MEDIUM TANK

 LIGHT INFANTRY, VERSATILE & RELIABLE

 AIR ASSAULT, LIGHT INFANTRY

 SPECIAL FORCES TRAINED FOR COASTAL ASSAULT

 INFANTRY, SPECIAL FORCES

  INFANTRY, FAST TANK

 MINE CLEARANCE, BRIDGING & TRANSPORT

Commander-in-Chief, Air Force:
Air Chief Marshal Trafford Leigh-Mallory

IST US ARMY

Commander: General Omar Bradley

VII CORPS
Commander: Major General J.L. Collins

4th Infantry Division "Ivy"
Commander: Major General Raymond Barton
Objective: First troops onto Utah Beach

9th Infantry Division "Old Reliables"
Commander: Major General Manton S. Eddy
Objective: Take and hold Utah Beach

79th Infantry Division "Cross of Lorraine"
Commander: Major General Ira T. Wyche
Objective: Take and hold Utah Beach

90th Infantry Division "Tough Ombres"
Commander: Brig-General Jay W. MacKelvie
Objective: Take and hold Utah Beach

30 Commando Assault Unit "Red Indians" (British)
Commander: Captain G. Pike
Objective: Take radar station at Douvres-la-Délivrande

70th Tank Battalion "Thunderbolts"
Commander: Lt-Colonel John C. Welborn
Objective: Support landing at Utah Beach

237th Combat Engineer Battalion
Commander: Major Herschel E. Linn
Objective: Clear obstacles at Utah Beach

299th Combat Engineer Battalion
Commander: Colonel Milton Jewett
Objective: Clear obstacles at Utah Beach

V CORPS
Commander: Major General Leonard T. Gerow

1st Infantry Division "The Big Red One"
Commander: Major General Clarence Huebner
Objective: Take and hold Omaha Beach

29th Infantry Division "Blue and Gray"
Commander: Major General Charles Gebhardt
Objective: Take and hold Omaha Beach

Ranger assault group
Commander: Lieutenant Colonel James Earl Rudder

2nd Ranger Battalion
Commander: Lieutenant Colonel James Earl Rudder
Objective: Capture battery at Pointe du Hoc

5th Ranger Battalion
Commander: Lieutenant Colonel Max Schneider
Objective: Capture battery at Pointe du Hoc

743rd Tank Battalion
Commander: Lieutenant Colonel John S. Upham
Objective: Support landing at Omaha Beach

UTAH

POINTE DU HOC

OMAHA

US troops look to the shore as their landing craft approaches Omaha Beach.

Image source: US Federal Government. Public domain

INLAND

82nd Airborne Division "All American Division"
Commander: Major General Matthew Ridgway
Objective: Secure left flank and rear of VI Corps

101st Airborne Division "Screaming Eagles"
Commander: Major General Maxwell D. Taylor
Objective: Secure left flank and rear of VI Corps

US Army Rangers at the cliffs of Pointe du Hoc.

Image source: National Archives USA. Public domain

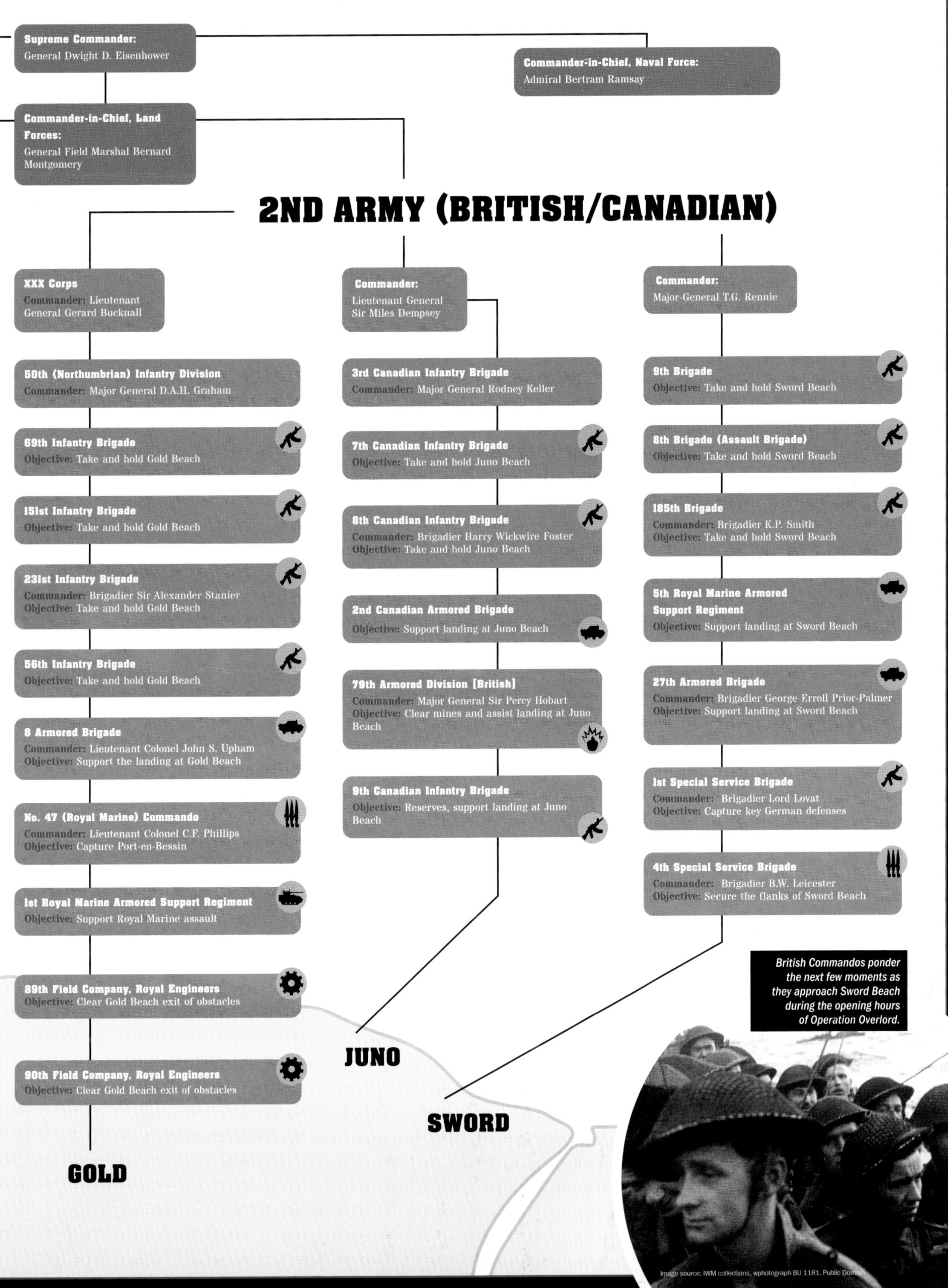
Supreme Commander:
General Dwight D. Eisenhower
Commander-in-Chief, Naval Force:
Admiral Bertram Ramsay
Commander-in-Chief, Land Forces:
General Field Marshal Bernard Montgomery
2ND ARMY (BRITISH/CANADIAN)
XXX Corps
Commander: Lieutenant General Gerard Bucknall
50th (Northumbrian) Infantry Division
Commander: Major General D.A.H. Graham
69th Infantry Brigade
Objective: Take and hold Gold Beach
151st Infantry Brigade
Objective: Take and hold Gold Beach
231st Infantry Brigade
Commander: Brigadier Sir Alexander Stanier
Objective: Take and hold Gold Beach
56th Infantry Brigade
Objective: Take and hold Gold Beach
8 Armored Brigade
Commander: Lieutenant Colonel John S. Upham
Objective: Support the landing at Gold Beach
No. 47 (Royal Marine) Commando
Commander: Lieutenant Colonel C.F. Phillips
Objective: Capture Port-en-Bessin
1st Royal Marine Armored Support Regiment
Objective: Support Royal Marine assault
89th Field Company, Royal Engineers
Objective: Clear Gold Beach exit of obstacles
90th Field Company, Royal Engineers
Objective: Clear Gold Beach exit of obstacles
GOLD
Commander:
Lieutenant General Sir Miles Dempsey
3rd Canadian Infantry Brigade
Commander: Major General Rodney Keller
7th Canadian Infantry Brigade
Objective: Take and hold Juno Beach
8th Canadian Infantry Brigade
Commander: Brigadier Harry Wickwire Foster
Objective: Take and hold Juno Beach
2nd Canadian Armored Brigade
Objective: Support landing at Juno Beach
79th Armored Division [British]
Commander: Major General Sir Percy Hobart
Objective: Clear mines and assist landing at Juno Beach
9th Canadian Infantry Brigade
Objective: Reserves, support landing at Juno Beach
JUNO
Commander:
Major-General T.G. Rennie
9th Brigade
Objective: Take and hold Sword Beach
8th Brigade (Assault Brigade)
Objective: Take and hold Sword Beach
185th Brigade
Commander: Brigadier K.P. Smith
Objective: Take and hold Sword Beach
5th Royal Marine Armored Support Regiment
Objective: Support landing at Sword Beach
27th Armored Brigade
Commander: Brigadier George Erroll Prior-Palmer
Objective: Support landing at Sword Beach
1st Special Service Brigade
Commander: Brigadier Lord Lovat
Objective: Capture key German defenses
4th Special Service Brigade
Commander: Brigadier B.W. Leicester
Objective: Secure the flanks of Sword Beach
SWORD

British Commandos ponder the next few moments as they approach Sword Beach during the opening hours of Operation Overlord.

Image source: IWM collections, wphotograph BU 1181. Public Domain

ANATOMY OF AN LCVP (landing craft vehicle personnel)

Created by a little-known manufacturer in New Orleans, the Higgins boat was the small landing craft that changed the war.

PROVING A POINT
Higgins' designs were constantly rejected by the US Bureau of Ships. In 1942, to see which vessel was best, a challenge was concocted to carry a 30-ton tank through rough water, and the Higgins boat proved its worth.

THE OPEN CARGO AREA HAD SPACE FOR A JEEP OR OTHER LIGHT VEHICLES

THE GATES TO HELL
The exception to the wooden construction was the metal ramp. As the primary defensive panel of the LCVP, once it was opened the soldiers would be exposed to direct attacks from the front.

LCVP HIGGINS BOAT

LENGTH: 36.2 FT (11.03 M)
SPEED: 14 MPH (22.5 KM/H)
CAPACITY: 36 TROOPS/A 6,000 LB (2,721 KG) VEHICLE / 8,100 LB (3,674 KG) CARGO
ENGINE: 225HP GRAY DIESEL ENGINE/HALL-SCOTT PETROL ENGINE
ARMAMENT: 2 X .30 CALIBER BROWNING MACHINE GUNS
NUMBER MADE IN WWII: 23,398

RAMP WINDOW

ENTRY AND EXIT
To get into the Higgins boat, the soldiers would climb down a cargo net hung from the troop transport. When the beaches of Normandy veered into view, they would leave the vessel by charging down the lowered ramp.

Image: Alex Pang

SWAMP ORIGINS

The prototype of the LCVP, the Eureka, was tested extensively on the US Gold Coast. Operating in just 18 inches (45 centimeters) of water, the vessel could run through vegetation and wooded areas with ease—ideal preparation for the French beaches.

ANTI-MINE DEFENSES

The craft was so light that it could float over hidden mines in the water. It was also so maneuverable that it could return from banks and shorelines with minimal damage to the bow or the propeller.

DOUBLE MACHINE GUNS

Higgins boats were designed for logistical landings rather than fire fights. The LCVP still needed some protection though, so it was equipped with two .30 caliber Browning machine guns to provide support and cover fire.

RAMP WINCH

STEERING POSITION WAS TO THE LEFT OF THE CRAFT

FUEL TANK

ENGINE

A CANVAS COULD BE PUT UP AS COVER IN ADVERSE WEATHER CONDITIONS

SHALLOW DRAFT

The LCVP could get much closer to the beaches of Normandy than almost anything else in the Allied navies. With no need for deep-water ports, the D-Day landings could be undertaken in the lightly defended parts of "Fortress Europe."

PROTECTING THE PROPELLER SHAFT

Under the Higgins boat, a wooden tunnel protected the propeller while aerated water allowed for faster speeds and improved maneuverability. A block of pine at the rear of the boat was made to be very sturdy to allow for frequent landings.

MAHOGANY WOOD CONSTRUCTION

To save costs, the majority of the boat was made from plywood or mahogany. Originally in the timber industry, Higgins was an expert at wooden boat construction and made the vessel light and cheap but also tough.

ARMOR PLATING

Illustration: Alex Pang

THE MAN BEHIND THE BOAT

Andrew Jackson Higgins was once a boat constructor in New Orleans, but all that changed with the advent of World War II. Funded by the US government, he developed the first designs for the boat that would later prove invaluable in the assault on Nazi-occupied Europe. Eisenhower is quoted as saying: "Andrew Higgins is the man who won the war for us. If Higgins had not designed and built those LCVPs, we never could have landed over an open beach. The whole strategy of the war would have been different." Hitler even labeled him the "New Noah" as he rued the Allied defeat of his Atlantic Wall.

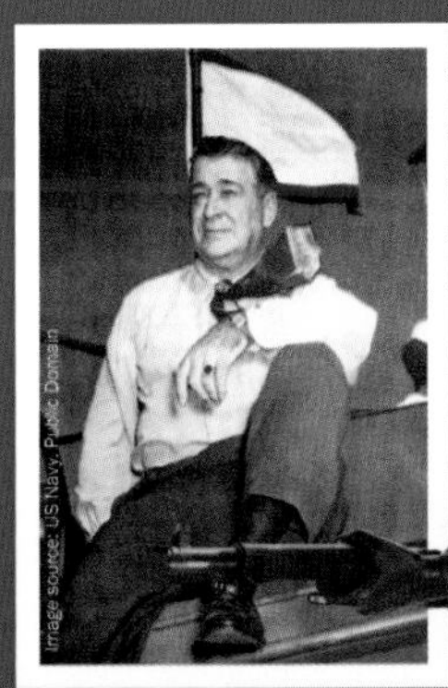

Image source: US Navy; Public Domain

Below: The impact of the Higgins boat is immortalized in memorials such as this one at Utah Beach.

THE BEACHHEAD AND BEYOND

Consolidating their foothold in Normandy, Allied forces pushed inland and kept pressure on the Germans immediately following the D-Day landings.

Image source: National Archives USA https://catalog.archives.gov/id/12003973, Public Domain

General Bernard L. Montgomery, commander of Allied ground forces for Operation Overlord, stepped into Normandy early on the morning of June 7, 1944, also known as D+1. He was quick to stress, along with his senior commanders—Generals Omar Bradley and Miles Dempsey of the American First and British Second Armies—that the need to keep the Germans off balance was critical.

With varying degrees of success, Allied troops had fought their way off the five D-Day invasion beaches during the previous 24 hours. Through the night they had cleared the way as best they could for reinforcements and the offloading of supplies and equipment that would be needed for further operations. They had also sent patrols across the countryside, scouting for German troop concentrations or preparations to retaliate. Now, Montgomery reiterated, it was time to consolidate the beachheads and to prevent German counterattacks from driving between them, a situation narrowly averted late on D-Day when the 21st Panzer Division had been forced to retire after thrusting between Juno and Sword beaches, making it all the way to the Channel.

Early priorities inland from Omaha Beach, where the American lodgment was most vulnerable, were simply to advance far enough to place the beachhead out of range of German artillery and obtain sufficient space to mount cohesive offensive operations. At all the landing sites, it was necessary to achieve all those objectives that had been left incomplete at the end of D-Day. From Omaha, the Americans of the 1st and 29th Divisions had to strike south and west, expanding their zone of operations and linking up with the 4th Division moving inland from Utah Beach, where the Germans had been unable to breach a defensive line thrown up by elements of the American 82nd Airborne Division along the River Merderet.

The capture of the transportation center of Carentan was vital to accomplishing the linkup between the Omaha and Utah beachheads. From there, the Americans were to thrust across the Cotentin Peninsula and cut off Cherbourg in preparation for the VII Corps of General J. Lawton Collins attempting to capture the deepwater port. If taken intact, Cherbourg would provide harbor facilities that would speed up the arrival on the continent of reinforcements and materiel.

The British had made significant progress but came up short in capturing the cities of Bayeux and Caen, cutting the road between them, and occupying the Carpiquet airport. Each objective was critical in controlling the flow of traffic southward in expanding the Gold, Juno, and Sword beachheads. Linking up with General Leonard Gerow's American V Corps, inland from Omaha Beach, was another task yet to be completed.

The Germans, of course, would have a say in just how successful each of these initiatives would be.

Renewed attacks from the secure Utah beachhead and from Omaha bore fruit on D+1 as the 4th Division made contact with the 82nd Airborne at Sainte-Mère-Église and glider troops arrived to reinforce the beleaguered paratroopers. Driving south from Omaha, the Americans gained four miles (six kilometers) to the banks of the River Aure. Meanwhile, a savage fight was brewing around Caen. The majority of the German armored reserve in Normandy, particularly the 12th SS Panzer Division Hitler Youth and the Panzer Lehr Division, had been held back on D-Day. Only Hitler's personal order could release them, and it came so late on June 6 that they had made little progress.

By the evening of D-Day, however, the 25th Panzergrenadier Regiment, vanguard of the 12th SS, was poised to strike. Colonel Kurt "Panzer" Meyer climbed to the top of a tower at the abbey of Ardenne on the outskirts of Caen. He watched tanks and troops of the Canadian 3rd Division advance towards Carpiquet airport and muttered, "Little fish! We'll throw

Right: General Bernard Montgomery, commander of Allied ground forces, talks with British soldiers in Normandy.

Image Source: IWM photograph B 6934 Public Domain

After it was secured, Omaha Beach became a beehive of activity as troops and supplies poured into Normandy.

them back into the sea in the morning!" When the Canadians advanced on D+1, Meyer unleashed an ambush that drove them back two miles (three kilometers) before naval and artillery fire slashed into the Germans and destroyed half their tanks.

The Canadian move was part of a thrust to capture Caen and the airfield that preempted a full-scale German counterattack aimed at the gap between the Canadian 3rd and British 3rd Divisions off Juno and Sword beaches. After the brutal battle, Meyer was left with only 17 tanks, and the Germans were so preoccupied with holding Caen that they had precious little to throw at the British 50th Division moving northwest of the city, where it took control of most of the Bayeux-Caen road.

On June 8 (D+2), Bayeux fell into British hands. A female operator at the town's telephone center called the headquarters of the German 84th Corps in Saint-Lô to report, "British tanks are now passing the soldiers' club. They are right in the middle of the town . . . I'm the last one here." Tanks under Lieutenant Colonel Stanley Christopherson of the Sherwood Rangers Yeomanry rumbled past her window, and the operator concluded, "Now the Tommies are driving past the building outside. You can hear for yourself, Herr Major!"

While progress was being made on the ground in some areas, Allied aircraft played havoc with German reinforcements. Any concentration of troops or vehicles that ventured from cover in daylight were relentlessly bombed and strafed. The 2nd SS Panzer Division Das Reich, hurriedly ordered to Normandy from the city of Toulouse in the south of France, was seriously slowed—unable to load its tanks aboard trains for at least ten days.

As the drama of Operation Overlord continued in Normandy, Hitler remained convinced that the main Allied thrust was yet to come and would still occur further north, at Pas-de-Calais, the shortest distance from England to the French coast. It was imperative to the Nazis, therefore, to hold Caen at any cost. The Germans concentrated their armored reinforcements around the city and paid the resulting price in the south and west. Although Montgomery had originally believed Dempsey's Second Army could take the city on D-Day, he later changed his perspective, asserting that his aim had been a battle of attrition, drawing the German reserves to the British sector to allow the Americans an opportunity to break out of their beachhead and battle through the treacherous bocage, or hedgerows, into open country for an eventual dash across France.

While the British 6th Airborne Division held the ground between the Rivers Orne and Dives until mid-month, Montgomery continued to hammer away at Caen, a prize only 120 miles (190 road kilometers) from Paris. On June 10 (D+4), considered by some historians as the date when the Allied lodgment in Normandy was finally safe from being pushed at least partially back into the sea, Montgomery launched a two-pronged attack to encircle Caen.

The British 51st Division and 4th Armored Brigade were to sweep southward from positions east of the River Orne and join forces with the 7th Armored Division, the famous Desert Rats, south of Caen. A timely 21st Panzer attack stymied the southward thrust,

ORDEAL AT ORADOUR-SUR-GLANE

En route to Normandy, troops of the 2nd SS Panzer Division Das Reich murdered the residents of a small French village.

Throughout the Normandy campaign, the French Resistance was active—cutting communication lines, destroying bridges, and killing Germans at every opportunity. As the 2nd SS Panzer Division Das Reich made its way to Normandy from the south of France, it was harried by Allied air strikes and harassed by the emboldened underground.

Oradour-sur-Glane, a tiny village in west-central France, lay in the path of Das Reich, and when the 4th SS Panzergrenadier Regiment Der Führer, under the command of Major Adolf Diekmann, entered the village on June 10, the officer was bent on reprisal. Apparently, resistance fighters had kidnapped an SS officer, and revenge for the crime was to be enacted on Oradour-sur-Glane.

Diekmann ordered the murders of 642 men, women, and children in the village. The men were prodded to outbuildings and barns, cut down by machine gun fire, and their bodies torched. The women and children were locked in the village church, which was set aflame. Those who managed to escape were gunned down in the open. Only one woman survived.

The tragedy of Oradour-sur-Glane was one of numerous atrocities committed by SS troops during the Normandy campaign. Diekmann was killed in action a short time later, but after the war, 65 of the 200 surviving SS men who perpetrated the massacre were put on trial. Twenty were found guilty of war crimes and sentenced to prison, the last being released in 1958. Two other trials have since occurred. One resulted in a life sentence; in the other, the charges were dropped.

Oradour-sur-Glane was never rebuilt.

Objects of everyday life, strewn about Oradour-sur-Glane, remain as reminders of the atrocity committed there.

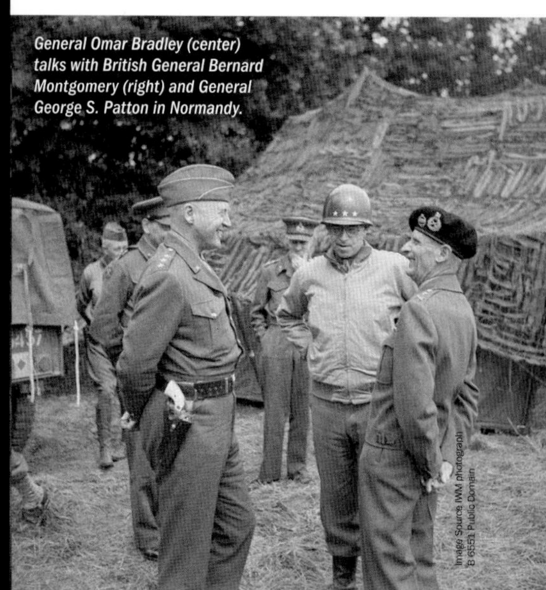

General Omar Bradley (center) talks with British General Bernard Montgomery (right) and General George S. Patton in Normandy.

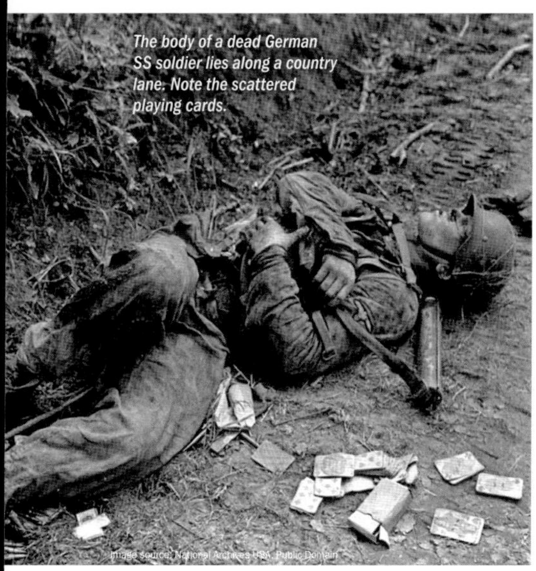

The body of a dead German SS soldier lies along a country lane. Note the scattered playing cards.

Right: After the 50th Division has moved inland, British soldiers inspect the wreckage of German strongpoint WN35 at Gold Beach.

Image Source IWM photograph B 5252. Public Domain

On June 7, 1944 (D+1), soldiers of the US 2nd Infantry Division march over the cliffs at Omaha Beach.

Image source: U.S. federal government, Public Domain

however, and the Desert Rats came to grief under the guns of Tiger tanks at Villers-Bocage on June 13 (D+7). Caen would not end up falling to the British for six agonizing weeks, and Carpiquet's airport would remain out of reach until early July.

To the west, the American VII Corps became bogged down in a slugging match, fighting yard by yard to transit the Cotentin Peninsula. They reached Montebourg, about 17 miles (28 kilometers) from Cherbourg, by June 12 (D+6). Cherbourg would not fall until the end of the month, its facilities made a shambles by the Germans. The V Corps, meanwhile, liberated the town of Isigny on June 9 (D+3), then linked up with British forces at Port-en-Bessin on June 10 (D+4), and occupied the town of Caumont, 10 miles (16 kilometers) inland from Omaha Beach, the following day.

Two battalions of the German 6th Parachute Regiment clung tenaciously to Carentan and withstood repeated assaults by the 101st Airborne Division. Carentan finally fell on June 13 (D+7), after four days of bitter fighting and the timely arrival of Combat Command A, 2nd Armored Division, which thwarted a German counterattack by the 37th SS Panzergrenadier Regiment. The last brawl at Carentan became known as the Battle of Bloody Gulch as the 502nd and 506th Parachute Infantry Regiments, 101st, were set upon by the enemy tanks and heavily armed panzergrenadiers. As the paratroopers neared breaking point, the 60 tanks of Combat Command A, supported by infantrymen of the 29th Division, arrived to halt the enemy drive. During the sharp engagement, 43 Germans were killed and 89 were wounded, along with four precious tanks.

With the fall of Carentan, the V and VII Corps finally converged, and the Allied front in Normandy stretched unbroken for 60 miles (96.5 kilometers) with a penetration of 10 miles (16 kilometers) at its shallowest point.

Although Field Marshal Erwin Rommel, commander of German Army Group B in Normandy, had wanted to shift the focus of his defense from Caen to the Cotentin Peninsula to protect Cherbourg, he was unable to do so. Furthermore, holding the British at bay around Caen and halting the Americans at the same time would prove an impossible task. German reinforcements arrived degraded from Allied air attacks and could only commit to fighting piecemeal out of necessity. By mid June, less than two weeks after D-Day, the German Army in Normandy faced inevitable defeat.

Conversely, the Allied buildup in France was continuing. As of June 11 (D+5), they had put 326,000 troops, 100,000 tons of supplies and equipment, and 50,000 vehicles ashore. Though the fighting had been costly and months of heavy combat lay ahead, one thing was certain: the Allies had established themselves in Normandy and were set to stay on the European continent.

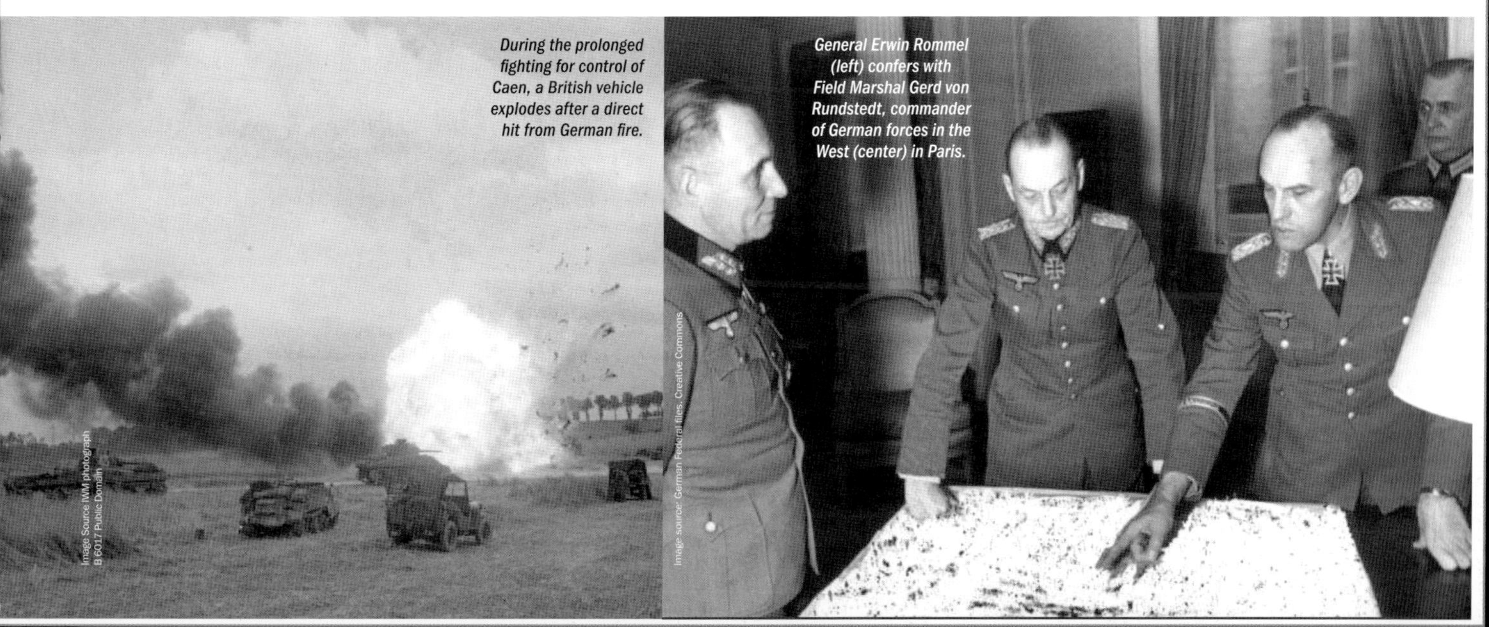

During the prolonged fighting for control of Caen, a British vehicle explodes after a direct hit from German fire.

Image Source IWM photograph B 6017 Public Domain

General Erwin Rommel (left) confers with Field Marshal Gerd von Rundstedt, commander of German forces in the West (center) in Paris.

Image source: German Federal files, Creative Commons

HOBART'S FUNNIES

They may have looked strange, but these specialized tanks played a vital role in overcoming all terrains in France and beyond.

As Britain prepared for D-Day, it had to overcome a multitude of problems in order for the operation to succeed. The beaches of Normandy and beyond were covered with both natural and man-made obstacles that would work in the enemy's favor. To combat this, a variety of unique tanks, known as Hobart's Funnies, were specially designed to give the Allies an advantage and ensure victory would fall in their favor.

DD TANK

Nicknamed "Donald Duck Tanks," this Sherman model was an amphibious swimming variant. The tank used a flotation screen and was powered to move through the water by a propeller. The DD tanks were rather fragile in rough seas, and in one instance during the Normandy landings, 27 of 29 tanks sank before reaching the shore.

FLOTATION SKIRT

An innovative design enabled the tank to "swim" to shore in shallow water. The skirt had issues in deeper water though, which was discovered at Omaha when seawater entered into the vehicle.

ARMORED ADVANCE

The DD was used with distinction at Juno Beach in particular, protecting infantry from German machine-gun fire. The design would also be used in later campaigns as well as Overlord, showcasing its versatility.

ATTACK POWER

A variation on the standard Sherman, the DD still wielded immense attack power and was effective in taking out the Normandy portions of the Atlantic Wall.

Image source: IWMCollection IWM Photo No: H 38084

ARMORED BULLDOZER

Designed to clear the invasion beaches of the various obstacles placed there by the Germans, this British innovation was a Caterpillar D7 Bulldozer equipped with armor. The first armored bulldozer used in war, it was adept at clearing rubble but too slow to keep up with conventional tanks.

"THE DD TANKS WERE RATHER FRAGILE IN ROUGH SEAS, AND IN ONE INSTANCE DURING THE NORMANDY LANDINGS, 27 OF 29 TANKS SANK BEFORE REACHING THE SHORE."

CHURCHILL CROCODILE

This modified Churchill tank came equipped with a devastating flamethrower. Although it reached Normandy after D-Day, its ability to project flame over long distances wreaked havoc in the German bunkers and trenches. It was a psychological weapon, with its mere appearance on the field enough to force soldiers to surrender immediately.

The flames from the Churchill Crocodile could reach up to 360 feet (110 meters) away.

CRAB FLAIL TANK

The Crab was another modified Sherman tank designed to clear minefields of obstacles. The tank was armed with a powerful mine flail powered by the main engine, capable of destroying barbed wire. It was also equipped with a pair of bins filled with chalk, which would mark the edges of the cleared route for troops to follow safely.

The Crab retained its 75-mm gun, which could be fired when the flail was not in use.

Image source: IWMCollection IWM Photo No. H 38080

CHURCHILL AVRE FASCINE CARRIER

Fascine bundles, comprising groups of sticks wired together, had previously been used in World War I to fill trenches, enabling tanks to pass over them. This tactic was used again to great effect in World War II with the Churchill AVRE. The tank was equipped with a fascine carrier and could be deployed to fill not only enemy ditches but also craters created by Allied bombs.

Fascines obscured the driver's view, meaning a crew member had to be outside to pass on directions.

SHERMAN BARV

Short for "beach armored recovery vehicle," this was a customized Sherman M4A4 tank. The turret was replaced by a boat-like framework and the entire tank was waterproofed. About 60 BARVs were used in Normandy to remove and rescue stranded vehicles.

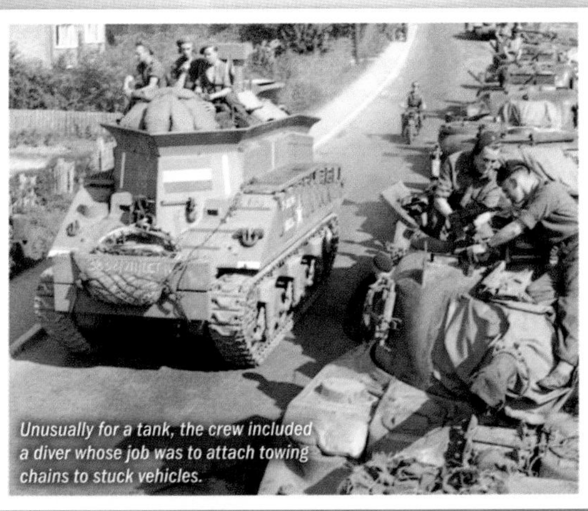

Unusually for a tank, the crew included a diver whose job was to attach towing chains to stuck vehicles.

The carpet-layer could lay down a 10 ft- (3 m-) wide mat.

CHURCHILL AVRE CARPET-LAYER WITH BOBBIN

The soft clay that covered the beaches of Normandy presented a problem for the tracked vehicles of the British Army, so a solution came in the form of the carpet-layer tank. The tank carried a canvas mat wound to a huge bobbin, which could be dropped and laid out, enabling vehicles to cross. The canvas was later replaced by a steel version.

General Percy Hobart was a member of the Royal Tank Corps, and the brother-in-law of Bernard Montgomery.

Image source: IWMCollection IWM Photo No: H 20697

Images: Alamy, DK Images, Getty Images

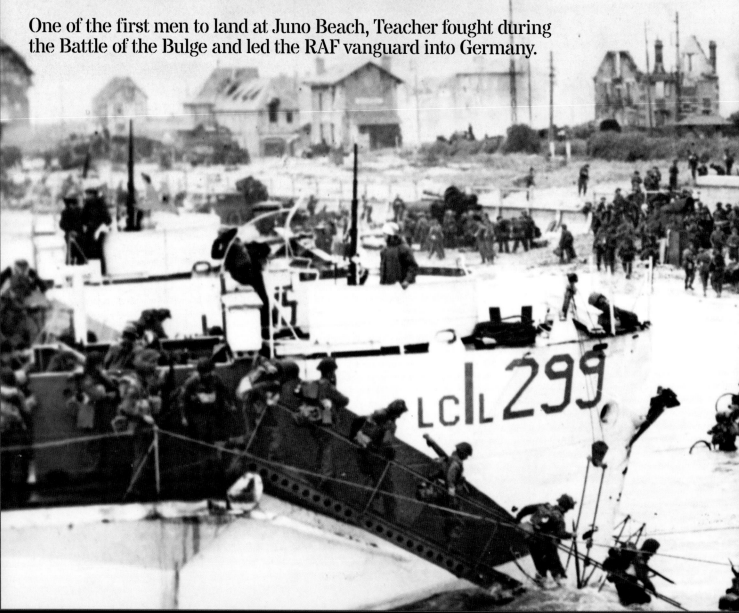

INTERVIEW WITH DAVID TEACHER MBE

Right: David Teacher at the very spot where he landed at Juno Beach 72 years before, June 6, 2016.

FROM THE ARCHIVES

D-DAY, BASTOGNE, AND BEYOND

BY TOM GARNER

One of the first men to land at Juno Beach, Teacher fought during the Battle of the Bulge and led the RAF vanguard into Germany.

June 6, 1944. Nearly 7,000 vessels containing 132,000 ground troops cross the English Channel to take part in the Allied invasion of Western Europe: the largest naval, air, and land operation in history. Nothing less than the liberation of a brutally suppressed continent is at stake and after years of intense planning, failure is not an option.

Five assault beaches on the Normandy coast must be taken, including one primarily reserved for Canadian forces: Juno Beach. However, in the vanguard of this sector is a 20-year-old British member of the RAF Beach Squadrons. Sitting in the cab of his truck and laden with supplies, the young driver is launched from his landing craft into deep water. The water rises almost to his chest but after putting his foot down on the accelerator, the engine roars into action and the vehicle lurches onto the beach.

Leading Aircraftman David Teacher was one of the first men to land on Juno Beach on D-Day and spent months afterwards in the same location ensuring that the logistical support for the Allies in France remained strong. His war continued to be dramatic beyond Normandy and as the march east continued, Teacher found himself fighting among American troops at Bastogne during the Battle of the Bulge before taking part in the invasion of Germany in 1945. We spoke to Teacher in 2017 to hear his story—a poignant tale of a young man's journey through war-torn Europe and the courage and horror that he witnessed.

Playing "Soldiers" in Palestine

Born into a Jewish family on December 29, 1923, in Hastings, Teacher moved to what was then the British Mandate of Palestine to live with his grandparents in 1934. Living in the small community of Karkur, Teacher experienced a multicultural environment that was nevertheless characterized by tensions the British authorities spent much time attempting to resolve. It was in Karkur that Teacher first encountered British

"THERE WERE THOUSANDS OF SHIPS AND LANDING CRAFT, BATTLESHIPS, DESTROYERS, AIRCRAFT FLYING OVERHEAD . . . THE NOISE WAS UNBELIEVABLE. WHEN THE NAVY STARTED BOMBARDING . . . IT WAS HORRENDOUS."

Canadian and British troops landing at Juno Beach, June 6, 1944. Teacher remembers the landings as well organized and thought highly of the Canadians.

armed forces: "Due to the circumstances in Palestine, as it was then, there were often riots between the Jewish people and the Arab people and the British police were very much involved. They had a station just outside Karkur where I was living, and eventually the Royal Ulster Rifles had a presence there and were given quite a large camp."

Far from viewing them as an occupying force, Teacher keenly interacted with the army: "I was there nearly every day of the week, going out on patrols and drinking beer with them. I learned to drive and learned to swear with them! I was 10 years of age and really had a ball enjoying myself. I also used to translate Hebrew and Arabic for them. I got into quite a lot of trouble with my grandparents."

Teacher moved back to England in 1938 and by the time war broke out in September 1939, he was living in Manchester and working as a mechanic. Having lived through the Manchester Blitz of 1940, Teacher was determined to join the war effort and signed on as an air cadet in order to later join the Royal Air Force. However, he recalls that his reasons for joining the RAF were unclear: "I don't really know why. I never wanted to fly but it was possibly the uniform. I didn't fancy the army that was for sure, and the navy was impossible to join or very difficult. So I was left with the air force and I was pleased I did, I had a wonderful time."

Training, the King, and "Monty"

Having been officially called up to serve in the British armed forces in September 1942, Teacher was assigned to the RAF and trained as a motor mechanic. By 1943 he was serving in Devon as part of Coastal Command but then volunteered to join a new outfit called Combined Operations. These units were specifically formed as part of the plans for the Allied invasion of Europe. As Teacher describes: "It was a way of getting the sea services to work together, instead of working against one another, or not being available when we wanted to make certain trials. So as a combined operation, we were always available to do whatever trials or maneuvers the hierarchy want: that was the start of the preparations for D-Day."

Right: American infantrymen fire at German troops in the advance to relieve the surrounded garrison in Bastogne.

Teacher would specifically be part of the RAF Beach Squadrons, which were an important element of the 2nd Tactical Air Force. For D-Day, the RAF had to provide close air support and fighter cover for the ground forces in the spearhead of the invasion. Aircraft had to be directed from the ground close to the front line and in order to provide that support, men and material were needed on the ground from the start. The role of the beach squadrons was to come ashore and establish themselves in designated areas to help with the large quantity of fuel, ammunition, equipment, and vehicles that was needed to sustain the RAF in the weeks after D-Day.

Training for this complex and crucial operation was intense: "We were 100 percent fit and then we used to practice a great deal of landings on all different types of surfaces: sands, grass verges, etc. This was general training for the invasion. We did a lot of unarmed combat because we were carrying a lot of gear—food, ammunition, petrol, and water—so we weren't able to carry any armaments. We weren't allowed to carry revolvers, so we would have had to carry Sten guns or rifles, which was impossible because of all the equipment we'd be carrying from the landing craft."

As part of No. 2 RAF Beach Squadron, Teacher was the main mechanic and serviced various vehicles such as Jeeps, motorcycles, and trucks. The latter would feature most prominently in Teacher's war experience particularly when the unit took possession of Bedford QL trucks, a vehicle he describes as "very reliable, I never had any trouble with it in all the 18 months that we had them." Teacher would experience D-Day driving a Bedford and during the preparations for the invasion, he spent much time practicing waterproofing his and others' vehicles for a beach landing.

Because of the importance of the training involved, Teacher came into contact with two of the most famous British figures of WWII: Field Marshal Bernard Montgomery and King George VI. On April 25, 1944, the latter inspected a large parade of over 5,000 troops at Hiltingbury Camp. Most of the men were Canadian with some British Army units and all were wearing khaki uniforms with the exception of Teacher's RAF unit. He recalls: "I remember King George VI particularly. We were training for some 12 months with the command and were just in khaki, when all of a sudden someone from air force hierarchy came down and said, 'These lads have got to be dressed in blue.' There was a big argument going on and he said, 'I'm very sorry but they are Royal Air Force,

"WE WEREN'T ALLOWED TO CARRY REVOLVERS, SO WE WOULD HAVE HAD TO CARRY STEN GUNS OR RIFLES, WHICH WAS IMPOSSIBLE BECAUSE OF ALL THE EQUIPMENT WE'D BE CARRYING FROM THE LANDING CRAFT."

After the Battle of the Bulge, Teacher had a brief rest in Brussels in February 1945. He is pictured (far left, holding glass) with his comrades in one of the few photographs taken during his war in Europe.

Teacher was still in his teens when this picture was taken of him in his RAF uniform in 1942.

Canadian soldiers landing at Juno on the outskirts of Bernières-sur-Mer, June 6, 1944. Bernières was located in Nan, the easternmost sector of Juno Beach.

"WE . . . HAD TO MAKE SURE THAT ALL THE TROOPS . . . DIDN'T RUN AMOK, BUT WENT THROUGH THE SAFE AREAS THAT HAD BEEN TAPED OFF. IT WAS VERY WELL ORGANIZED. IT WASN'T LIKE IN FILMS WHERE THEY DASH OFF THESE LANDING CRAFT AND RUN."

Below: Canadian soldiers of the Winnipeg Rifles head for Juno Beach aboard LCA (Landing Craft Assault) vessels.

Below: Canadian infantrymen aboard landing craft HMCS Prince Henry moving towards Juno Beach. Teacher's task was to ensure their landing went smoothly.

Below: Canadian reinforcements landing on Juno Beach from HMCS Prince Henry. Teacher was already on the beach.

NORMANDY
JUNE 6, 1944

The Allied Commonwealth landing beaches on D-Day consisted of Gold, Juno, and Sword beaches. Juno was spearheaded by the Canadian 3rd Division and surrounded by the British-led Gold and Sword beaches. Each beach was split into codenamed sectors with Juno consisting of "Love," "Mike," and "Nan." David Teacher landed in "Mike" sector, which meant that he drove his Bedford QL into the heart of the Commonwealth landing grounds at Courseulles-sur-Mer.

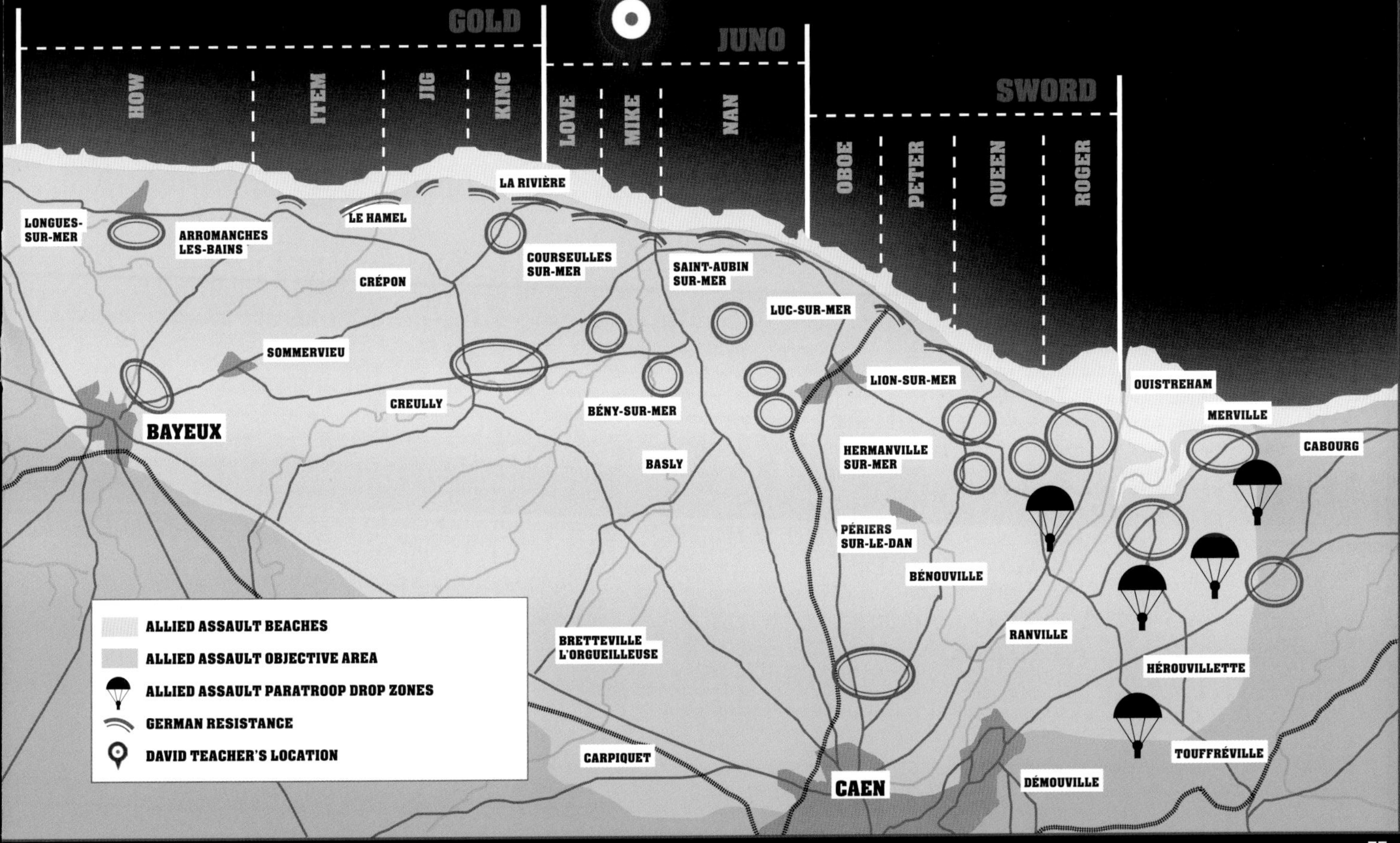

and RAF uniform is blue, so they will wear blue, end of story.' So we were issued with brand-new kit and it was about this time that the king came and inspected us all. We (about a group of 30 men) stood out like a sore finger, so the king wanted to know what this bit of blue was doing among all the khaki. He drove over in his Jeep and dismounted. We opened ranks and he inspected each one of us. We were highly delighted because it was one up for the RAF on the army! It was fabulous."

By contrast, Teacher's memories of Montgomery, the commander of all Allied ground forces for the invasion, were mixed: "He was a very moody man; one day he would be very sociable, another he wouldn't speak to anybody. He was always encouraging us and very optimistic that everything would go well. He was right at the end of the day but he made a lot of mistakes. He wouldn't listen to advice, he was always right, and he always did what he wanted to do."

By the summer, all preparations were complete for Operation Overlord and Teacher drove his Bedford truck to Southampton on June 5, 1944. His was the last of three Bedford trucks (and the only one belonging to the RAF) to reverse onto a landing craft, which meant that he would be first off when it landed for the invasion. However, despite months of training and speculation, Teacher didn't know what his destination would be: "We had no idea where we were landing, not even when we got there. We weren't told anything. I was waiting in a landing craft for about four hours before we went ashore and the coxswain wouldn't say where we were. I don't even know if he knew, certainly he wouldn't tell me if he did."

D-Day

Amidst a choppy sea on June 6, 1944, Teacher sat on top of a truck and observed the vast armada he was part of: "It was unbelievable. You could not realize what was going on. There were thousands of ships and landing craft, battleships, destroyers, aircraft flying overhead . . . the noise was unbelievable. When the navy started bombarding a couple of hours before we went ashore, it was horrendous."

As the flotilla made its way south, Teacher remembers wanting to start what he had trained for months to do: "I just wanted to get on with it. I was just keen to get ashore and get started. We'd been trained repeatedly and now it was a case of putting it all into practice and seeing how well it went. As it happens, it went very well indeed. The weather caused more damage than the enemy."

The official orders for the Beach Squadrons on D-Day were as follows: "No. 1, 2, and 4 RAF Beach Squadrons will work with the Army Beach Organization to supervise the discharge of RAF personnel, vehicles, and stores, and movement to the forward area of all units." The "discharge" area for Teacher would be on Juno Beach.

Juno formed part of five Allied assault beaches along the Normandy coast. Two of these beaches, Omaha and Utah, were to be taken by the

"I JUST WANTED TO GET ON WITH IT. I WAS JUST KEEN TO GET ASHORE AND GET STARTED."

Mike Sector on Juno Beach around the time that Teacher landed at 8:20 a.m. on June 6, 1944. One of the dots on the beach near the landing craft is Teacher's Bedford QL truck.

"WE HAD NO IDEA WHERE WE WERE LANDING, NOT EVEN WHEN WE GOT THERE. WE WEREN'T TOLD ANYTHING."

Americans, with the Commonwealth forces set to secure the remaining three. Teacher witnessed landing craft being thrown in the air and survived an unexploded bomb that landed 20 feet (six meters) away from him. Less than half a mile away from his position, there was close-quarter fighting with bayonets.

This intense scenario was Teacher's first experience of combat but his thorough training served him well: "You revert back to your training and you do what you were told to do. We were very well trained and we kept to the training moves and migrations and got through. In fact it went very easily. At around 4 p.m. the Germans tried to attack, without any success. We had a couple of casualties then, but they were our only battlefield casualties of the campaign." This particular German attack was a heavy air bombardment with anti-personnel bombs in the beach maintenance area.

By the end of June 6, 21,400 Allied soldiers had landed on Juno Beach but 1,200 had become casualties. Such was the German firepower it is estimated that in the first assaults each Canadian soldier had a 50-50 chance of survival. Nevertheless by the end of the day the Canadians had cleared exits off the beach and linked up with the British at Gold Beach. Teacher remembers them as, "Excellent lads. They were all young boys but very high-spirited, eager, and very nice to get on with."

The RAF's own ground statistics for Juno on D-Day were impressive: 657 RAF personnel disembarked along with 75 tons of stores and 146 M T vehicles were landed. However, Teacher would not leave the area for months: "We weren't allowed off the beach. For three months we just took equipment in, food, ammunition—anything that was required to serve the army." The Commonwealth beaches were codenamed after fish: Gold (fish), Sword (fish), and Jelly (fish). In the latter's case it was rumored that Winston Churchill crossed out "Jelly" and replaced it with the word "Juno" after the Roman goddess.

The beach was a six-mile (10-kilometer) stretch of coast centered around the small fishing village of Courseulles-sur-Mer and split into three sectors known as "Love," "Mike," and "Nan." Unlike Gold and Sword beaches, which were primarily assaulted by the British, Juno was in the hands of the Canadian 3rd Division. Their task would be to link up with Gold to the west and Sword to the east. Nevertheless, before the bulk of the Canadians could land, the beach units—including Teacher's—had to disembark and establish themselves.

Teacher vividly remembers the dicey start to his own landing in "Mike" sector at 8:20 a.m. on June 6: "I was one of the first to shore. It was very noisy, but the coxswain said, 'I'm sorry Dave, but I'm going to have to drop you in deep water.' I said 'How deep?' He said, 'I'm afraid to say very deep. Come on, let's get going,' and he dropped the front part of the landing craft. I went into the sea and went down and down. It actually stopped sinking when the water was up to my chest. So I put it in gear, four-wheel drive, and drove it to shore without any problems at all."

Once he had landed, Teacher drove to a sandy clearing known as a "DVP" (Drowned Vehicle Park) where all broken-down vehicles were to be stored. He left his Bedford there and returned to the beach: "We were in control of the equipment that came through Juno Beach. We also had to make sure that all the troops that came ashore didn't run amok, but went through the safe areas that had been taped off. It was very well organized. It wasn't like in films where they dash off these landing craft and run . . . Obviously there were those who got injured, but generally speaking it went very well."

As a mechanic Teacher would also fix broken-down vehicles and move them on as quickly as possible. Nevertheless, he was under fire from the Germans who counterattacked using 88-mm guns and aerial bombardment.

Teacher remained on Juno Beach from June 6 until it was closed on September 6, 1944. The unit was shelled almost every day as the Germans could fire with 88-mm guns

Right: A heavily armed German machine-gunner carrying ammunition boxes in the Ardennes, December 1944. Their tenacious fighting offensive put severe strain on the Allies in Belgium.

The wreckage of a German tank, destroyed near Bastogne during the Battle of the Bulge. Teacher often fought near the American 101st Airborne Division.

BEDFORD QL TRUCK

The truck that David Teacher drove on D-Day was a highly adaptable and functional vehicle.

Manufactured by Bedford Vehicles, a subsidiary of Vauxhall Motors, the QL was one of the most widely produced trucks of the war with 52,247 being manufactured between 1941-45. Bedford was contracted by the British War Office to produce a three-ton 4x4 general service truck in 1939. It took only a year to develop from prototype to production, which was an impressive feat in a time of national crisis.

The QL was designed to use its four-wheel drive on rough terrain but it could also convert to front-wheel drive on hard roads to ease the wear on tires and the gearbox. It was known for its flexibility and could be used in a variety of roles. A QL could act as a troop carrier, field kitchen, tanker, cargo, communications, and breakdown recovery vehicle. It could also be adapted to take attachments such as a Bofors gun tractor, fire tender, anti-aircraft guns, and could even be converted into an office or signal van.

Teacher's association with the QL was not unusual as the RAF was one of its major operators and many were used as fuel tankers with swinging booms to refuel aircraft. This was somewhat ironic as the QL had a low fuel economy.

"WE HAD NO LEAVE, YOU COULDN'T WRITE LETTERS, AND EVERYTHING WAS HEAVILY CENSORED."

from miles away. There were also continual problems with flies that were attracted to dead bodies. To compound matters, Teacher was constrained by censorship: "It was still very secretive. We had no leave, you couldn't write letters, and everything was heavily censored. We also weren't allowed any contact with the local population at all. That was it, we just got on with what we had to do."

Nevertheless, by the time Teacher left Juno, the combined operations units had discharged a total of 20,650 tons of stores, disembarked 30,728 personnel, and landed 8,644 vehicles. Along with similar impressive feats from the other beaches, there was now no going back, and Teacher's own war in Europe was far from over.

Battle of the Bulge

After a short spell in England, Teacher was transferred to No. 2742 Squadron, RAF Regiment. Initially designed for defensive security purposes, 2742 Squadron was reconfigured to become a reconnaissance unit. Teacher's job was to maintain and drive the vehicles of the squadron that belonged to "A" flight. These included a Bedford truck, one Jeep and BSA motorcycle, an American Dodge truck, and five Humber Super Snipe cars.

Teacher quickly returned to the Continent in September, and by December he was recovering in a Brussels hospital after a motorcycle accident. The 2742 Squadron was supposed to spend Christmas 1944 in Ghent, but only a week after leaving the hospital, Teacher's unit was assigned to work with the US 8th Corps at Bastogne. The Belgian town was close to the Luxembourg border and only 50 miles (80 kilometers) away from German territory. Teacher arrived on December 17 and his sudden deployment was a surprise: "We weren't told where we were going, and were given 30 minutes' notice to set off. The weather was terrible, it was just starting to snow, and we finished up in the Bulge." It was unfortunate timing as the Battle of the Bulge had just begun.

This huge battle was the last major German offensive campaign in Western

Below: QL trucks proved to be so reliable that they remained in service with the British armed forces until the early 1960s.

Right: David Teacher with a Bedford truck similar to the ones he drove on D-Day.

THE BRITISH AT THE BULGE

Although the battle in the Ardennes was primarily fought between the US Army and the Wehrmacht, thousands of British troops also took part.

It is estimated that along with 500,000 American soldiers, approximately 55,000 troops of the British Army (including Canadians) fought in the Battle of the Bulge.

On December 19, 1944, Supreme Allied Commander Dwight D. Eisenhower placed all Allied forces north of Givet and Prum under the command of Field Marshal Bernard Montgomery. British troops from XXX Corps halted the advance of the 2nd Panzer Division on the River Meuse on December 24 and heavy casualties were incurred in three days of fighting from January 3, 1945. By January 8, the German High Command realized that their attack had failed, but fighting continued against their rearguard. Montgomery then ordered XXX Corps back to the Netherlands eight days later.

Although he would later exaggerate the British contribution to the battle, their defense of the northern sector was a valuable contribution. Casualties were also high with around 1,400 killed, wounded, or missing.

Montgomery and Eisenhower (right), 1944. The two allies clashed during the Battle of the Bulge with Montgomery undiplomatically quipping that American troops made great fighting men when given proper leadership

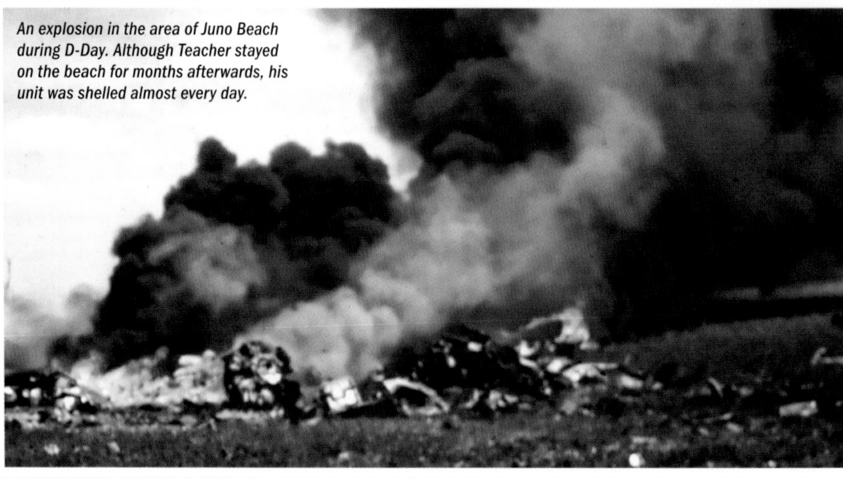

An explosion in the area of Juno Beach during D-Day. Although Teacher stayed on the beach for months afterwards, his unit was shelled almost every day.

Europe and Hitler's last gamble to halt the Allied advance. The overall plan was to drive a wedge through Allied forces, break them in two, and recapture the port of Antwerp. In an eerie repeat of the Battle of France, the Germans completely surprised thinly defended Allied lines in the Ardennes forest and the resulting advance made a literal "bulge" on military maps. Half a million German soldiers, including 13 infantry divisions and seven armored divisions, were aided by poor weather conditions that prevented Allied air attacks from assisting the beleaguered troops on the ground. The vast majority of Allied troops in the Ardennes were American but around 55,000 troops serving in the British armed forces, including Teacher, also fought in the battle.

Bastogne was an important strategic crossroads in the Ardennes and approximately 11,000 American troops quickly became besieged by around 54,000 German soldiers from December 20. 2742 Squadron's task was to seek out German units and report their position in the area near Bastogne. Teacher was largely positioned around Marche-en-Famenne, 20 miles (32 kilometers) northwest of Bastogne from December 21: "We were near the 101st Airborne Division: we were only yards from them in many places. It's strange to think what a small world it is!"

Fighting conditions during the battle were notoriously difficult: "We were in or near Bastogne for weeks . . . it was cold, wet, and miserable. We had no food or heat. The snow was six feet (1.8 meters) deep. The temperature was extremely low and we were in summer uniform. It wasn't pleasant."

Teacher and the other members of 2742 relied on the Americans to keep the squadron going: "We were depending on the Americans for food and fuel. As I was the driver and mechanic, it was my job to bring up rations and supplies. I saw more of the Yanks than most people did. They were very nice lads, doing a great job under difficult conditions. It was organized chaos. There was no day or night, it was just cold, dark, wet, and miserable."

No fires were permitted during the battle and Teacher still had to run the engines of his vehicles every 15 minutes to prevent the fuel freezing in temperatures as low as -1 degree Fahrenheit (-18 degrees Celsius). Nevertheless, despite the conditions Teacher's diligence did not go unnoticed and it was noted in the squadron's records: "Vehicle maintenance in these testing conditions has been first class." Teacher puts it more modestly, "We came out of the battle in late December 1944, early January 1945, after four-and-a-half weeks of fighting. It was a long stretch. We were under constant attack and those four weeks were the worst experience of my service, but we survived."

The Invasion of Germany

Bastogne was eventually relieved on December 26, 1944, and Teacher left the battlefield a few days later. After a brief rest in Ghent and Brussels, 2742 Squadron was ordered to prepare for the invasion of Germany. On March 15, 1945, Teacher crossed the River Rhine into Germany: "We were the first RAF ground unit to cross the Rhine but obviously aircraft had been over in the sky beforehand."

Teacher was understandably nervous: "We were all very concerned. We'd fought the enemy without really seeing them, and we wondered how determined they would be to defend their own Fatherland." However, he was surprised when armed resistance fell away inside Germany: "As it turns out, it was a doddle by comparison to the rest of the war. They did not put up a great fight in Germany itself; they kept surrendering and the biggest problem then was taking prisoners."

Nevertheless, Teacher was not spared the full horrors of Nazi brutality. When Buchenwald concentration camp was liberated by American forces in April 1945, Supreme Allied Commander Dwight D. Eisenhower insisted that all Allied personnel within the vicinity had to go past the camp. Some 250,000 people had been imprisoned at Buchenwald between 1937-45 and although exact mortality figures can only be estimated, at least 56,000 prisoners were murdered, including 11,000 Jews. When the Americans liberated the camps they found 21,000 emaciated and starved prisoners as well as piles of dead bodies. Eisenhower wanted as many men as possible to see the camp because he believed, "the day will come when some son of a bitch will say this never happened."

Eisenhower views the bodies of prisoners in Buchenwald concentration camp, April 12, 1945. He ordered every Allied personnel within the vicinity, including Teacher, to pass through the camp to prevent Holocaust denial.

More details about David Teacher's life and military career can be found in his 2016 autobiography ***Beyond My Wildest Dreams.***

"EISENHOWER WANTED AS MANY MEN AS POSSIBLE TO SEE THE CAMP BECAUSE HE BELIEVED, 'THE DAY WILL COME WHEN SOME SON OF A BITCH WILL SAY THIS NEVER HAPPENED.'"

Teacher was one of those ordered to witness the horror and although he is Jewish, he is keen to note that the camp's victims did not just include Jews: "We went past Buchenwald just after it had been liberated; we were probably one of the first of the general bulk of the army to see what went on. I don't think it makes a difference being Jewish or not. There were atrocities committed to non-Jewish people as well. Anyone who wasn't Aryan was rubbish, and treated as such."

His experience at Buchenwald reinforced his already low opinion of the Germans and the brutalities they inflicted on civilians: "They were a determined lot, but to me the only good German was a dead German . . . We saw some terrible atrocities that they had committed: burning churches, women and children being tortured, and general maltreatment. The thing that upset me was that afterwards they used to run around firing their weapons in the air, it wasn't nice."

By VE Day on May 8, Teacher and the RAF Regiment was approximately 50 miles (80 kilometers) from Berlin and he was relieved that the Russians would take the German capital: "We had no choice. We were told the Russians would get there first, and to be honest we were quite happy about it because of the casualties. The Russians had lost 250,000 men just taking Berlin and those could have been our casualties. So those were lives saved. The Russians were more than happy to do it." Having been through so much since D-Day, Teacher (still only 21 years old) was relieved the war had ended: "It was a great relief when the fighting was over. It was inevitable it was going to happen and there was no doubt about how it was going to end, so the sooner it ended the better."

After a short spell back home, Teacher was posted to the Azores en route to the Far East but the Japanese surrendered and he was eventually demobbed in December 1946.

Recognition

In the years since the war, Teacher has been heavily involved in charity work and was subsequently awarded an MBE for his work with ex-service organizations in Greater Manchester. In 2015 he was also awarded the Legion of Honor by the French government after President François Hollande officially recognized all surviving British veterans who fought for the liberation of France between 1944-45.

Since 2015, Teacher has volunteered at Imperial War Museum North in Stretford, Manchester and speaks to school parties and adults, averaging around 2,000 people per month. He enjoys hearing the varied and occasionally humorous questions from schoolchildren: "The main thing is about food, 'What did you get to eat?' and sometimes I'm asked, 'How did you charge your mobile phone?' They are very receptive; some are very knowledgeable and others are curious. I go twice a week to IWM North, its very enjoyable."

As for his own dramatic experiences during the war, Teacher's main memories are positive despite the frequently horrific events he endured: "I enjoyed every minute of it. I enjoyed the comradeship, including the hardships, because we all went through it together. I enjoyed my service career immensely; it's something I would do again if I had to—I wouldn't hesitate. It was a wonderful way of life, no doubt about it."

Images: Alamy

THE FRENCH RESISTANCE & D-DAY

Sabotage, espionage, intelligence gathering, and small-scale combat were among the many contributions made by the French Resistance before and during the Normandy assault.

BY WILL LAWRENCE

The message arrived over the airwaves on June 1, 1944, courtesy of the French service of the BBC. It was a warning for the French Resistance to prepare en masse. Running contrary to the Allied predilection for carefully disguised codes, it said simply: "The moment of battle is approaching." All over France, members of the Resistance, German security forces, and ordinary citizens huddled around radios waiting to hear what might come next. Could the moment of liberation be nigh?

The confirmation came four days later on June 5 as personal messages rang across radios all over France, asking the Resistance to spring into action. The messages were sent countrywide so that the enemy would not know the identity of the primary landing grounds. In Normandy, the Allies' true destination, the voice said: "The dice are down." All across the region, the freedom fighters sprang into action, cutting communications lines.

The Germans did not respond. Admittedly, false alarms had echoed across the Channel throughout the spring, but it must be noted that neither the Germans, nor indeed the Supreme Headquarters Allied Expeditionary Force (SHAEF), placed that much faith in the influence of the French Resistance. The London-based Special Operations Executive (SOE) parachuted in money and weapons throughout the war, hopeful that the Resistance would be useful providing intelligence and military support after D-Day, but hopes were not high. In the run-up to D-Day, the SOE was in contact with almost 140 active stations in France and during the spring of 1944 it estimated the French Resistance movement at around 350,000 active members. However, it also believed that only around 100,000 had serviceable firearms and that only 10,000 of these had enough ammunition to sustain more than one day's combat. Consequently, the SOE considered that during the D-Day operations the Resistance would be best suited to intelligence-gathering and sabotage rather than long-form guerrilla warfare.

Though Normandy was the Allied choice for the D-Day landings, the actual number of active Resistance members operating in the region was relatively small. It has been said that the most active as a fighting force was the Surcouf group at Pont-Audemer. There were 200 fighters in the Bayeux area and further inland, in and around the forests of Orne, there were around 1,800 Resistance members of whom around one-third were thought to be armed. Despite the relatively small numbers of armed fighters in the area, a steady supply of information passed back across the Channel, with workers in the local laundries identifying the exact German divisions stationed nearby, and plotting out German minefields.

The supply of information from the Resistance led to a number of notable successes. The data used by the British to take

Liberation of Paris, August 25, 1944. Gendarmes, soldiers, and Resistance fighters escort German prisoners in front of the opera house.

Right: Fighters study weapons dropped by parachute in the Haute Loire, including a Sten Mk II, Ruby, Colt, and Le Francois pistols and Colt and Bulldog revolvers.

The Resistance sabotage the Marseille-Paris railway in Romanèche on August 30, 1944.

control of the bridge over the Orne at Bénouville, for example, which was seized via a daring glider attack, came from members of the Resistance.

Indeed, the Résistance-Fer, a covert organization of French railwaymen, proved especially effective at both intelligence gathering and sabotage. They were able to provide information on German unit strengths: the 12th SS Panzer Division, for example, was estimated at full strength by the railwaymen as they had been told that 84 trains were required to move them. They then concentrated their efforts on helping regular Resistance groups blow up trains as they passed through tunnels, making the salvation operations especially difficult. They also regularly diverted German troop trains down the wrong lines.

According to the historian Antony Beevor, heavy lifting cranes became a prime focus, with the Résistance-Fer guiding air and sabotage attacks, while engines were targeted in the yards and train tracks were constantly exploded. The Résistance-Fer halted much rail traffic within Burgundy and eastern France, right up to the German border. Beevor reports that around Dijon, 37 railway lines were cut, prompting terrible reprisals against the French workers. Hundreds were executed and thousands more were carted off to concentration camps.

In one instance, the railroad attacks caused a traffic jam of 51 trains backed up around Lille, and these made easy pickings for Allied bombing sorties. Damage to rail tracks not only hindered troop movement, it also placed extra strain on the German war machine. By 1944 Hitler was desperately short of fuel, and forcing the Germans to move by road ate up precious reserves.

Similarly, rubber was also in short supply and tank tracks had a limited life span. Using this up on basic movement was a poor use of a precious resource. The Resistance set about the German road movements with heavy tacks and glass scattered on the roads as part of the Tortoise Plan.

The Resistance attacks on the railways were all part of the carefully laid Green Plan, which unfolded alongside three other sabotage plans. French telecommunications workers at the PTT were responsible for the Violet Plan, targeting landline communications by cutting important cables. This forced German forces to communicate by radio, which was targeted by the Allied decoders using Ultra. The Blue Plan, meanwhile, sabotaged strategic power lines, while the Bibendum Plan chose to target troop transport.

Back in London, SHAEF planned the operational activities of the special forces who would parachute behind enemy lines and work with Resistance groups on the ground. In the first few days after the Allied landings, SAS and SOE teams were dropped all over France in a bid to cause as much havoc as possible. One great success, involving both the SAS and the Resistance, came on June 10 when a group of local French fighters approached the 50-strong SAS force in the forest of Verrières in the Vienne, who had landed three days earlier.

"THE RÉSISTANCE-FER HALTED MUCH RAIL TRAFFIC WITHIN BURGUNDY AND EASTERN FRANCE, RIGHT UP TO THE GERMAN BORDER."

The Resistance members brought news of huge German petrol stocks laid up at a railways junction at Châtellerault, 35 miles (56 kilometers) north. The SAS sent out one Lt. Stephens, who dressed as a Frenchman and rode out on a bicycle with two local fighters to reconnoiter the area. It was a dangerous journey—in the wake of the landings, the region was awash with Germans on high alert—but it was fruitful and Stephens saw line upon line of tanker wagons brimming with vital fuel supplies (which, it was later discovered, was designated for the deadly "Das Reich" 2nd SS Panzer Division). There were 11 gas trains halted in the sidings around 3,000 feet (900 meters) east of the junction, and these were covered with heavy camouflage netting and had thus far escaped Allied air assault.

Stephens and his colleagues made it back to camp the following night, and within hours a radio message had called in an air strike. The trains and their precious cargo were destroyed, and the 2nd SS Panzer Division arrived on the Normandy battleground much later than intended. The Germans responded with a large assault against the SAS camp, and Stephens and many others paid the ultimate price; they were captured and executed a few days later. But this mission proved a masterclass of coordinated action between intelligence forces, special forces, and the Resistance.

Elsewhere, news of the Allied landings prompted several acts of foolhardiness from Resistance groups. On June 8, one group seized the industrial town of Tulle, killing more than 50 German soldiers, an action that prompted terrible reprisals. The aforementioned "Das Reich" 2nd SS Panzer Division, comprising 15,000 men and more than 1,400 vehicles, roared into the region and retook the town. Appalled by their humiliation at the hands of "terrorists" a few days before, the

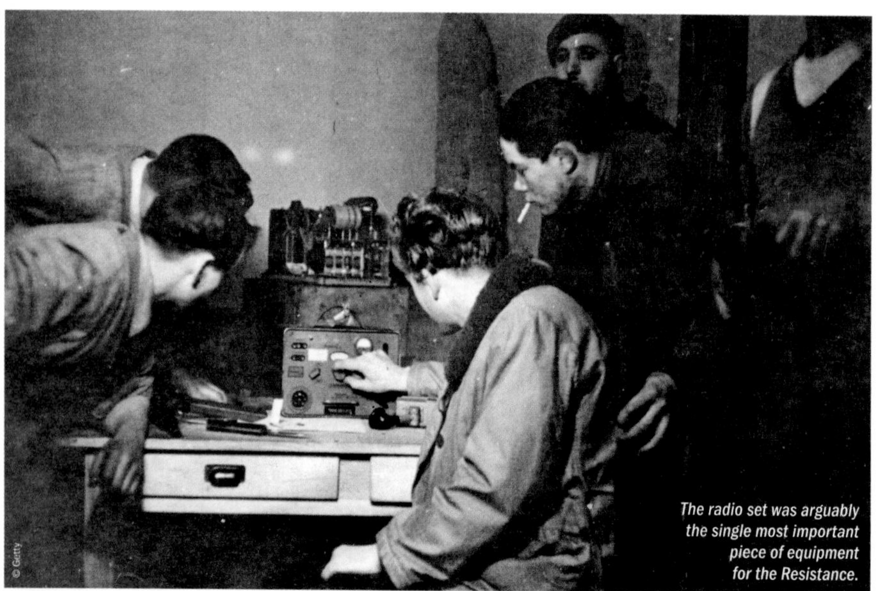

The radio set was arguably the single most important piece of equipment for the Resistance.

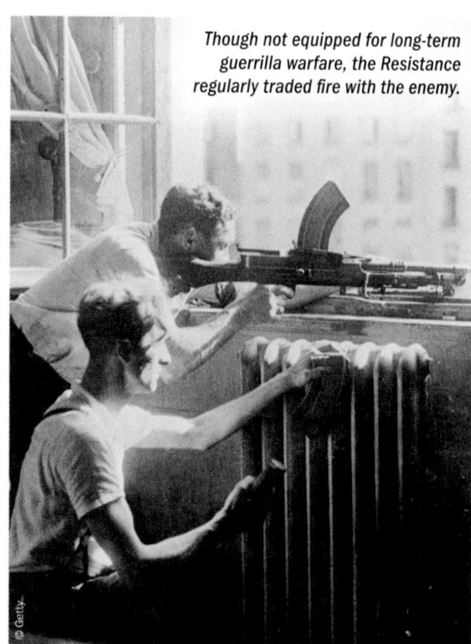

Though not equipped for long-term guerrilla warfare, the Resistance regularly traded fire with the enemy.

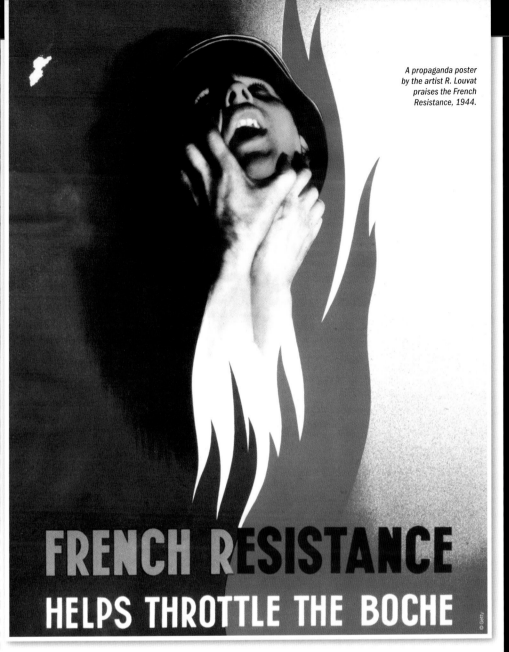

A propaganda poster by the artist R. Louvat praises the French Resistance, 1944.

FRENCH RESISTANCE
HELPS THROTTLE THE BOCHE

© Getty

Germans began hanging innocent men. More than 200 civilians died. On June 10 "Das Reich" extended reprisals further north with another massacre at Oradour-sur-Glane.

Another group of 28 Resistance fighters managed to hold up an entire column from "Das Reich" for 48 hours near Souillac. Almost all of these men fell in battle but, thanks to the combined efforts of the Resistance, the SAS, and Allied bombing, it took the feared 2nd SS Panzer Division 17 days to reach the front line, two weeks later than planned. Given the lack of experience among so many of the Germans fighting on the Western Front, depriving the front line of such battle-hardened and vicious troops may have proved pivotal.

In the months after D-Day, the Resistance expanded enormously. One fighter from the Grenoble region, on hearing of the Normandy landings, declared: "The underground Resistance is over! Open Resistance begins!" In the words of a leading historian of the Resistance movement, "Hundreds of thousands of men and women who had previously remained at home—out of fear, uncertainty, or simple ignorance as to how to join the Resistance—put on armbands . . . and helped liberate their country."

There was some disdain shown towards these latecomers by those who had risked so much during the occupation. They were often dubbed *resistance du mois de septembre*. Those who resisted in June 1944 and who helped the Allies establish their foothold in France had run a grave risk. The Allied commanders who had doubted the Resistance could no longer find fault in their courage or their resolve. The French Resistance played its part in the liberation of its country.

The freedom fighters took grave risks, and many were captured and executed by the occupying forces.

© Getty

MAQUIS SURCOUF

These fighters were the most militarily active of the Resistance groups in Normandy at the time of the D-Day landings.

This Maquis, or group of Resistance fighters, was founded and led by Robert Leblanc, who worked as grocer at Saint-Étienne-l'Allier. It was put together over the course of 1942-43 with the help and complicity of Father Meulan, a local parish priest. The Maquis Surcouf was the most militarily active of all the small groups in the Normandy region and was tightly organized, its actions unfolding in the region of Vièvre and Lieuvin.

At its apex in June 1944, the group numbered almost 250 men, though combat losses saw the numbers dwindle. The group's balance sheet as of the end of August 1944 recorded 104 Germans killed, more than 270 taken captive, along with several hundred machine guns captured. It also claimed the recovery of 10 motorcycles, four trucks, and five automobiles. In a high-profile mission, the group claimed the life of the infamous Gestapo collaborator Violette Morris, who they shot in an ambush in April 1944.

Leblanc's courage during the course of the occupation and liberation of France saw him awarded the National Order of the Legion of Honor, the War Cross with Palms, the Combatant's Cross of the Resistance, and the Bronze Star Medal of the United States. The group has been commemorated by several monuments, including one that stands on the road between Épaignes and Lieurey. The town of Épaignes also sports a monument in memory of four members of the Maquis Surcouf shot by the Germans.

Robert Leblanc was the founder and charismatic leader of the Maquis Surcouf.

Creative Commons; Credit Robert Leblanc

HEROES OF OVERLORD

THE SUCCESS OF THE ALLIED OPERATION WAS OFTEN DOWN TO SMALL BUT CRUCIAL ACTS OF HEROISM.

JOHN G. BURKHALTER

YEARS ACTIVE: 1942-69
FORCE: UNITED STATES ARMY
RANK: LIEUTENANT COLONEL

Burkhalter was an unlikely soldier—in 1935, he was named senior pastor of a Baptist church in Florida, however, he decided to combine his faith with his military career. He was assigned to the 1st Infantry Division in 1943 and landed on Omaha Beach on D-Day. A letter that he wrote to his wife was printed in the Miami Daily News, bringing the public a true account of the horrors experienced by those fighting on the beaches.

Burkhalter's regiment formed part of the front line and he described the soldiers alongside him as having great courage.

As he witnessed men being killed by artillery shells, he prayed intensely, saying that "danger was everywhere; death was not far off." Witnessing death all around him, the pastor crawled up the high hills along the beach with his fellow soldiers. When the battle was over, he administered blessings to the dead Allied and German troops.

Burkhalter went on to fight in the battle of the Bulge, where he sustained multiple head injuries. After the battle he was declared "missing in action" (MIA) until he turned up in a French hospital. For his immense bravery he was awarded the Purple Heart, Bronze Star, and the Silver Star.

Image source: Public Domain, US Government

Major General Matthew B. Ridgway (left) decorates Brigadier James Hill with the US Silver Star.

Image source: IWM Collection, IWM Photo No: BU 2310

JAMES HILL

YEARS ACTIVE: 1931-48
FORCE: BRITISH ARMY
RANK: BRIGADIER

In the days before D-Day, Brigadier Hill was placed in charge of the 3rd Parachute Brigade in the 6th Airborne Division. Formed solely for the Normandy landings, the brigade was full of volunteers who had no parachute experience, and Hill set about training them. He drove the men hard, including the clerks and telephone operators, urging them to practice in the dark and sending them on two-hour marches carrying 60 pounds (30 kilograms) of equipment.

In order to keep morale up, he introduced parachuting dogs and encouraged the men to go to church—something they later thanked him for. Before they went into the fray, he said to his men: "Gentlemen, in spite of your excellent training and very clear orders, don't be daunted if chaos reigns—because it certainly will."

When the brigade landed on the night of D-Day, Hill found himself in 4.5 feet (1.4 meters) of water due to an inaccurate landing. He gathered the men he could find (about 42) and they tied themselves together. As enemy aircraft passed over, Hill threw himself on the man in front as the brigade was pummeled.

Although he was hit, Hill survived, but there was only one other man who was able to stand. After giving morphine to the injured, Hill pushed on knowing that as commander he had a responsibility to pursue the objective. He marched for four-and-a-half hours to get to the original planned landing location, and once he discovered his battalion had achieved their objectives, he finally allowed the doctors to treat his severe wounds.

Refusing to allow much time for his recovery, Hill threw himself back into command and led a counter-attack during a German assault. The bodies of the men of his brigade who had died were thrown into a big shell hole by the Germans, however, the area was soon recaptured and Hill made sure to unearth them and give them the burials they deserved.

Mynarski's Lancaster bomber was shot down while flying over northern France.

Mynarski was 27 when he died.

Image source: IWMCollection IWM Photo No: CHP 975

ANDREW MYNARSKI

YEARS ACTIVE: 1940-44
FORCE: ROYAL CANADIAN AIR FORCE
RANK: PILOT OFFICER

After the D-Day attacks, on June 12, 1944, Mynarski was flying aboard a Lancaster bomber preparing for a raid on northern France. Although the crew reached their target, they were spotted by the enemy and the plane was pummeled with cannon fire.

The men were ordered to bail out, but as Mynarski went to leave, he noticed that one of the officers, Pat Brophy, was stuck in his turret. Mynarski immediately went back through the flames to help Brophy, using whatever he could get his hands on to free the trapped pilot. Noticing that Mynarski's parachute and flight suit were both on fire, Brophy signaled him to leave. Mynarski eventually complied; when he reached the door, he turned, saluted and said "good night, sir" before jumping.

Due to his burning parachute lines, Mynarski dropped rapidly, and although he survived the impact, he was severely burned. He was taken to a German field hospital but died of his wounds. By a miracle, Brophy managed to survive the crash, and when he learned of Mynarski's death, told the story of his valiant efforts to save him. Mynarski was posthumously awarded the Victoria Cross for "valor of the highest order."

SAM GIBBONS

YEARS ACTIVE: 1941-45
FORCE: UNITED STATES ARMY
RANK: CAPTAIN

Although he is now remembered for his work in the political world, Gibbons postponed his law education to serve as a second lieutenant, and eventually captain, after the outbreak of World War II. He was a member of the 501st Parachute Infantry Regiment when it landed near Carentan, France, on D-Day.

Aged just 24, Gibbons landed in a field and followed the sound of metal clickers to find his fellow paratroopers. On June 13, the battalion went head to head in a battle against German tanks as the main German force moved towards Carentan. The relentless battle raged from 6 a.m. to 10 p.m., with only 400 of the 600 paratroopers who began that day still alive by the end. Against tremendous odds, the men managed to restore their line of defense. From where Gibbons was positioned, he saw a dozen burning tanks. For his brave actions, he was awarded the Bronze Star, and the conflict was later immortalized in the war drama *Band of Brothers*. Many who knew him best said that he went into politics not to win wars, but to make them unnecessary.

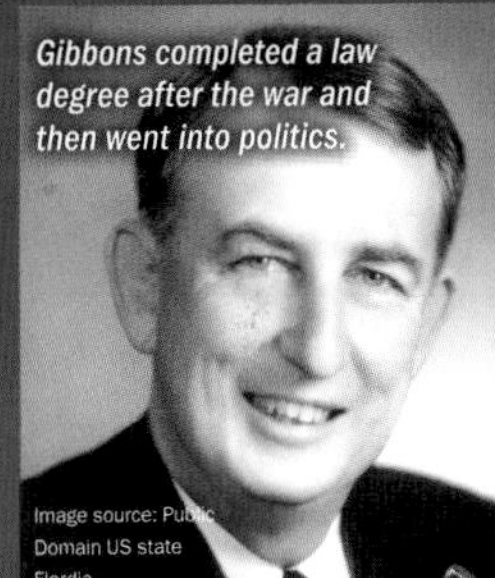
Gibbons completed a law degree after the war and then went into politics.

Image source: Public Domain US state Flordia

DAVID JAMIESON

YEARS ACTIVE: 1939-48
FORCE: BRITISH ARMY
RANK: CAPTAIN

Jamieson's army career began early when he worked as a volunteer in the Territorial Army in 1939 aged just 19. Despite his young age, he was quickly promoted to second lieutenant. However, when his battalion went to France in 1940, he was considered too young to accompany them. Nevertheless, the intrepid young soldier soon followed, and by the time he turned 23, he had been promoted to captain of the 7th Battalion of the Royal Norfolk Regiment. On August 7-8, Jamieson was in command of a company just south of Grimbosq, Normandy, a position he filled by being the only officer remaining. The area offered the Germans useful cover to prepare their counterattacks, so the company soon found itself under fire from the 12th Panzer Division. The men faced overwhelming odds against a slew of attacks from Tiger and Panzer tanks. Jamieson was witnessed mounting a British tank to relay information to the commander inside, all under heavy enemy fire. Through 36 hours of bitter fighting, and sustaining multiple wounds, the young captain motivated his men with determination and a cool head. Seven German counterattacks were repulsed and the enemy suffered great losses, largely thanks to Jamieson's noble and courageous leadership, for which he later received the Victoria Cross.

STANLEY HOLLIS

YEARS ACTIVE: 1939-44
FORCE: BRITISH ARMY
RANK: COMPANY SERGEANT MAJOR

Born in Middlesbrough, young Stanley Hollis worked in his father's fish-and-chip shop as a boy. When he was old enough, he joined the merchant navy, but he was struck with blackwater fever and forced to return home. With two young children to support, he became a lorry driver, but he joined the army with the Green Howards shortly before war broke out and quickly rose through the ranks to become a company sergeant major.

After landing at the beaches on D-Day, Hollis went with his commander to investigate two German pillboxes. Hollis fearlessly rushed into one pillbox and took all but five of the Germans prisoner. He quickly dealt with the second, taking 26 prisoners.

Just hours later, he discovered that two of his men had been left behind after an unsuccessful raid. Simply saying "I took them in, I will try to get them out," he went back alone. Facing enemies armed with machine guns, he distracted their attention with a grenade. Although it failed to go off, it gave him enough time to run in, shoot them down, and rescue his men.

In recognition of his gallantry, Hollis was the only soldier to be awarded a Victoria Cross on D-Day.

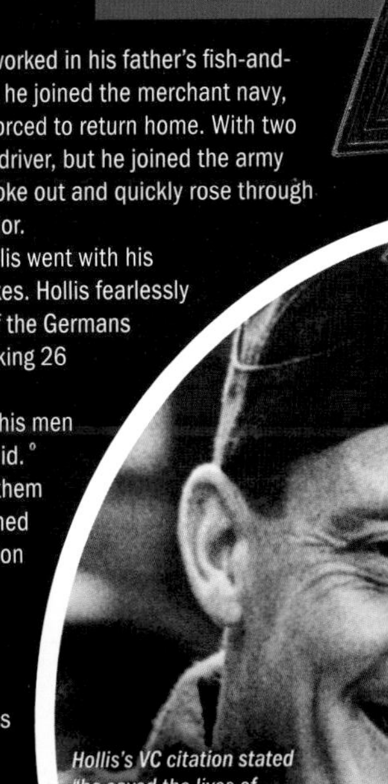
Hollis's VC citation stated "he saved the lives of many of his men."

© Alamy

THE GERMAN RESPONSE

Despite the valiant efforts of the Waffen-SS, poor leadership from the top fatally hampered the German retaliation to D-Day.

BY **WILL LAWRENCE**

Hitler knew that an Allied attack in the west would decide the war. If he could repel an invasion, it would take the Allies years to rearm and to rebuild their armies. He would then be free to unleash all his fighting power in the east for a final showdown with Russia. The Eastern Front was proving intolerable and his armies there were close to breaking point. Between July 1943 and May 1944, the war in the east had seen the destruction of 41 divisions.

By June 1944, he had 59 divisions in Western Europe. If the Allied landings were quashed, he could send these against the Russians, while, he figured, within a year his jet aircraft and secret weapons would be significantly developed. Victory in Europe would bring total victory to the Reich.

"THE SPEED AND MANEUVERABILITY OF TANKS, WHICH COULD STEM AN ATTACK UNTIL INFANTRYARRIVED . . . WOULD BE PIVOTAL."

It was towards the end of 1943 that Hitler recognized the Western allies as a serious threat. The war in Africa had seen the British regain their confidence as a fighting force following their defeat in France during the opening stages of the war, while the Americans had gained vital battlefield experience during their first exchanges in the Western Theater. His much-vaunted Atlantic Wall, meanwhile, a streak of fortresses and naval defenses. designed to run from Norway to the Spanish frontier, had not been completed. In some sectors, work had not even begun.

In November 1943, came Führer Directive No. 51, in which he recognized the imminent danger in the west and pledged to no longer deplete his forces there in favor of the war in the east. He went further, proclaiming, "I have therefore decided to reinforce its defenses, particularly those places from which long-range bombardment of England [with pilotless missiles] will begin."

Hitler boosted the German Army Command in the West (Oberbefehlshaber West, or OB West)—comprising Army Groups B and G under Field Marshal Gerd von Rundstedt—by concentrating on the reinforcement of its panzer and panzergrenadier divisions. In January 1944, there were 24 panzer divisions on the Eastern Front and eight elsewhere; courtesy of Directive No. 51 by June 1944 the split was 18 in the east and 15 elsewhere.

The deployment of panzer divisions in the west was critical. The rest of OB West was practically immobile. The Atlantic Wall (where it was completed), designated "fortresses" at vital ports and beach defenses were manned by troops that were not supposed to leave their stations, while the other sections of the army groups lacked mechanized transport and fuel. They were almost entirely reliant on the French railway system, which was susceptible to air attack and sabotage, while German artillery and supply units relied on horsepower. With the exception of bicycle reconnaissance companies, the German forces while marching were no swifter than Europe's medieval armies. The speed and maneuverability of tanks, which could stem an attack until infantry arrived to reinforce and counter, would be pivotal.

The mighty Panzer Lehr Division was recalled from Hungary to Châtres and the 21st Panzer Division was brought into Caen. The panzer forces would also, to some degree at least, compensate for the lack of quality among OB West's foot soldiers. There was a pair of potent parachute divisions in Brittany and both the 352nd and 91st Infantry Divisions, each assigned to coastal positions were of sound quality, but Hitler's past insistence on concentrating his crack troops in the east, where the threat was actual rather than imminent, meant that many of the troops left to defend the west were formed from divisions that had been shattered in the Russian conflict, or which were either too old or too medically unfit for service against the Red Army. His forces in Europe also included defectors from Russia, Italy, and Poland, and some units were bolstered by forced laborers and conscripts from the occupied territories.

In a bid to remedy the situation in the west he appointed Erwin Rommel, the "Desert Fox," to

Hitler hoped the Atlantic Wall would keep Britain and America at bay but many compared it to the ill-fated Maginot Line.

Though Hitler wanted to hold the French ports, his commanders knew they'd have to surrender Cherbourg.

GERMAN COMMANDERS IN THE WEST

FIELD MARSHAL GERD VON RUNDSTEDT

The Commander-in-Chief of German Army Command in the West, comprising Army Groups B and G, at the time of the Normandy landings, Rundstedt served in WWI before commanding Army Group South in the invasion of Poland. He commanded Army Group A during the Battle of France and Army Group South during the invasion of Russia. Hitler became frustrated by his defeatism and replaced him in Normandy with Field Marshal von Kluge during July 1944.

FIELD MARSHAL ERWIN ROMMEL

Cutting his teeth in World War I, Rommel distinguished himself as the commander of the 7th Panzer Division during the invasion of France. He earned a nickname, "the Desert Fox," during distinguished service in the North Africa campaign before he was appointed to the command of Army Group B in January 1944.

FIELD MARSHAL GÜNTHER VON KLUGE

Kluge commanded the 4th Army during the invasion of Poland, the Battle of France, and the invasion of Russia. He was promoted to command Army Group Center during the Russian counter before replacing Rundstedt as the Commander-in-Chief of OB West. Though he was not actively involved in the plot, he committed suicide after the failed attempt on Hitler's life.

Allied air superiority played a pivotal role in Germany's Normandy defeat.

"THE GERMAN SLUGGISHNESS IN RESPONDING TO THE FIRST ALLIED MOVEMENTS OF D-DAY HAS PASSED INTO THE LEGEND OF WAR."

take charge of the Atlantic Wall in December 1943. The wily field marshal immediately got to work laying millions of mines and countless obstacles across the beaches of France. Germany's main concern was uncertainty over where the Allies would land. The Allied deception plans had proved particularly effective, though during the spring of 1944 Hitler did allude to the probability of a Normandy landing. In January 1944, he appointed Rommel to command Army Group B in a bid to add some steel and tactical common sense.

Rommel was a veteran of mobile warfare and knew how to operate under Allied air superiority. He was hampered, however, by the fact that his direct superior, Rundstedt, did not. The OB West's commander-in-chief had never fought a battle without German air superiority. Rundstedt believed that armor held in reserve could be committed from a central zone once the location of the landings was known. But Rommel knew from his experience in North Africa that rumbling tank columns were easy prey for enemy aircraft. The *Luftwaffe* was in no position to provide adequate air cover. On the eve of the invasion, the Allies had amassed 12,000 aircraft to support the invasion. On the Channel coast on the morning of June 6, 1944, the *Luftwaffe* could scramble fewer than 170 fighters.

Unfortunately for Rommel, Hitler's bid to resolve the dispute between his two top commanders did little to alleviate the problem. He split the six panzer divisions in Army Group

The Hitler Youth of 12th SS Panzer won a formidable reputation in the battle for Normandy.

Panzer Divisions like the 21st were made up of too many Mark IVs and not enough Panthers or Tigers.

B evenly between Rommel and Rundstedt, with the provision that the latter's divisions would not be committed without the approval of Hitler's operations staff. With the 21st Panzer Division (under Rundstedt's command) providing the only armor close to the Overlord beaches in Normandy—armed with Mark IV tanks instead of Panthers and manned largely by conscripts—Rommel's bid to launch a swift counterstrike with skillful, armored units was doomed from the outset.

In the words of historian Max Hastings, "The German sluggishness in responding to the first Allied movements of D-Day has passed into the legend of war." The *Luftwaffe* had failed to mount significant air patrols and its meteorologists had deemed June 6 an unlikely day for attack due to bad weather. The vessels the German navy had in the region provided no hint of the incoming attack, and they had even failed to spot the proliferation of Allied minesweepers operating off the Normandy coast on the evening of June 5.

In a further blow, the German forces were temporarily deprived of their senior commanders. When the first Allied paratroopers began to descend, Rommel was in Germany celebrating his wife's birthday. Rundstedt, an old campaigner, is said to have regularly ignored his alarm calls, while Hitler was going to bed after a long chat with Eva Braun and Goebbels about cinema and the state of the world. General Edgar Feuchtinger, the commander of 21st Panzer, was absent from duty with rumors circulating that he was out visiting a female friend. Even as news seeped through, Hitler was not informed—the *Oberkommando der Wehrmacht* (OKW, or High Command of the Armed Forces) believed these were Allied diversionary tactics and they did not want to wake him. He was not presented with firm evidence of the invasion until six hours after the first landing craft had unloaded.

Some local commanders responded as best they could with General Richter of 716th Division, for example, moving out against the Allied paratroopers, but the delays in dispatching armored units were extremely costly. The chance of a swift German riposte seeped away. The nearest tank unit to the Normandy beaches, the 21st Panzer Division, finally got permission from the dithering OKW to move at 6:45 a.m. Delays in the command chain held up the order for another two hours.

CAPTAIN WITTMANN: PANZER ACE COMMANDERS

The daring exploits of a Tiger tank commander stand among the greatest single-handed actions of the war.

On June 13, during the Battle of Villers-Bocage, *Obersturmführer* Michael Wittmann and his Tiger tank emerged from a small wood and launched a devastating attack. He led a group of five Tigers from the 101st SS Heavy Panzer Battalion, the first reinforcements to plug the gap in the German line. He had already earned a fearsome reputation on the Eastern Front, recording 137 tank kills, and when he spotted a squadron of British Cromwell tanks idling on a high-banked stretch of road, his battle lust ignited. Without waiting for his other tanks, he roared out from his concealed position and fired shell after shell at the British armor with his Tiger's heavy 88-mm cannon, blasting the Cromwells to pieces.

He then rammed another vehicle from the road and drove into the village of Villers-Bocage where he destroyed three more tanks, only missing a fourth when the driver reversed into a garden. A Sherman Firefly, which boasted a more powerful gun than a Cromwell, managed to hit Wittmann's Tiger but only caused superficial damage. Wittmann returned fire and brought a building crashing down on the Sherman's turret. In just five minutes, the "Panzer Ace" had smashed the spearhead of the British 7th Armored Division.

Wittmann then rearmed and refueled and, alongside his other Tigers and an infantry group, joined the battle around Hill 213. He returned to Villers-Bocage that afternoon with sections of the 2nd Panzer Division but was beaten back; this time the British were prepared. He died in an ambush on August 8.

Field Marshal Rommel commanded Army Group B, but was frustrated in his efforts by Hitler's meddling.

When the tanks finally rolled, they were ordered to probe between the Sword and Juno beaches and to halt the British advance on Caen. Long diversions and conflicting orders took the 21st out on the open roads, exposing them to Allied air attacks. Having set out with 104 Mark IVs, there were no more than 60 in combat by the late afternoon. General Erich Marcks famously told one of his commanders that if the 21st failed to throw the British back into the sea, "We shall have lost the war."

His words were prescient. When the 21st took on the British, it found that its Mark IVs were no match for the Staffordshire Yeomanry's anti-tank Fireflies—Shermans equipped with long 17-pounder cannons. These tanks were thought to be the equal of the Tiger, and they destroyed 13 Mark IVs within minutes.

The Germans' failure to commit more armor at this early stage was crucial to the Allied success. Marcks tried desperately to bring the 12th SS Panzer Division of the Hitler Youth into combat, but again the OKW dithered and the main body did not move out until nightfall. Over June 7 and 8, the 12th SS Panzer inflicted heavy losses on the Canadian bridgehead, west of Caen, but they failed to punch all the way through to the sea.

The highly skilled Panzer Lehr Division eventually linked up with 12th SS Panzer on June 9, and with the remnants of the 21st to form the defense around Caen, both Panzer Lehr and the Hitler Youth fought like tigers. Still, Hitler refused to bolster the 7th Army with units from the 15th, 1st, and 19th Armies, by the threat of a second invasion elsewhere in France. Only grudgingly did he allow 9th and 10th SS Panzer Divisions to move into Normandy. While Allied bombing hindered their progress, they made a telling contribution to halting the British assault on Caen. Air power and the efforts of the Resistance also played a decisive role in holding up the arrival of the most notorious of all the units to fight in Normandy: the 2nd SS Panzer Division, "Das Reich," had built a brutal reputation in the east.

By late June there were 14 German divisions, including eight Panzer divisions, in Normandy. After the fall of Cherbourg, they succeeded in establishing a defensive line. It did not last, but it brought welcome relief to Hitler who had seen his forces in the east battered by Operation

The Battle of the Falaise Gap was a disaster for Germany with thousands of troops killed or captured.

Bagration, which carried the Russian line 300 miles (480 kilometers) westward to the edge of Warsaw. Rundstedt, however, knew that his forces were in a perilous position and he urged Hitler to sue for peace. He was immediately replaced by Field Marshal Günther von Kluge.

The only strategic option open to the Germans was a coordinated fighting retreat, sapping Allied strength with each retirement. Hitler, however, refused to countenance any such move, leaving his forces subject to naval bombardment, and he still refused to surrender southern France, which would have allowed Army Group G to join the battered Army Group B in Normandy.

"THE GERMANS' FAILURE TO COMMIT MORE ARMOR AT THIS EARLY STAGE WAS CRUCIAL TO THE ALLIED SUCCESS."

Rommel still believed that a second invasion would come and he spent much time visiting the 15th Army, nudging the 116th Panzer Division ever closer to the coast instead of redeploying it to Normandy. With a lack of air reconnaissance and no insight into their enemies' intentions, the German war effort was severely disadvantaged. Hitler continued to mistrust most of his commanders and refused to let them respond to situations as they saw fit. He dictated their strategy from afar, visiting Normandy just once, and his choices were almost always misguided.

Still the German forces in Normandy held on, stifling the Allied advance for two months despite poor leadership from above and a striking lack of reinforcements. General Quesada of the American Air Force wrote that, "One's imagination boggled at what the German army might have done to us without Hitler working so effectively for our side." The German line was fatally broken in late July when heavy air bombing preceded a huge American push, codenamed Cobra. The once mighty Panzer Lehr Division was reduced to 14 tanks, an indicator of how the battle for Normandy had sapped the strength of German forces.

It was against this testing backdrop that there was a failed attempt by German officers to assassinate Hitler inside his Wolf's Lair field headquarters near Rastenburg. If the Führer doubted his senior staff before the plot, he severely mistrusted them afterwards. He harbored grave doubts over the loyalty of his men on the Western Front. To test them, and to try and reverse the situation in France, he ordered a counterattack on the enemy flank as the Americans pushed into Brittany.

Operation Lüttich saw four armored divisions spearhead the attack—116th, 2nd, 1st SS, and 2nd SS Panzer—with four more (11th and 9th from the south of France and 9th SS and 10th SS from Caen) joining the assault when they arrived. "The object remains to keep the enemy confined to his bridgehead," Hitler said as he committed some 1,400 tanks to battle, "and there to inflict serious losses upon him in order to wear him down and finally destroy him."

In total, 10 German tank divisions took on ten Allied in the second largest armor battle of the entire war (Kursk in July 1943 saw 12 German panzer divisions take to the field). It was a brutal, sprawling clash, fought over 800 square miles (2,070 square kilometers), tank versus tank. The Battle of the Falaise Gap, which opened with a clash on the night of August 6 was an unmitigated disaster for Hitler.

The Germans had more experienced tank crews and better machines than the Allies, but the pounding they had received over the previous two months had taken its toll on their strength, and poor leadership let them down. Only the resolution and fervor of 12th SS Panzer, the Hitler Youth Division, prevented the total destruction of Army Group B. The German resistance continued—Hitler would launch one last great armored offensive—but the die was cast. His western forces would not recover. The battle for Normandy was lost.

BEYOND THE BEACHES

VILLERS-BOCAGE 99

With a beachhead in occupied France established, Allied and German forces made a desperate scramble to grab strategic positions.

BREAKING OUT FROM NORMANDY 118

The Allies faced a monumental task as they pushed on to Paris.

SAS D-DAY MISSIONS 108

The SAS parachuted into France with instructions to cause havoc, cut railway lines, and kill Germans.

FRIENDLY FIRE OFF NORMANDY 124

WWII naval veteran Claude Sealey reveals a deadly encounter with his own countrymen in a notorious but little-known incident off northern France.

WHAT IF D-DAY HAD FAILED? 136

The consequences of a failure on D-Day would have been felt for decades to come.

132 THE IMPORTANCE OF D-DAY

With the future of Europe hanging in the balance, success was essential.

140 DESTINATION NORMANDY

Discover some of the most important landmarks in European history.

The village of Villers-Bocage still lies in ruins months after the fierce clash, October 1944.

NORMANDY, FRANCE JUNE 13, 1944

VILLERS-BOCAGE

With a beachhead in occupied France established, Allied and German forces made a desperate scramble to grab strategic positions that saw opposing armored divisions forming the tips of the spears.

BY **MIKE HASKEW**

As Allied forces stormed ashore along the Norman coast of France on June 6, 1944, all ready to begin the arduous campaign to liberate Western Europe from Nazi occupation during World War II, the primary D-Day objective of the British 3rd Infantry Division was the port of Caen.

As one of the largest cities in Normandy, Caen was a communications hub at the center of a major road network, connected to the English Channel through a canal. Its seizure would anchor the left flank of the Allied perimeter and deny the defending Germans the advantage of the river and canal, which would otherwise present major obstacles to inland expansion of the D-Day beachhead.

General Bernard Law Montgomery, commander of Allied ground forces in Normandy, envisioned the capture of Caen within hours of British ground forces storming ashore at Sword Beach, the easternmost of the five D-Day landing beaches. However, stiff German resistance from the veteran 21st Panzer Division, the 12th SS Panzer Division Hitlerjugend and the 716th Infantry Division had stymied progress towards the city and with that, Montgomery's belief that it could be captured on D-Day proved overly optimistic.

A week after the Normandy landings, Allied troops were slugging their way inland against fierce German opposition, but Caen remained firmly under enemy control despite numerous efforts by

British forces to take the city in a direct assault. For Montgomery though, an opportunity had developed, as the US 1st Infantry Division pushed southward from Omaha Beach, compelling German forces to retreat and opening a gap west of Caen between the 352nd Infantry Division and Panzer Lehr, a crack German armored division.

Operation Perch

Montgomery's staff altered Operation Perch—its plan for the early ground phase of the Normandy campaign—hoping to take advantage of the recent development in the enemy's front line. A pincer movement might outflank Panzer Lehr and envelop Caen, forcing its stubborn German defenders to retire or risk being surrounded. While the 51st (Highland) Infantry Division attacked in the east, the 7th Armored Divison—the "Desert Rats," who had achieved fame with Montgomery's Eighth Army in North Africa—was to swing southeastward and capture the town of Villers-Bocage, just more than 16 miles (27 kilometers) southwest of Caen, along with nearby high ground identified on maps as Point 213.

On June 10, the refocused Operation Perch commenced with the advance of the 7th Armored Division, while the 51st (Highland) Division stepped off the next day. Although some initial gains were made east of Caen, a powerful counterattack from 21st Panzer stopped that British thrust cold, eventually forcing the Highlanders to retire to the banks of the Orne. Still, the prospects for the western pincer's success remained.

As the 7th Armored Division advanced, Major General Fritz Bayerlein—the capable commander of Panzer Lehr—realized the predicament his division faced and ordered a ferocious counterattack that bogged the western drive down around the village of Tilly-sur-Seulles. On the morning of June 12, Lieutenant General Miles Dempsey, commander of the British Second Army, traveled to 7th Armored headquarters to meet with Major General George "Bobby" Erskine, the division commander, who suggested that Panzer Lehr might still be outflanked if 7th Armored disengaged from the fight at Tilly-sur-Seulles and struck toward Villers-Bocage from further west.

Rolling Towards Villers-Bocage

Within hours, the 22nd Armored Brigade—the vanguard of the Desert Rats—was on the move towards Villers-Bocage with the tanks and armored cars of the 8th and 11th Hussars covering its flanks. As darkness fell around them, Brigadier Robert "Looney" Hinde, leading, called a halt to the advance after reaching the Caumont-Villers-Bocage road, just five miles (eight kilometers) from his objective. Early on the morning of June 13, tanks of the 4th County of London Yeomanry and troops of Company A, 1st Battalion, The Rifle Brigade, rolled into Villers-Bocage against only token resistance. French civilians turned out in large numbers to welcome them.

Wary of the fact that a German counterattack was likely, since control of the road network emanating from Villers-Bocage was tactically significant for the Germans as well, Brigadier Hinde ordered the tanks of A Squadron, County of London Yeomanry, and Company A, The Rifle Brigade, to occupy Point 213. About one mile (1.6 kilometers) northwest of Villers-Bocage, the high ground commanded the approaches to the town and National Highway 175 toward Caen.

Although his tankers were exhilarated by the rapid run to Villers-Bocage, Lieutenant Colonel Viscount Arthur Cranley, commanding the 4th County of London Yeomanry, was worried. German reconnaissance vehicles had been spotted and enemy soldiers were seen making a hasty getaway in a staff car. Soon enough, the enemy would be coming back and occupying Point 213 would invite a counterattack against the exposed position.

Nevertheless, Cranley left four tanks of his regimental headquarters in Villers-Bocage before hurrying off to take stock of A Squadron's new posting. B Squadron was positioned to the west of the town, guarding the intersection along the road that led to the village of Caumont.

Just after 9 a.m., the leading elements of the 4th County of London Yeomanry and the accompanying infantry reached Point 213. The

"ALTHOUGH HIS TANKERS WERE EXHILARATED BY THE RAPID RUN TO VILLERS-BOCAGE, LIEUTENANT COLONEL VISCOUNT ARTHUR CRANLEY, COMMANDING THE 4TH COUNTY OF LONDON YEOMANRY, WAS WORRIED."

A Waffen SS MG42 and Panther tank take up defensive positions around Caen, ready to repel the allied advance, 1944.

Right: German reinforcements race towards Normandy in an attempt to bolster the coastal defenses against the anticipated invasion.

OPPOSING FORCES

VS

BRITISH ARMY 22ND ARMORED BRIGADE	GERMAN ARMY SS HEAVY TANK BATTALION 101
LEADER Brigadier Robert "Looney" Hinde	**LEADERS** SS *Obersturmbannführer* (lieutenant colonel) Heinz von Westerhagen
INFANTRY 1/7th Battalion Queen's Royal Regiment (West Surrey); 1st Battalion Rifle Brigade	**ARMOR** 1st Panzer Company, SS *Hauptsturmführer* (captain) Rolf Mobius; 2nd Panzer Company, SS *Obersturmführer* (1st lieutenant) Michael Wittmann
ARMOR 4th County of London Yeomanry; 5th Royal Tank Regiment	

bulk of the British armor and infantry halted along the road, awaiting orders for deployment to consolidate their hold on the high ground. More than two dozen tanks and halftracks lined the road, along with numerous troop carriers. Sentries were posted but their field of vision was limited due to the terrain and thick woods in the area.

Tigers Unleashed

In the wake of the D-Day landings, the relative few German panzer formations in Normandy were alerted. One of these, the 1st SS Panzer Corps, had started towards the fighting early on June 7. Ravaged by Allied fighter-bombers along the route, the corps lost a significant number of armored vehicles, and by the morning of June 13, SS Heavy Tank Battalion 101, its last uncommitted reserve advancing from Beauvais, had been reduced from an original strength of 45 tanks to fewer than 20.

Most of the German armored battalion's vehicles, however, were the 56-ton Tiger I heavy tank, mounting a high-velocity 88-mm cannon that was superior to the 75 mm and 17-pounder (76-mm) guns of the new British Cromwell and Sherman Firefly tanks in the field. Although plagued by mechanical difficulties, the Tiger was a daunting foe in combat. Hits from Allied shells were often deflected harmlessly away by its thick armor plating, and the range of the formidable 88-mm weapon allowed the Germans to engage enemy targets at standoff distances.

On that morning, two companies of Tigers from SS Heavy Tank Battalion 101 had reached the vicinity of Villers-Bocage. The 1st Company was under SS *Hauptsturmführer* (captain) Rolf Möbius, and the 2nd Company was led by *Obersturmführer* (first lieutenant) Michael Wittmann. Already a leading panzer ace and holder of the Knights Cross with Oak Leaves, Wittmann had well over 100 kills on the Eastern Front to his credit. Accounts vary as to the actual strength of the two panzer companies and the details of the engagement that followed. However, the ensuing battle contributed to the growing legend that was *Obersturmführer* Michael Wittmann—possibly even exaggerating his role in the fight for Villers-Bocage.

Wittmann's Tiger company had taken positions along a ridge south of Point 213, to offer support to either Panzer Lehr or the 12th SS Panzer Division.

Right: A Tiger tank lies abandoned after being taken out of action during the battle—evidence against the supposed invincibility of this model.

Image source: German Federal Archive

© Getty

The young Tiger ace was astonished when British armored vehicles appeared throughout Villers-Bocage. He later recalled: "I had no time to assemble my company; instead I had to act quickly, as I had to assume that the enemy had already spotted me and would destroy me where I stood. I set off with one tank and passed the order to the others not to retreat a single step but to hold their ground."

Just as the British tankers and infantrymen on the road to Point 213 were ordered to resume their advance to the high ground, three Tiger tanks, those of Wittmann, SS *Oberscharführer* (company sergeant major) Jürgen Brandt, and SS *Untersturmführer* (2nd lieutenant) Georg Hantusch were seen advancing parallel to the British column along a path adjacent to the highway but screened by a tall hedgerow. Apparently, the two other German tankers had moved forward with Wittmann, despite his order for them to remain where they were.

As the other two Tigers attacked the British armor at Point 213, Wittmann emerged from a wooded area onto National Highway 175, where he destroyed a Cromwell at close range and then blasted a Sherman Firefly, its blazing hulk blocking the British column. He turned and worked his way down the line of armored vehicles strung out along the road. In short order, the Tiger's 88-mm gun and its two 7.92 mm MG 34 machine guns destroyed eight halftracks and four troop carriers.

Struggle in the Streets

Leaving a trail of destruction on the highway, Wittmann then rolled down the Rue Georges Clémenceau towards the eastern edge of Villers-Bocage. Three M5 Stuart light tanks of the 4th County of London Yeomanry Reconnaissance Troop, their 37-mm guns no match for the thick armor protecting the Tiger, were stationed at the intersection with the road to Tilly-sur-Seulles.

No doubt, the reconnaissance squadron leader, Lieutenant Rex Ingram, knew that his situation was perilous. Nevertheless, he ordered the driver of his 15-ton Stuart into the road—directly in the path of Wittmann's oncoming Tiger—in an attempt to delay the German tank's advance

SS Obersturmführer Michael Wittmann strikes a jaunty pose atop his Tiger tank.

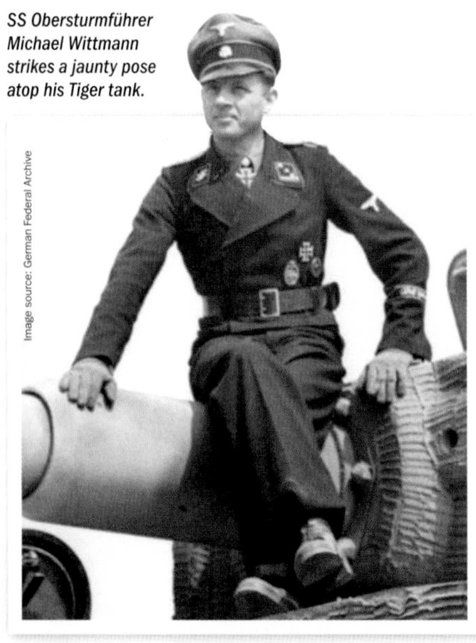

Image source: German Federal Archive

GOLD

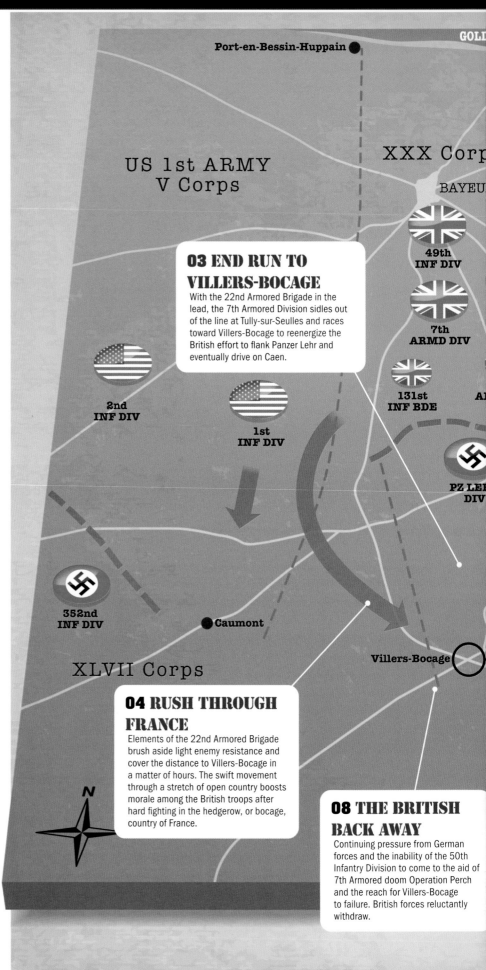

Port-en-Bessin-Huppain

US 1st ARMY
V Corps

XXX Corps

BAYEUX

49th INF DIV

7th ARMD DIV

131st INF BDE

2nd INF DIV

1st INF DIV

PZ LEHR DIV

352nd INF DIV

Caumont

Villers-Bocage

XLVII Corps

N

03 END RUN TO VILLERS-BOCAGE

With the 22nd Armored Brigade in the lead, the 7th Armored Division sidles out of the line at Tully-sur-Seulles and races toward Villers-Bocage to reenergize the British effort to flank Panzer Lehr and eventually drive on Caen.

04 RUSH THROUGH FRANCE

Elements of the 22nd Armored Brigade brush aside light enemy resistance and cover the distance to Villers-Bocage in a matter of hours. The swift movement through a stretch of open country boosts morale among the British troops after hard fighting in the hedgerow, or bocage, country of France.

08 THE BRITISH BACK AWAY

Continuing pressure from German forces and the inability of the 50th Infantry Division to come to the aid of 7th Armored doom Operation Perch and the reach for Villers-Bocage to failure. British forces reluctantly withdraw.

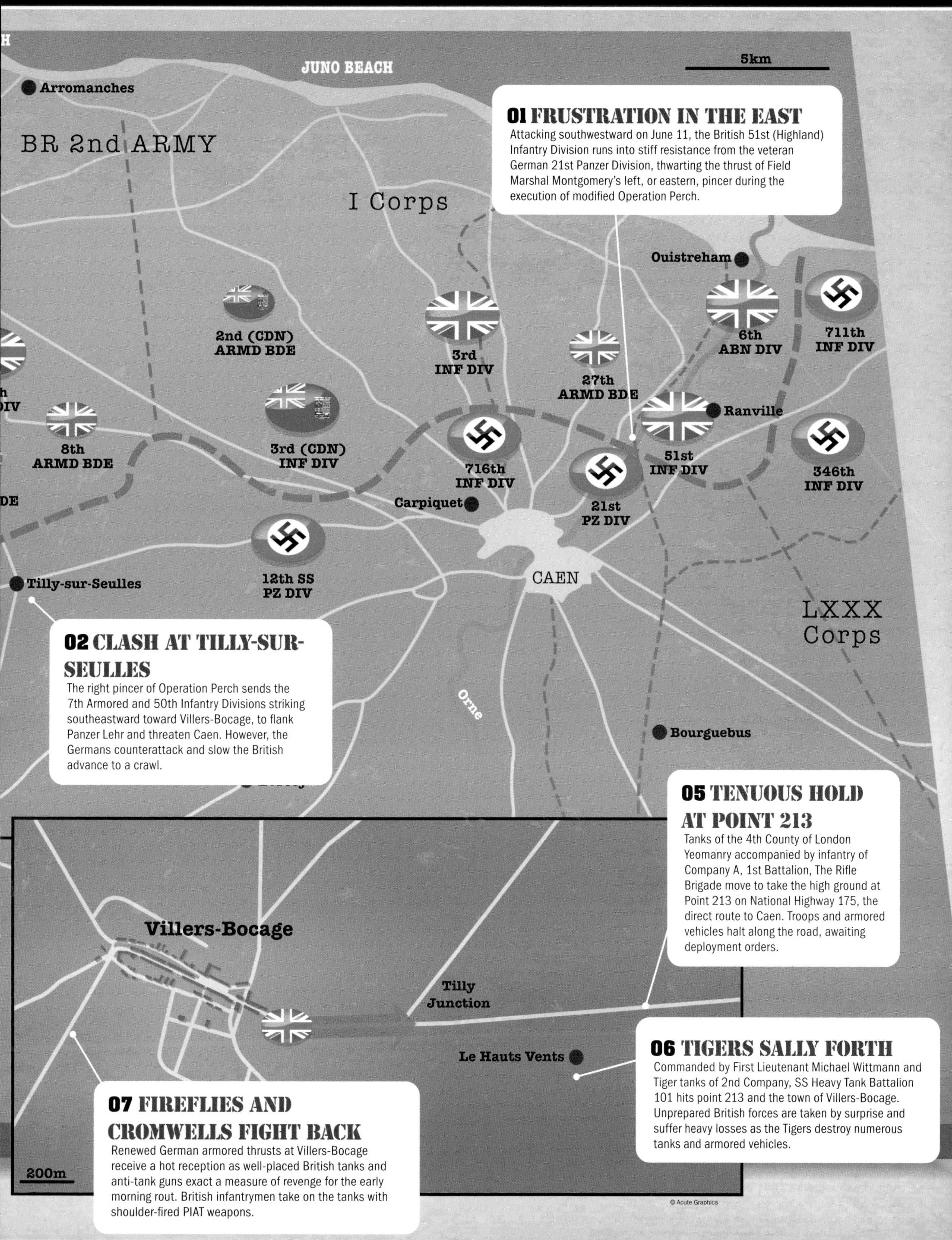

01 FRUSTRATION IN THE EAST

Attacking southwestward on June 11, the British 51st (Highland) Infantry Division runs into stiff resistance from the veteran German 21st Panzer Division, thwarting the thrust of Field Marshal Montgomery's left, or eastern, pincer during the execution of modified Operation Perch.

02 CLASH AT TILLY-SUR-SEULLES

The right pincer of Operation Perch sends the 7th Armored and 50th Infantry Divisions striking southeastward toward Villers-Bocage, to flank Panzer Lehr and threaten Caen. However, the Germans counterattack and slow the British advance to a crawl.

05 TENUOUS HOLD AT POINT 213

Tanks of the 4th County of London Yeomanry accompanied by infantry of Company A, 1st Battalion, The Rifle Brigade move to take the high ground at Point 213 on National Highway 175, the direct route to Caen. Troops and armored vehicles halt along the road, awaiting deployment orders.

06 TIGERS SALLY FORTH

Commanded by First Lieutenant Michael Wittmann and Tiger tanks of 2nd Company, SS Heavy Tank Battalion 101 hits point 213 and the town of Villers-Bocage. Unprepared British forces are taken by surprise and suffer heavy losses as the Tigers destroy numerous tanks and armored vehicles.

07 FIREFLIES AND CROMWELLS FIGHT BACK

Renewed German armored thrusts at Villers-Bocage receive a hot reception as well-placed British tanks and anti-tank guns exact a measure of revenge for the early morning rout. British infantrymen take on the tanks with shoulder-fired PIAT weapons.

into the town. A single 88-mm round caused the British tank to erupt in flames. The Tiger shunted the blazing wreck aside and blasted at least one more of the light tanks.

Wittmann then directed his lumbering Tiger down the main thoroughfare in Villers-Bocage and a few yards beyond the road junction, the four Cromwells of the regimental headquarters came into view. Apparently, several of the crewmen were actually outside of their vehicles when the encounter began. The first Cromwell, commanded by the regimental executive officer, Major Arthur Carr, was damaged and attempted to back out of the line of fire. Two more British tanks, under Lieutenant John L. Cloudsley-Thompson and Regimental Sergeant Major Gerald Holloway, were both destroyed.

As Cloudsley-Thompson's crew bailed out of its burning Cromwell, Captain Pat Dyas, the regimental adjutant, reversed his tank and backed ponderously into a garden, obscured from Wittmann's view. The action had developed so rapidly that Dyas's gunner, away from the vehicle on a nature call, had no time to return to the tank. Positioned for a killing shot, Dyas was powerless to act as the big Tiger rumbled past, its broadside completely exposed to him.

Continuing down the Rue Georges Clémenceau, Wittmann spotted two observation post tanks of the 5th Royal Horse Artillery as they tried to avoid contact, backing around a corner into the Rue Pasteur. Due to its observation role, the Sherman commanded by Major Dennis Wells was quite defenseless, mounting a wooden decoy gun rather than a real main weapon; the Cromwell was most likely unarmed as well. Captain Paddy Victory continued backing his Cromwell into a side street behind the Sherman at the rear entrance to the Hotel du Bras d'Or. A moment later, Wells's tank was blown up by an 88-mm shell from Wittmann's Tiger.

Captain Victory tried to escape, but his transmission gears locked up. As Wittmann passed by, the Cromwell crew grasped a fleeting hope that they had remained unseen. But the Tiger stopped, reversed for a moment, then pumped a round into the British tank just below its turret. The crew bailed out, but Captain Victory returned to the disabled Cromwell and destroyed its interior the best that he could before slipping away.

While Wittmann shot up these British tanks and moved steadily westward towards the center of Villers-Bocage, Lieutenant Charles Pearce escaped from the area in a scout car and alerted B Squadron to the presence of the marauding Tiger on the other side of the town. After winning a momentary reprieve, Captain Dyas began tracking Wittmann through the streets of Villers-Bocage.

"CAPTAIN VICTORY TRIED TO ESCAPE, BUT HIS TRANSMISSION GEARS LOCKED UP. AS WITTMANN PASSED BY, THE CROMWELL CREW GRASPED A FLEETING HOPE THAT THEY HAD REMAINED UNSEEN."

As Dyas followed his Tiger, Wittmann ran into a Sherman Firefly of B Squadron under the direction of Sergeant Stan Lockwood. Lockwood was the first British tanker to hear Lieutenant Pearce's alarm; he turned his Firefly from the Place Jeanne d'Arc onto the Rue Georges Clémenceau and got the drop on Wittmann, firing a 17-pounder shell that inflicted slight damage on the big Tiger. In turn, Wittmann swerved into a brick wall, causing it to collapse on top of Lockwood's Sherman.

Captain Dyas sensed an opportunity, rolling his Cromwell forward and firing two 75-mm rounds that hit the Tiger, but failed to penetrate its armor. In seconds the tables were turned. The Tiger's turret swung around, its cannon belched flame, and the resulting hit killed the Cromwell gunner and driver while missing Dyas—stunned, but remarkably uninjured.

Wittmann knew that other B Squadron tanks were closing in. He turned back down the Rue Georges Clémenceau and proceeded only a few yards before the crash of a shell caused the Tiger to lurch to a halt in front of the Huet-Godefroy clothing store. A single round from a six-pounder anti-tank gun had accomplished what numerous British tanks had failed to do. Fired from an alley between the Rue Jeanne Bacon and Boulevard Joffre, the anti-tank round disabled a drive sprocket. Wittmann and his crew abandoned their Tiger, expecting that it might be recovered later and made their way four miles (seven kilometers) to Panzer Lehr headquarters at Chateau d'Orbois, where Wittmann described the situation around Villers-Bocage to the officers present.

Chaos at Point 213

While Wittmann was devastating the British armor in Villers-Bocage, Brandt and Hantusch drove on to Point 213 and added to the carnage. Within the hour, a third Tiger, commanded by *Unterscharführer* Kurt Sowa, joined the assault and by 10 a.m., reconnaissance troops and armored vehicles of the 4th Panzer Company, SS Heavy Tank Battalion 101 reached the one-sided battle. Half an hour later, the Germans were rounding up scores of prisoners and consolidating their hold on National Highway 175 between Villers-Bocage and Point 213.

The morning action ended with a staggering tally of destruction. Twenty Cromwells, four Sherman Fireflies, and three Stuart tanks were thought to have been destroyed, along with numerous troop carriers and other vehicles. The Fireflies of B Squadron, 4th County of London Yeomanry prepared for a renewed battle that would surely come, while the 1/7th Battalion, Queen's Royal Regiment also occupied positions in Villers-Bocage. Anti-tank guns studded the British defensive cordon.

Despite their losses, the British still menaced the flank of Panzer Lehr and there was hope at the headquarters of the 7th Armored Division and its parent XXX Corps that the 50th Infantry Division might break through at Tilly-sur-Seulles and support the drive through Villers-Bocage and perhaps even to Caen. However, the vigor of the morning Tiger assault had shattered the spearhead of the British offensive and the initiative lay squarely with the Germans, who sensed the potential for a solid local victory.

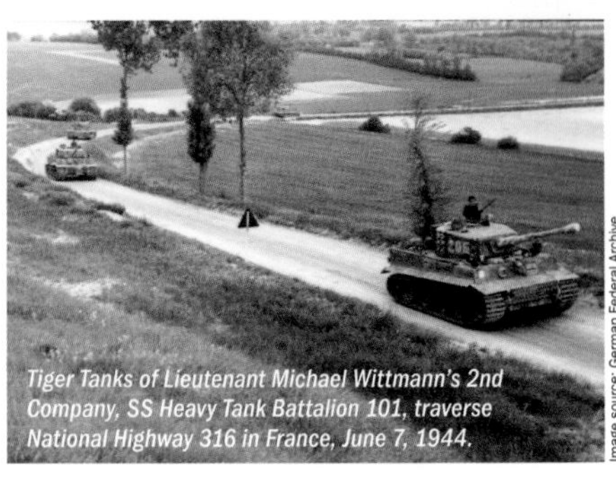
Tiger Tanks of Lieutenant Michael Wittmann's 2nd Company, SS Heavy Tank Battalion 101, traverse National Highway 316 in France, June 7, 1944.

Image source: German Federal Archive

Its hatches thrown open, a destroyed Pz.Kpfw. IV tank of Panzer Lehr sits amid the rubble in Villers-Bocage

Image source: German Federal Archive

Captain Victory's Cromwell was immobilized when attacked by Wittmann's Tiger tank.

Image source: IWM: B8633

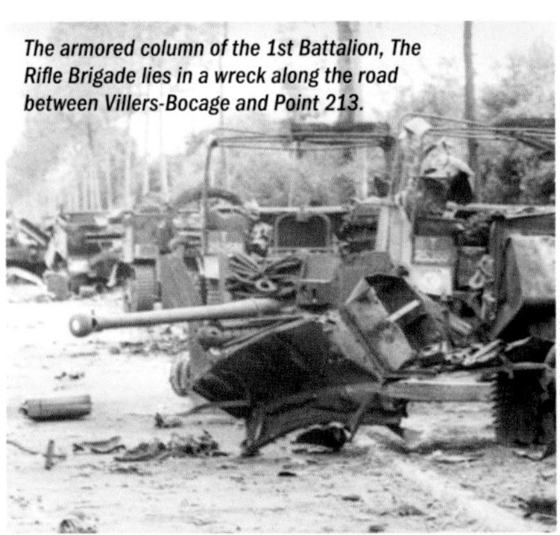
The armored column of the 1st Battalion, The Rifle Brigade lies in a wreck along the road between Villers-Bocage and Point 213.

Image source: German Federal Archive

Image source: German Federal Archive

The blackened hulk of a Cromwell tank, one of more than 30 British armored vehicles lost at Villers-Bocage, rests abandoned.

"THE TIGER'S TURRET SWUNG AROUND, ITS CANNON BELCHED FLAME, AND THE RESULTING HIT KILLED THE CROMWELL GUNNER AND DRIVER."

An artist's impression of the battle from the London Illustrated News. The British tank pictured is an older design, possibly a Covenanter.

Below: After recapturing the town in August, British engineers fill a Tiger with land mines to destroy it.

A short time after Wittmann's arrival at Chateau d'Orbois, Captain Helmut Ritgen was moving to block potential British routes of advance north of Villers-Bocage, with 15 Pz.Kpfw. IV tanks of the 2nd Battalion, Regiment 130, Panzer Lehr. Ritgen soon ran into some intense fire from concealed anti-tank guns, lost one Pz.Kpfw. IV, and was ordered to regroup near Villers-Bocage. Subsequently, he sent four tanks roaring in from the south, while ten more renewed their advance along Rue Georges Clémenceau, the British claimed a pair of Pz. Kpfw. IVs. At around 1 p.m., Panzer Lehr's armor tried to take the town again, losing two more Pz.Kpfw. IVs in the process.

The 1/7th Battalion, Queen's Royal Regiment held the railway station and other key positions in and around Villers-Bocage and put up stiff resistance. British and German infantrymen fought street-to-street and house-to-house before the defenders pulled back to positions along the edge of town. A British roadblock in the center of Villers-Bocage concealed several six-pounder

"BOTH SENIOR COMMANDERS SEEMED UNCHARACTERISTICALLY DETACHED, FAILING TO ASSERT STRONG LEADERSHIP AND DECISION-MAKING DURING THE FIGHT."

An Allied Sherman recovery tank towing a crippled Sherman behind it during the Battle of Caen.

Right: The lightning fast advance of the Germans on the morning of June 13 led some British tanks, like this Cromwell, to be abandoned.

"BRITISH AND GERMAN INFANTRYMEN FOUGHT STREET-TO-STREET AND HOUSE-TO-HOUSE BEFORE THE DEFENDERS PULLED BACK TO POSITIONS ALONG THE EDGE OF TOWN."

anti-tank guns, at least one Sherman Firefly, and several Cromwells, which lay in wait for any German tanks advancing towards the town square.

While the initial Panzer Lehr forays into Villers-Bocage were rebuffed, Wittmann sped back towards Point 213 and conferred with Möbius prior to a renewed effort against the town by the Tigers of 1st Company, SS Heavy Tank Battalion 101. Möbius then moved his Tigers into Villers-Bocage along the Rue d'Evrecy and linked up with the remaining Pz. Kpfw. IVs of Panzer Lehr near the town.

The German commanders distributed their tanks to attack from multiple directions, but by the time the combined assault commenced, the British were waiting in ambush. As the lead Tiger trundled down National Highway 175 into the town, a nearby Firefly unleashed a 17-pounder shell that missed. Quickly after, a six-pounder gun found the mark and knocked out the big tank.

Immediately, three more Tigers came into view, veering away in an attempt to outflank the British positions, and the fight developed into a bushwhacking melee reminiscent of something from the Wild West. One of these Tigers fell victim to an anti-tank gun, while an infantryman destroyed another with a PIAT (Projector, Infantry, Anti-Tank) spring-loaded, shoulder-fired weapon. Another second shot from a PIAT disabled the last of this Tiger trio.

Yet another Tiger, its commander well aware of the commotion to his front, stopped short of the British trap in the town square and waited. An opportunistic Firefly crew took a shot at the Tiger through the windows of a corner building and the round glanced off the German tank's gun mantlet. The Tiger began to churn down the street as its driver accelerated. A Cromwell emerged from behind, killing the behemoth with a shot to its vulnerable rear. At the same time, the Firefly that had spooked the Tiger blasted another Pz.Kpfw. IV.

Meanwhile, outside the city limits other units of the 7th Armored Division repulsed German attacks along a north-south line in the vicinity of Amaye-sur-Seulles and Tracy-Bocage.

Although some historians have disputed the presence of elements of the 2nd Panzer Division during the fighting at Villers-Bocage, others assert that as many as two panzergrenadier battalions entered the town on June 13, pressing the infantry of the 1/7th Battalion, Queen's Royal Regiment until the tanks of B Squadron began to cut down German troops in heaps with their machine guns.

Nevertheless, by 6 p.m. the enemy had advanced close to the 1/7th Battalion headquarters and reluctantly, the decision was made to withdraw from the town. Under a covering barrage from the 5th Royal Horse Artillery and the heavy guns of the US V Corps, the British pulled back. The Germans harassed their movement until well after dark.

Overnight, Hinde reinforced a defensive box on high ground at Point 174, one mile (1.6 kilometers) west of Villers-Bocage, and Panzer Lehr, along with the few remaining Tigers of SS Heavy Tank Battalion 101, assailed the position the next day. Artillery of the US 1st Infantry Division helped beat back the initial German thrusts, but simultaneous attacks in the afternoon succeeded in breaching the defensive box and rendering artillery support useless since British and German troops were intermingled. Just as the German assault threatened the 22nd Armored Brigade headquarters, it was finally beaten back.

Although Hinde remained confident that the 22nd Armored Brigade could hold its salient at Villers-Bocage, the 50th Division remained tangled with Panzer Lehr, unable to move up in support. Therefore, the 22nd Armored Brigade was pulled back and consolidated with the Allied line to the north and west, effectively ending the British bid for Villers-Bocage.

In the aftermath of the battle, the capabilities of the British field commanders, including Brigadier Hinde, Major General Erskine, and Lieutenant General G.C. Bucknall commanding XXX Corps, were debated. The tactical deployment of the 22nd Armored Brigade was questioned and the troops of the 50th Division were not the only potential reinforcements available. None of these commanders made a formal request for support from the 50th Division or any other units that might have intervened.

Equally, Dempsey and Montgomery cannot escape some responsibility. Both senior commanders seemed uncharacteristically detached, failing to assert strong leadership and decision-making during the fight. Within weeks of the failed offensive, Hinde, Erskine, and Bucknall were relieved of command. Dempsey later admitted that, "... the whole handling of the battle was a disgrace."

Casualties were substantial on both sides, with 217 British dead and the loss of more than 40 tanks and armored vehicles. A Squadron, County of London Yeomanry lost all 15 of its Cromwells, Fireflies, and Stuarts. As many as 15 German tanks, including six irreplaceable Tigers, were destroyed and although dozens of Germans were killed, the exact number is unknown. British forces hammered away at Caen for two months before capturing the city, and Villers-Bocage remained in German hands until the first week of August. Perhaps the greatest casualty of Operation Perch and the affair at Villers-Bocage was that the chance to race for Caen slipped through British grasp.

SAS

D-DAY MISSIONS

As Operation Overlord began, the SAS parachuted into France with instructions to cause havoc, cut railway lines, and kill Germans.

BY GAVIN MORTIMER

As the British forces landed on the Normandy beaches, the SAS had already caused havoc for the Nazis across France.

When David Stirling was granted permission to expand the SAS in September 1942, he appointed his brother, Bill, as commanding officer of the second regiment. Bill was the eldest of five children, and David's senior by four years. The siblings shared a similar military background (Scots Guards and commandos), but differed in personality.

One wartime SAS officer who knew them both, Anthony Greville-Bell, recalled: "I was very fond of Bill. He was a very deep, intelligent and well-read man. Bill was cleverer than David. [He] was more charismatic and more physical, the younger brother, and was outwardly very good at dealing with higher-ups and getting what he wanted. Bill was much quieter and more intellectual, and in terms of dealing with authority I think he was better than David."

Nonetheless, the brothers agreed on how the SAS should be deployed in any given theater of war, and after David's capture in January 1943, Bill became more determined than ever to adhere to the principles outlined by his brother when, in 1941, he'd produced a plan for a special forces unit to operate behind enemy lines in North Africa.

In the summer of 1943, lieutenant colonel Bill Stirling had clashed with the HQ 15th Army Group about how 2SAS should be used in Italy, but that was just a foretaste of the bitter row that erupted the following March when the Supreme Headquarters Allied Expeditionary Force (SHAEF) issued the SAS Brigade with its operational instructions for D-Day.

They tasked the SAS brigade (which now comprised 1SAS, 2SAS, two French regiments, 3 & 4, and a company of Belgian soldiers) to parachute into Normandy between the landing beaches and the German reserves 36 hours in advance of the main invasion fleet. Their job would be to prevent three panzer divisions of reserves from reaching the beaches once the invasion began.

Bill Stirling was aghast when he read the operational instructions. It was a suicide mission, and a type of warfare for which the SAS was not trained. Paddy Mayne, commanding officer of 1SAS, shared Stirling's sentiments but the big Irishman was better suited to fighting the enemy than his own top brass. "Paddy was useless with dealing with senior officers because if they did something to annoy him, he threatened to punch their noses," said Tony Greville-Bell.

In a strongly worded letter to SHAEF, Stirling expressed his grave misgivings about the operational instructions and demanded that the SAS operate in France as they had in the desert, in the principles set down by his brother.

Before Bill Stirling could send the letter, however, Lieutenant General Frederick "Boy" Browning intervened on behalf of the SAS, advising the chief of staff, 21 Army Group, that it would be preferable if the SAS Brigade was dropped deeper into France to attack German lines of communication, train the resistance, and waylay reinforcements en route to Normandy.

Stirling sent his letter nonetheless, in order to put on record his anger with what he considered as the constant misunderstanding of the SAS by the top brass. The letter infuriated many within SHAEF, but Stirling refused to retract his criticism.

Instead he resigned, and his decision to fall on his sword was not in vain. On May 28, 21 Army Group issued an amended order for the SAS Brigade to replace the original order two months earlier. Now the SAS Brigade would carry out 43 missions in France, all but one (Titanic, involving a six-man party dropping into Normandy to spread confusion with dummy parachutes), entailing the insertion of SAS units deep behind enemy lines to attack the Germans.

"BILL STIRLING WAS AGHAST WHEN HE READ THE OPERATIONAL INSTRUCTIONS. IT WAS A SUICIDE MISSION, AND A TYPE OF WARFARE FOR WHICH THE SAS WAS NOT TRAINED."

Left: Lieutenant colonel Brian Franks replaced Bill Stirling as CO of 2SAS and later parachuted into France to join the ill-fated Operation Loyton.

Right: Paddy Mayne was one of the SAS originals, replacing David Stirling as CO of 1SAS following the latter's capture.

OPERATION HOUNDSWORTH

Causing chaos across France, A Squadron cut off vital German resource and communication lines.

The first major mission into Occupied France was code named Houndsworth and involved A Squadron. Their task was to cut the railway lines between Lyon and Paris, train the numerous local groups of Maquis, and generally make nuisances of themselves.

The boys in A Squadron considered themselves a cut above the rest of the SAS brigade. They were veterans of the desert; a few—like Johnny Cooper, Jeff Du Vivier, Reg Seekings, and their commanding officer, Bill Fraser—were even "Originals," among the 66 men recruited by David Stirling in 1941.

But it was one of the recent additions to the squadron, Captain Ian Wellsted, who got Operation Houndsworth underway on the night of June 5. As the Allied invasion fleet sailed for the Normandy beaches, Wellsted and four others parachuted into the thickly forested, rolling countryside of the Massif du Morvan, west of Dijon. Their task was to ensure the area was safe for the arrival of a second 20-strong SAS party under the command of Bill Fraser, which duly dropped without incident on June 11.

By June 22, the remaining 46 men of A Squadron were safely inserted into the Morvan, with Fraser's HQ camp established at Vieux Dun and a second base approximately 10 miles (16 kilometers) south, not far from the village of Montsauche, under the command of Alex Muirhead and Ian Wellsted. The local Resistance group, Maquis Bernard, camped in the forest close to Wellsted's men and he recalled that, "although full of enthusiasm, none of the Maquisards, even the most military of them, had any idea of true discipline and were liable easily to be discouraged. Their true worth depended entirely upon the capacity of their leader and the use of their local knowledge."

On June 24, the Maquis tipped off the SAS that a convoy of Germans and White Russians [Soviets fighting for Germany] was on its way to ambush what they believed to be "Canadian paratroopers." Forewarned, the SAS turned from the hunted to the hunter. "We just toddled off to a road that they would have to pass back to their camp," wrote sergeant John Noble. "We waited four hours on that road until at long last they came. We were spread over 200 yards along the road and on a prearranged signal we opened up. Their order of march was a truck with a 20-mm [cannon] on it, a private car, another truck with a 20 mm, followed by a motorcycle. I had the first truck to deal with."

By the time Wellsted arrived at the scene, Noble's bren gun had done its work. "The leading German lorry was blazing furiously," recalled Wellsted. "The windscreen was shattered and the bodies of the men in the cab lolled grotesquely in their seats . . . beyond the first truck was a small civilian car. It, too, was stopped and derelict, and a huddled form twitched on the road beside it." Once the last of the resistance had been overcome, the SAS vanished into the forests, leaving behind a scene of death and destruction. The German retaliation was swift and savage. The next day, eight truckloads of soldiers burned the villages of Montsauche and Planchez to the ground, raping and killing with impunity.

On June 26, a force of around 300 Germans and White Russians attacked the forest where they believed the SAS to be hiding. But there were no guerrilla fighters and their prey slipped away, having gunned down dozens of Germans as they moved clumsily through the trees.

For the rest of June and into the beginning of July, heavy rain fell in the Morvan and there was little activity, either from the SAS or the Germans. Then on July 5, the SAS received a resupply of food and equipment, including three jeeps dropped by parachute. One of the jeeps was given to Johnny Wiseman, who with a signaler and a couple of other men, departed in the direction of Dijon, where over 30,000 Germans were stationed. Their

"ONCE THE LAST OF THE RESISTANCE HAD BEEN OVERCOME, THE SAS VANISHED INTO THE FORESTS, LEAVING BEHIND A SCENE OF DEATH AND DESTRUCTION."

Right: Paddy Mayne (left) arrived in France on August 7 with Mike Sadler (right), and the pair first paid a visit to Bill Fraser in Houndsworth.

The men of Houndsworth familiarize themselves with a mortar prior to their successful attack on Autun.

Aircraft dropped several jeeps to the SAS during Operation Houndsworth, but the parachute on this one failed to open. Captain Ian Wellsted is center.

mission was to select targets and call up RAF air strikes, which they did with considerable success.

Back in the Morvan, the arrival of the jeeps provided the SAS with the means to range far and wide in harassing the enemy. In the most audacious attack, Wellsted and Muirhead targeted a synthetic oil factory at Autun, 25 miles (40 kilometers) from the SAS camp. "Mortar bombs were plumping most satisfactorily into the factory area at the range of 700 yards and dense clouds of steam were seen rising from broken pipes," wrote Muirhead. "Then with a roar the 7 Vickers K opened up at 200 yards spraying the whole area with tracer and incendiary. Each gun pouring two full pans into the rising steam."

Several times, sabotage parties cut the railway lines to Paris, slowing the Germans as they transported men and munitions towards the heavy fighting in Normandy.

The most successful such operation was led by the desert veteran, Jeff Du Vivier, who in late July laid three pressure charges under a 50-yard (45-meter) stretch of track. It was a complex and time-consuming job for Du Vivier and his two comrades, but their patience was rewarded when a munitions train appeared a few hours later.

The engine was destroyed and 10 of the 40 wagons were blown off the line, damaging several anti-aircraft guns. Best of all, noted Du Vivier in his report after the action, the Germans were left "very frightened and demoralized" by the sabotage.

Fittingly, the final ambush was carried out by A Squadron's CO, Bill Fraser, who on September 3 attacked and killed seven German officers. Five days later, the squadron arrived in England having been replaced by Tony Marsh's C Squadron. In their three months in France, Fraser's men had killed or wounded 220 Germans, derailed six trains, destroyed 23 motorized vehicles, and damaged a synthetic oil refinery. Their casualties were two dead and seven wounded.

The Nazis called them "terrorists," but the SAS were World War II's most effective special forces unit. Tough, fit, disciplined, and intelligent, the SAS killed 7,733 Germans during operations in France.

Illustration: Jean-Michel Girard, The Art Agency

"THE ENGINE WAS DESTROYED AND 10 OF THE 40 WAGONS WERE BLOWN OFF THE LINE, DAMAGING SEVERAL ANTI-AIRCRAFT GUNS."

BEHIND ENEMY LINES

Crucial to the allied effort, various SAS squadrons entered German territory and caused mayhem for the enemy, destroying weapons, supplies, and communication and transport lines.

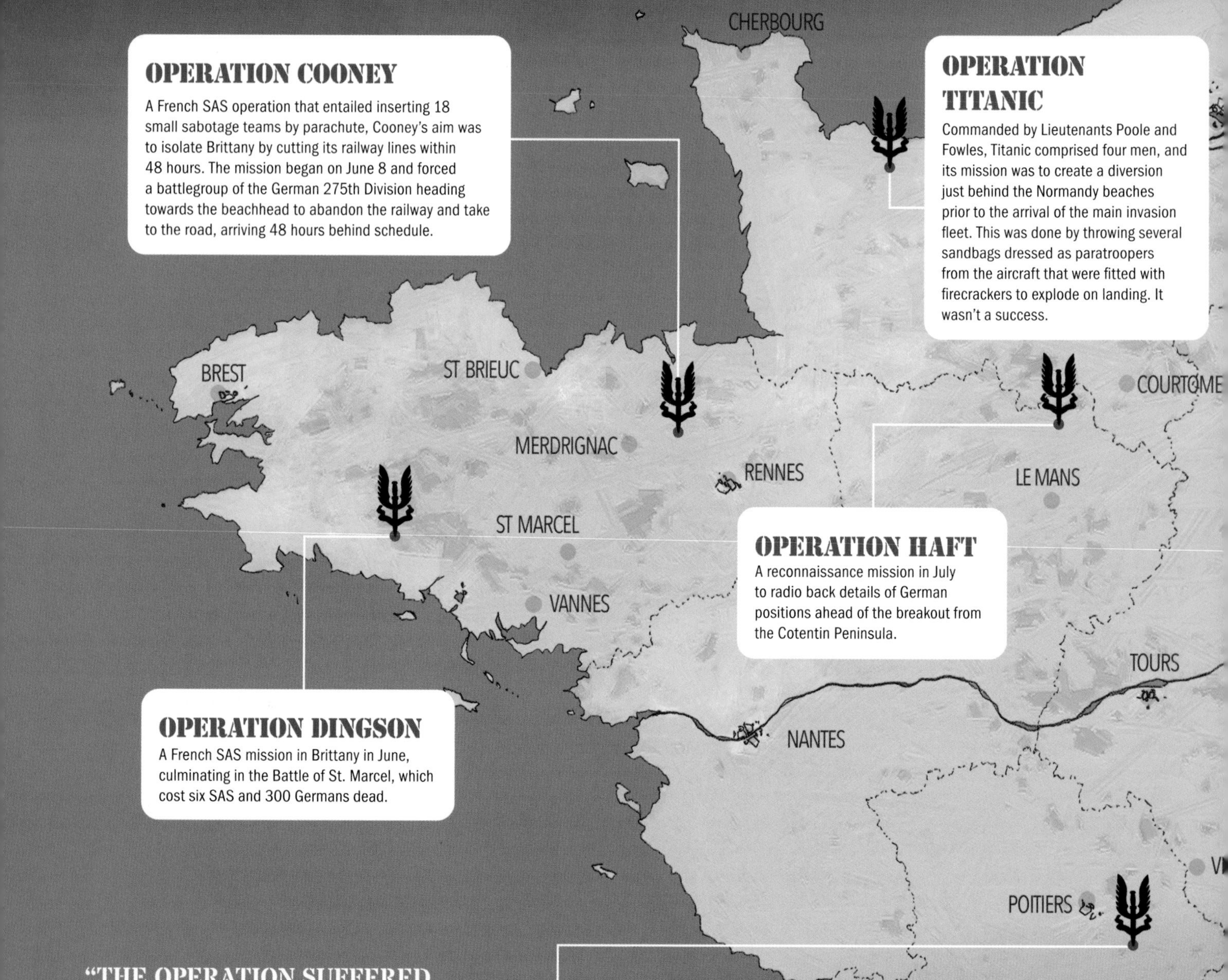

CHERBOURG
BREST
ST BRIEUC
MERDRIGNAC
RENNES
ST MARCEL
VANNES
LE MANS
COURTOME
TOURS
NANTES
POITIERS

OPERATION COONEY

A French SAS operation that entailed inserting 18 small sabotage teams by parachute, Cooney's aim was to isolate Brittany by cutting its railway lines within 48 hours. The mission began on June 8 and forced a battlegroup of the German 275th Division heading towards the beachhead to abandon the railway and take to the road, arriving 48 hours behind schedule.

OPERATION TITANIC

Commanded by Lieutenants Poole and Fowles, Titanic comprised four men, and its mission was to create a diversion just behind the Normandy beaches prior to the arrival of the main invasion fleet. This was done by throwing several sandbags dressed as paratroopers from the aircraft that were fitted with firecrackers to explode on landing. It wasn't a success.

OPERATION HAFT

A reconnaissance mission in July to radio back details of German positions ahead of the breakout from the Cotentin Peninsula.

OPERATION DINGSON

A French SAS mission in Brittany in June, culminating in the Battle of St. Marcel, which cost six SAS and 300 Germans dead.

"THE OPERATION SUFFERED FROM THE PROXIMITY OF LARGE NUMBERS OF ENEMY TROOPS AND AT DAWN ON JULY 3, THE CAMP WAS OVERRUN WITH THE GERMANS CAPTURING 31 SAS SOLDIERS, ALL OF WHOM WERE EXECUTED."

OPERATION BULBASKET

Commanded by Captain John Tonkin, Bulbasket was a 1SAS operation that began on the night of June 6 when the men parachuted into the countryside south of Poitiers. From the start, the operation suffered from the proximity of large numbers of enemy troops and at dawn on July 3, the camp was overrun with the Germans who captured 31 SAS soldiers, all of whom were executed.

Right: To supply the SAS parties with jeeps required four huge 90-foot (24-meter) parachutes for each vehicle.

Map: Rocio Espin

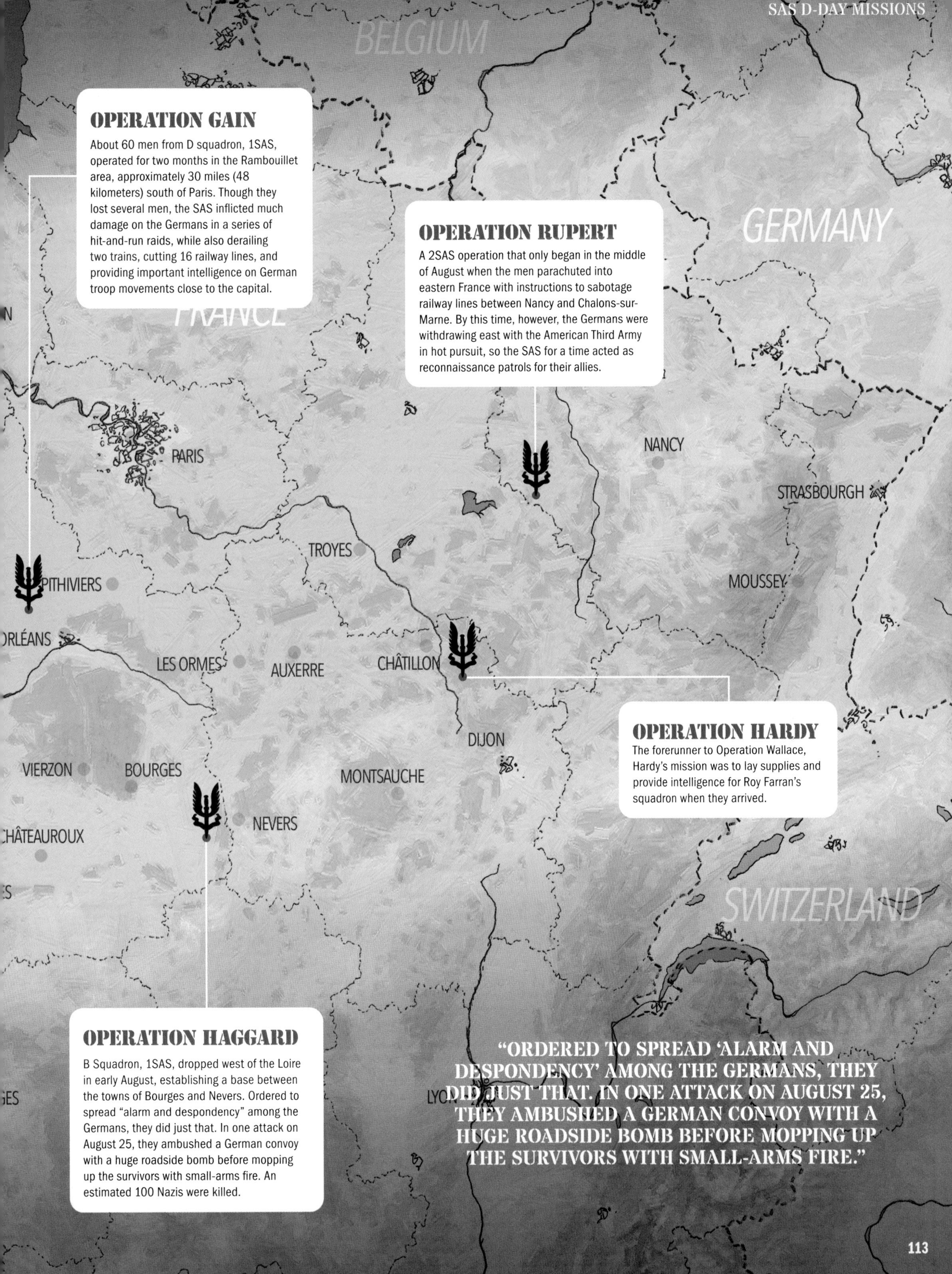

OPERATION GAIN

About 60 men from D squadron, 1SAS, operated for two months in the Rambouillet area, approximately 30 miles (48 kilometers) south of Paris. Though they lost several men, the SAS inflicted much damage on the Germans in a series of hit-and-run raids, while also derailing two trains, cutting 16 railway lines, and providing important intelligence on German troop movements close to the capital.

OPERATION RUPERT

A 2SAS operation that only began in the middle of August when the men parachuted into eastern France with instructions to sabotage railway lines between Nancy and Chalons-sur-Marne. By this time, however, the Germans were withdrawing east with the American Third Army in hot pursuit, so the SAS for a time acted as reconnaissance patrols for their allies.

OPERATION HARDY

The forerunner to Operation Wallace, Hardy's mission was to lay supplies and provide intelligence for Roy Farran's squadron when they arrived.

OPERATION HAGGARD

B Squadron, 1SAS, dropped west of the Loire in early August, establishing a base between the towns of Bourges and Nevers. Ordered to spread "alarm and despondency" among the Germans, they did just that. In one attack on August 25, they ambushed a German convoy with a huge roadside bomb before mopping up the survivors with small-arms fire. An estimated 100 Nazis were killed.

"ORDERED TO SPREAD 'ALARM AND DESPONDENCY' AMONG THE GERMANS, THEY DID JUST THAT. IN ONE ATTACK ON AUGUST 25, THEY AMBUSHED A GERMAN CONVOY WITH A HUGE ROADSIDE BOMB BEFORE MOPPING UP THE SURVIVORS WITH SMALL-ARMS FIRE."

OPERATION WALLACE

Heading towards Auxerre, C Squadron fought a company of the Afrika Korps and took down a train.

The officer who replaced Bill Stirling as commanding officer of 2SAS was lieutenant colonel Brian Franks. Charming and debonair, he nonetheless grew increasingly frustrated as the summer of 1944 wore on at the lack of opportunities for his regiment. A couple of missions were aborted at the last minute because of concerns about the operational area, and when the first parties did insert in August, they were soon overrun by the American Third Army, now on its dash east across France.

So when Major Roy Farran and 60 men of C Squadron, 2SAS, disembarked from their Dakotas at Rennes airfield in 20 jeeps, they were determined to waste no time in taking the fight to the Germans.

It was August 19 when they motored away from Rennes towards Auxerre on the start of Operation Wallace. Four days later, the SAS had their first contact with the enemy when they encountered a company of tanned Afrika Korps, recently arrived from Italy and still in their tropical battledress of khaki shirts and blue shorts. "Everything had seemed so peaceful," recalled sergeant major Harry Vickers. "When we heard the explosion, we turned the bend and saw Farran getting everyone organized."

Farran was a veteran of many a firefight and knew the importance of seizing the initiative. He ordered one section to cover their right and then sent Vickers' section, with their four brens, into the hedgerow on their left. The Afrika Korps soon attacked, believing their superior numbers would prevail. "I started to spray the hedge with bullets, and as I did so I could hear the Germans shouting rude things at us," said Vickers.

The fight lasted an hour and cost the Germans dozens of casualties. The SAS lost no one and withdrew to find another route to Auxerre. By the end of August, they had reached their operational area and began hunting out Germans. Vehicles were destroyed, roads were mined, billets attacked, and on one occasion a train strafed as it chuffed down the line

On August 30, they ambushed a convoy of 30 trucks as they approached the German garrison in the Chateau Marmont in Chatillon. Vickers, awarded a Distinguished Conduct Medal for his courage during the attack, was the first to open fire from a distance of 20 yards (18 meters). In his memoirs, Farran described how "the first five trucks, two of which were loaded with ammunition, were brewed up and we were treated to a glorious display of fireworks."

Vickers, years later, recalled it "as all a bit bloody." The SAS suffered one fatality in the ambush; the Germans lost nearly 100 men.

Operation Wallace continued to inflict heavy casualties on the Germans in the first week of September; the aggression and mobility of the SAS helped by the growing confusion in the enemy ranks as they began their withdrawal to the east.

On September 7, Vickers opened fire on two German staff cars he saw speeding down the road, killing a battalion commander and his second in command. The following day, the SAS destroyed five German petrol tankers. On September 13, they launched a mortar attack on the enemy held town of Langres, raining down bombs from a commandeered Peugeot. "It had a sliding roof in the first place," recalled Bob Walker-Brown, the officer who led the assault. "We enlarged it, took out the back seat, and stuffed the mortar on top of a lot of sandbags. It says a lot for the Peugeots of the time."

Three days later, Farran made contact with the US Seventh Army, bringing to an end to Operation Wallace. In his report he estimated that he and his men had killed or wounded 500 Germans, destroyed 59 motorized vehicles, plus a train, and blown up 100,000 gallons of enemy fuel. 2SAS casualties were seven dead and seven wounded. "This operation proves that with correct timing and in suitable country, with or without the active help of the local population, a small specially trained force can achieve results out of all proportion to its numbers," he concluded.

"HE ESTIMATED THAT HE AND HIS MEN HAD KILLED OR WOUNDED 500 GERMANS, DESTROYED 59 MOTORIZED VEHICLES, PLUS A TRAIN, AND BLOWN UP 100,000 GALLONS OF ENEMY FUEL."

A VETERAN OF OPERATION KIPLING

Alexander "Alec" Borrie was born in London in 1925 to a veteran of World War I who had survived four years in the trenches. When he was 14, Borrie left school and became an apprentice joiner, and during the Blitz he was involved in repairing bomb-damaged buildings. In 1942, aged 17, he enlisted in the British army and was posted to the Highland Light Infantry.

WHEN AND HOW DID YOU JOIN THE SAS?
In 1943, my battalion was posted to the Orkney Islands to guard against German raiding parties. Nothing happened and eventually in January 1944 the battalion was disbanded. We were given the choice of joining the Commandos, Parachute Regiment, or the SAS; I chose the SAS, not really knowing what they did.

WHAT HAPPENED NEXT?
I was interviewed by the commanding officer, who was Paddy Mayne, and once accepted, I was ordered to Darvel in Scotland where 1SAS was based. I later found out that I was one of only 30 from 300 to be chosen by Mayne. By the time we'd finished the parachute training at Ringway, the number was down to about 15 men.

CAN YOU DESCRIBE SOME OF THE SAS TRAINING?
A lot of exercises in the Scottish countryside learning how to navigate and also endurance marches. We learned about explosives, how to blow trains off lines, and we even got to drive a steam train in case once we were in France we ever needed to move it up the line.

WHEN DID YOU GO TO FRANCE?
I was in C Squadron, commanded by Major Tony Marsh, and we went in to replace A Squadron [see Operation Houndsworth] on Operation Kipling. On August 19, the squadron, plus about 20 jeeps, landed in Dakotas in Rennes and motored down to near Orleans. It took us about three days and I was in a section under the command of Lieutenant Roy Close.

WHEN DID YOU FIRST SEE ACTION?
I've heard it said we went on a seven-day patrol. I don't remember it like that, I recall we just drove around looking for targets. We got word that there were three German trucks driving along the Nevers road, so Roy Close decided we'd ambush them on a bend where a rough gravel track led up towards some woods. As the trucks came into view we opened fire, destroying the vehicles and killing about 15 Germans.

WHAT HAPPENED NEXT?
What we didn't know was that the convoy had an armored escort. So the next thing it all went off, this heavy machine gun's knocking great lumps out of the trees around us. Roy Close yelled, "back up the track." But the jeeps were stacked one behind each other so it wasn't easy. One ended up in a ditch and another, Close's, got stuck over a log with its wheels spinning. I was driving the third jeep. We managed to free the log and the two jeeps sped off, leaving the third behind.

ANY CASUALTIES?
The reason the jeep went into a ditch was because its driver, Joe Craig, got a bullet through his hand. We cleaned the wound by pulling a cloth covered with sulfonate cream right through the hole. It healed beautifully.

DID THE GERMANS GIVE CHASE?
No, but not long after, we passed through the village of

Right: Johnny Cooper, one of the SAS Originals, at the wheel of his jeep, which he's christened "Constance" in honor of his girlfriend.

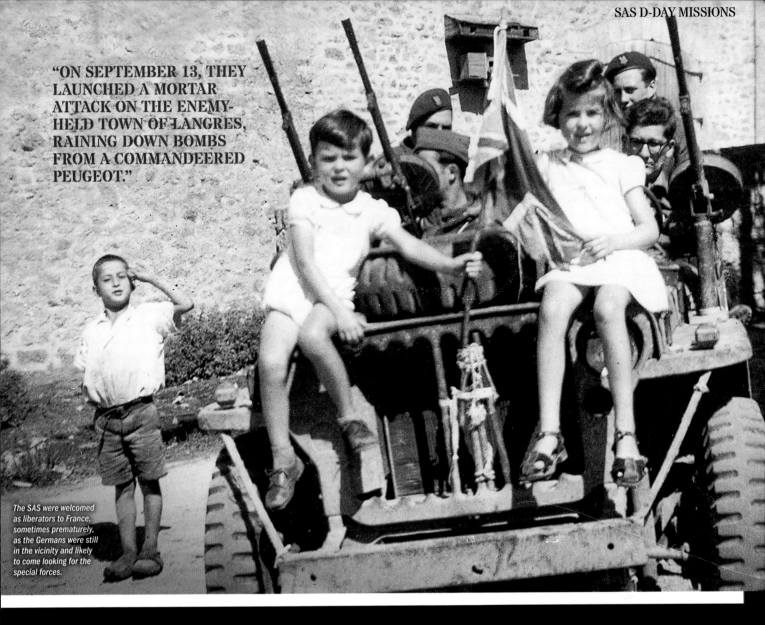

"ON SEPTEMBER 13, THEY LAUNCHED A MORTAR ATTACK ON THE ENEMY-HELD TOWN OF LANGRES, RAINING DOWN BOMBS FROM A COMMANDEERED PEUGEOT."

The SAS were welcomed as liberators to France, sometimes prematurely, as the Germans were still in the vicinity and likely to come looking for the special forces.

Chatillon-en-Bazois and the people treated us as liberators. They threw flowers at us and wanted to have a party. We tried to tell them that we hadn't liberated them and they should get back in their houses because the Germans were near.

HOW DID THE REST OF THE PATROL GO?

We just continued to drive around looking for targets. We had a couple more shoot ups, but by this stage of the war, we were running out of targets because the Germans were fast retreating east.

Eventually we got ordered down to Dijon, I believe to look for any German snipers who had been left behind.

WERE YOU AWARE THE GERMANS HAD ORDERS TO EXECUTE ANY SAS SOLDIERS THEY CAPTURED?

We were told about the order, and so we knew what would happen if captured. When you're 19, you think that might happen to others but not you.

DID YOU COME THROUGH THE WAR UNSCATHED?

No, on April 14, 1945, my jeep drove over a landmine as we advanced into Germany. My sergeant, Sandy Davidson, who had just become a dad, was killed and another trooper was badly burned. I spent several weeks in the hospital recovering from wounds to my right leg.

Tony Marsh (left) and Roy Close.

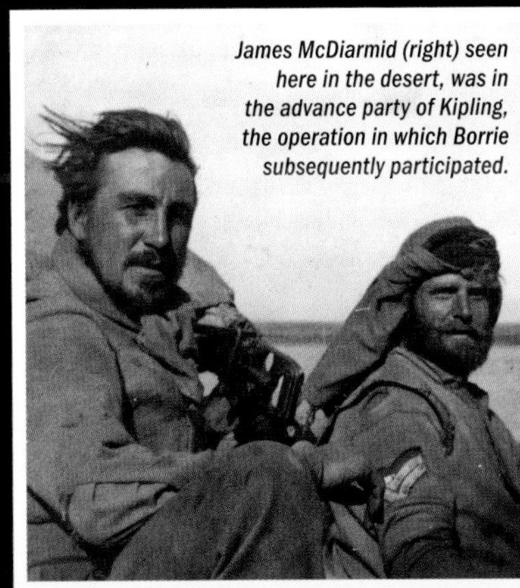

James McDiarmid (right) seen here in the desert, was in the advance party of Kipling, the operation in which Borrie subsequently participated.

Below: Paddy Mayne, a pre-war rugby international for Ireland, takes the SAS in scrum practice during a lighthearted training session in Darvel (April 1944).

(l-r) Major Pat Hart, Paddy Mayne, and Roy Farran wait for their transport at Stavanger airport in Norway, in the summer of 1945.

OPERATION LOYTON

With the Vosges reinforced to stop the oncoming 3rd Army, the SAS were charged with attacking the withdrawing Nazis.

With Operation Wallace having run its course, Roy Farran had hoped to lead his men east to link up with another 2SAS mission, code named Loyton. But word reached him that the Nazis, determined to stop the Third Army advance towards Germany, had brought in reinforcements who were well dug in along the east bank of the Moselle River. Additionally, the Americans, in their dash across France, had stretched their supply line to breaking point. Instead, Farran led his squadron to Paris to enjoy a week's leave in the French capital.

The men on Operation Loyton, meanwhile, were involved in a deadly game of cat and mouse with the Germans. The SAS advance party had parachuted into the rugged region known as the Vosges in late August with orders to attack the enemy as they withdrew into Germany. The drop zone was a meadow encircled by forest and near the village of La Petite Raon: "Not the best landing for me as I could see that I was drifting towards the trees and pulling hard on my rigging lines didn't help," recalled Dusty Crossfield. "I crashed through the branches and came to rest swinging gently with no idea of the distance between me and the ground. I punched my quick release and dropped heavily to the deck—it must have been about 15 feet (4.5 meters). Someone was running towards me and I reckon I had my colt 45 out faster than John Wayne, but the quick cry of '*Tres bien, Angleterre*' saved the lad from being shot."

Among the Maquis reception committee was 21-year-old Henri Poirson. "One of the British, sergeant Seymour, hurt his ankle on landing so we had to carry him back to our camp," he said. "The next day, captain Druce [the SAS commander] decided they needed a new base because there were so many Germans in the area it was becoming dangerous."

As the SAS moved through the forest, they encountered an enemy patrol and in the ensuing firefight, two British soldiers were killed and two were captured, one of whom was Seymour.

By the end of August, 34 more SAS soldiers had been inserted by parachute, including lieutenant colonel Brian Franks, and a number of jeeps. That provided the British with mobility and firepower, but as Druce recalled: "The Germans had sent a division from Strasbourg to find us and we were pretty oppressed." Nonetheless, the SAS embarked on a series of offensive patrols, shooting up any enemy vehicle they encountered on the winding forest roads. In the most spectacular raid, Druce attacked a unit of SS troops as they formed up in the village square of Moussey, machine-gunning them with the jeep's Browning and inflicting many casualties. The Germans retaliated by transporting the male population of Moussey to concentration camps; only 70 of the 210 returned.

The SAS were also learning that they had dropped into a region where history had divided the people's loyalties. Some villagers in the Vosges considered themselves French, but others had German blood, and were only too willing to pass on information to the Nazis. On September 24, Poirson was arrested by the SS as he arrived at the timber yard where he worked as a lorry driver. "They put me up against a wall and were going to shoot me, but then an officer appeared and said 'no, not this one,'" he recalled.

Poirson believes he knows who betrayed him, and he thinks they gave his name to the Germans only after a promise he wouldn't be executed. Instead, Poirson was put on a train east, first to Auschwitz, where he spent several weeks taking the bodies of the dead to the incinerator, and then Dachau, where he remained until the camp was liberated by the Americans.

By the start of October, Franks had concluded that with the American advance stalled, Operation

"SOME VILLAGERS IN THE VOSGES CONSIDERED THEMSELVES FRENCH, BUT OTHERS HAD GERMAN BLOOD, AND WERE ONLY TOO WILLING TO PASS ON INFORMATION TO THE NAZIS."

Henri Poirson, seen here in 2016, was a member of the Resistance who fought with the SAS in Operation Loyton and was subsequently captured and sent to Auschwitz.

The SAS participate in a service of commemoration for the victims of Moussey killed in German concentration camps.

Loyton had no further purpose. It had been a botched operation from the start, a mix of misfortune and bad planning by SHAEF. So, on October 6, Franks split his men into five parties and instructed them to withdraw west, through an area rife with Germans. "The colonel saw us all off and scrounged a packet of fags from me as he wished us goodbye and good luck," recalled Crossfield, who left in a party of five, one of whom was Jock Robb. "All went well for us over the next couple of days despite some very close calls with the enemy," said Crossfield. "We then came up against a fairly wide river [the Meurthe], and as we undressed to swim across, I became aware that Jock was doing nothing. He then told me that he was staying where he was because he couldn't swim. He'd lied during training and got through somehow without being found out. It was too difficult a crossing for me to ferry him over and I was damned if I was going to leave a good pal. So I got dressed again and we decided to find our own way by a different route back to safety." The pair eventually made it through the German lines, where they were reunited with Franks and the others who had returned safely.

However, 31 soldiers on Operation Loyton didn't make it back. Caught individually or in small groups, they were questioned, tortured, and then executed.

"DRUCE ATTACKED A UNIT OF SS TROOPS AS THEY FORMED UP IN THE VILLAGE SQUARE OF MOUSSEY, MACHINE-GUNNING THEM WITH THE JEEP'S BROWNING AND INFLICTING MANY CASUALTIES. THE GERMANS RETALIATED BY TRANSPORTING THE MALE POPULATION OF MOUSSEY TO CONCENTRATION CAMPS."

Below: The graves in Moussey cemetery of the three of the SAS soldiers caught and executed by the Germans.

Images: Alamy, Getty

BREAKING OUT FROM NORMANDY

After the brutal work of establishing footholds on the Normandy beaches, the Allies faced another monumental task in breaking out into the open countryside beyond.

BY **DAVID SMITH**

The Germans in Normandy were in no mood to run, however optimistic the crew of this tank may have been.

Allied planes like the Hawker Typhoon were the bane of German infantry and armor during the Overlord campaign.

The inability to achieve a quick breakout following the successful landings on D-Day caused concern among Allied commanders and has led some historians to question whether too much emphasis had been placed on simply getting ashore. D-Day had certainly presented an immense challenge, but breaking out of the defensive cordon set up by the Germans was proving equally hard.

The failure at Villers-Bocage had left Montgomery with a major problem. The Germans had brought up units to plug the gaps in their line that the Allied general had tried to exploit, and whispers about Montgomery's performance were starting to grow. Monty himself believed that VII Armored Corps was underperforming and suspected they resented being given hard fighting, having already "done their bit" in the Mediterranean Theater. Villers-Bocage had marked the end of any hope of a rapid breakout for the British and Canadians in the east, meaning that, from now on, they would have to grind their way forwards.

It wasn't just German resistance holding up the Allies. Nature herself seemed to be against them, as a major storm blew up on June 19 and wrecked the American Mulberry harbors, while seriously damaging the British one. An estimated 140,000 tons of supplies were lost during the "great storm," further complicating what was already a tenuous logistical position.

Facing the strongest German units in Normandy, and having been given a taste of their stubbornness in defense, Montgomery was determined to launch an assault on a bigger scale. Operation Epsom would attempt to punch a hole in the German defenses that could then be quickly exploited.

Dominance in the Air

Air superiority was a massive advantage for the Allies. Their interceptors kept *Luftwaffe* planes at bay, while medium and heavy bombers could attack German defensive positions almost with impunity. As long as the contested land lay close to the coast, naval vessels could also bring their big guns to bear, putting almost intolerable strain on German units. If the drone of aircraft engines was heard overhead, German soldiers did not have to look up and wonder whose side they were on. Despite these huge pressures, however, the Germans held their positions in a masterful display of defensive organization.

Epsom called for 60,000 men, 600 tanks, and 700 pieces of artillery to move forwards, supported by naval gunnery and air attacks. The assault started at 7:30 a.m. on June 25. Four days later, however, it was over.

A German counterattack, incorporating 9th and 10th SS Panzer Divisions, was effective, but not as effective as the British believed it to have been. As the British became unnerved (demonstrating how the Germans had got into the heads of their Allied opponents), the offensive lost momentum and had to be called off. More than 4,000 men had been lost.

Key among the issues hampering the British was the failure to properly integrate the operations of armored units and infantry. Tanks repeatedly outstripped their infantry support, making them extremely vulnerable to German infantry equipped with anti-tank weapons, as well as the superior German tanks themselves, not to mention the formidable 88-mm guns of the German artillery arm.

The Allies were also coming to the painful realization that their men did not fight with the determination of the Germans. Feeling that they were on an unstoppable march to victory, the British, Canadian, and American troops were less committed than their desperate foes, who were battling for their very survival.

The Germans were also not alone in suffering from attrition. British battalions were being broken up to reinforce others, though there was also a steady stream of new arrivals to replace losses.

"VILLERS-BOCAGE HAD MARKED THE END OF ANY HOPE OF A RAPID BREAKOUT FOR THE BRITISH AND CANADIANS . . . FROM NOW ON, THEY WOULD HAVE TO GRIND THEIR WAY FORWARDS."

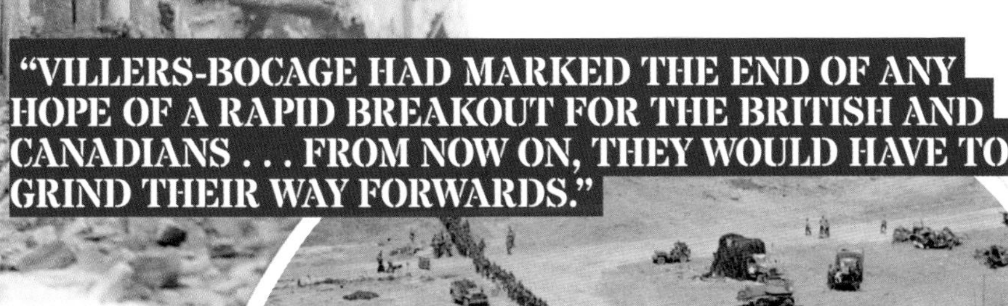

Right: A steady flow of men and materiel gradually tipped the balance in favor of the Allies after the D-Day landings.

Image source: U.S. federal government

Success in the West

While Montgomery was making heavy work of it in the east, the Americans were enjoying real success to the west. This was partly due to the fact that the enemy formations they faced were not of the same quality as those massed around Caen. The Americans, however, did have their own problems. The hedgerows of Normandy were proving to be a nightmare.

THE BOMB PLOT

Hitler was slipping into destructive paranoia even before a group of his own officers attempted to kill him.

© Getty

Above: Hitler had always been free with his advice to his generals, and he only interfered more after the failed assassination attempt.

The plot that failed to kill Hitler had consequences for those fighting in Normandy. An atmosphere of paranoia descended on the German high command, especially noticeable in Hitler himself, but also among his generals, who either grew suspicious of their colleagues or feared themselves under suspicion.

Many officers were disgusted, considering the plot an act of treachery. A rift opened between the regular army and SS, with mistrust increasingly common. With morale crashing among common troops, many believed the plot ultimately cost the thousands of German lives at the front.

Hitler even used the plot as proof that his own plans were reasonable. The lack of anti-tank weapons in Normandy, he argued, was due to sabotage in the supply chain by the quartermaster general, one of the men implicated in the attempt. Some even began to suspect the tying up of forces around Pas-de-Calais was the work of traitors, rather than the result of the success of Operation Fortitude.

Hitler's paranoia would lead to a greater role in military decision-making for the remainder of the campaign, and a stubborn refusal to allow his men to disengage when all hopes of success were at an end.

"Although there had been some talk in the UK before D-Day about the hedgerows," Brigadier James Gavin commented, "none of us had really anticipated how difficult they would be."

It had taken until June 13 for the Americans to link their bridgeheads on Utah and Omaha beaches, and their overriding concern was then to take the port of Cherbourg. A usable harbor was considered of critical importance even before the great storm wrecked one of the Mulberries. The struggle to land enough supplies, especially artillery ammunition, was hampering American operations.

Progress was possible, however, in part due to the weakness of their enemy. German units in the west were equipped with captured French and Czech tanks, rather than the more formidable Tiger and Panther models. On June 22, having made rapid progress (at least when compared to the British), the Americans began their assault on Cherbourg.

Reinforcements were heading for Normandy, but rail lines and roads were subject to constant attack. The bulk of the infantry made their way on foot and were left behind by armored units.

The precious panzers were also forced to undertake defensive duties, serving as strongpoints in prepared positions. They were still a problem for the Allies in this role, but it was not the best use of their capabilities. Losses mounted steadily as the British continued to attack in the east and most of the German commanders soon realized that their position was hopeless in the long term.

The V-1 flying bomb campaign, which started on June 13, was a morale-boost for German troops, but a month later, Erwin Rommel could see nothing but futility in continuing the struggle around Normandy.

"The tragedy of our position is this," he noted. "We are obliged to fight on to the very end, but all the time we're convinced that it's far more vital to

"EISENHOWER WAS DESPERATELY DISAPPOINTED [AFTER OPERATION GOODWOOD FAILED] AND CAME CLOSE TO FIRING MONTGOMERY, WHOSE REPUTATION WAS AT ITS LOWEST EBB."

The Germans surprisingly withdrew men from their outer defenses and concentrated on holding the fortified positions in the city. During fierce street fighting, in which the Americans basically had to learn on the job, the German grip on the town was steadily weakened. All resistance in Cherbourg ended on June 27, but by then the port had been comprehensively destroyed. The Americans had been denied their prize, which would not be fully operational again until the end of September.

The German Resistance

The German response to the landings was seriously hampered by Allied air superiority.

stop the Russians than the Anglo-Americans from breaking into Germany." Some in the German Army even harbored hopes of making common cause with the British and Americans to fight the Russians.

Forlorn faith was just about all the German troops had to hold on to by this point, but they could rely on weapons that were generally superior to those wielded by the Allies. In the field of tanks, especially, the Germans held a decisive advantage. They also had a far superior machine gun in the MG 42 and a much more effective infantry-held anti-tank gun (the *Panzerfaust*), as well as the terrifying *Nebelwerfer*, a multi-barreled mortar.

© Getty

Allied planes, such as the Hawker Typhoon, were the bane of German infantry and armor during the Overlord campaign.

Left: A tank modified with "tusks" to enable it to plough through the hedgerows of Normandy.

Image source: U.S. National Archives and Records Administration

All of these advantages could be relied upon to keep the scales balanced while the fighting front was condensed. A million men (it would eventually increase to two million) squared off on a front that was just 100 miles (160 kilometers) long in Normandy, and the cramped nature of the battlefield prevented the Allies from exploiting their major strength, which was their overwhelming superiority in numbers of tanks and other vehicles. The campaign became a question of how long the Germans could keep the Allies bottled up.

The success of Operation Fortitude had its part to play. Rommel remained convinced that a second landing was imminent and forces remained tied up around the Pas-de-Calais.

The hedgerows of Normandy made excellent natural defenses for the Germans and were dreaded by the Americans who had to deal with them.

A "Real Showdown"

A month after landing, Montgomery believed the British 2nd Army was as strong as it was ever going to be and planned an operation on a much bigger scale. He needed to achieve something, as mutterings about his performance were getting louder. Air Marshal Arthur Tedder (deputy supreme commander under Eisenhower) believed the British general had lost sight of the urgency of the situation.

"It seemed clear to me that Montgomery did not attach sufficient importance to the pressing time factor," Tedder complained. "Few weeks of summer remained. Our urgent need was to get across the Seine."

Operation Goodwood would utilize the strength of three armored divisions in an attack that Montgomery touted as being a "real showdown." Controversy would dog the operation, mainly because the British commander appeared to move the goalposts after the attack failed. Having spoken with his superiors in enthusiastic terms about the prospects of achieving a breakout, he afterwards insisted his main aim had been to tie up German resources to give the Americans in the west an easier time.

Goodwood failed at a price of more than 400 tanks and 5,500 casualties. Eisenhower was desperately disappointed and came close to firing Montgomery, whose reputation was at its lowest ebb. Thankfully for the Allies, things were going better to the west.

Battle Among the Hedgerows

The problematic hedgerows facing the Americans were about to be partially nullified by the invention of a new tank modification. Hundreds of Shermans (as well as other models) were converted to incorporate new steel "tusks" at the front, which could sheer through the hedges in two or three minutes. Restoring some much-needed mobility to the America forces, these "rhinos" were utilized in the next big move.

Operation Cobra was planned along a much narrower front than was usual for the Americans—just four miles (6.4 kilometers). Air attacks and 1,000 artillery pieces supported the offensive, which was scheduled to open on July 24. Bad weather put the start date back a day, but after preparatory strikes by fighter-bombers and then an attack by 1,800 heavy bombers of the American 8th Air Force, the assault commenced.

Damage inflicted by the "Great Storm" of June 1944, which destroyed the American Mulberry harbor.

The superb, one-use Panzerfaust was superior to any hand-held anti-tank gun in the Allied arsenal.

© Getty

The Germans were already beaten, and surrendering in substantial numbers, by the time the Falaise Gap controversy blew up.

As was all too common with the Allied bombers, however, some of their payloads had gone astray. As a result, there were more than 600 casualties among the Americans before they even took their first step, but brushing off this dispiriting start, they made steady progress. With 15 American divisions advancing against just 11 battered German ones, a breakout was always in the cards, but the fact that the German defenses were not as well organized here helped immensely. Isolated pockets were bypassed and the American advance gathered momentum. It was the inevitable result of the Allies gaining strength while the Germans steadily lost it. Eventually, a tipping point was reached and the dam broke.

Morale in many German units was low by this point, and there was also confusion following the assassination attempt on Hitler, which took place on July 20. In a state of turmoil, the Germans found any response to the breakout to be all but impossible.

"The enemy air superiority is terrific," complained Field Marshal von Kluge, "and smothers almost every one of our movements." The battlefield was suddenly transformed, and it seemed that progress might now be rapid.

The Americans then surprised everyone, not least their British and Canadian allies, by making a right turn into Brittany rather than a left turn to roll up the German defenses. Two corps headed for Brest, hoping to capture a port in better condition than the one at Cherbourg. Under the command of the fire-breathing General George Patton, progress was rapid—this was exactly the sort of free-wheeling, fast-moving operation the American army was built for. German units retreated into Brest and started to work on demolishing the harbor facilities.

The Germans Strike Back

Elsewhere, the Germans made one last roll of the dice, organizing a small offensive, Operation Lüttich. With direct input from an increasingly deranged Hitler, the offensive was ill-conceived and Allied fighter-bombers broke up the advance almost immediately.

The failure of Lüttich further weakened the German defensive line. By chance, the German attack coincided with a Canadian operation, Totalize, aiming for Falaise. Kluge had stripped some units in front of the Canadians to strengthen his Lüttich offensive, but despite this, the Canadians performed poorly. American bombers again inflicted friendly fire casualties (around 300 Canadians were killed or wounded) and momentum was lost after an advance of just six miles (10 kilometers). Totalize was called off within three days.

Such was the growing Allied strength, however, that another Canadian operation, Tractable, was mounted just four days later, on August 14. The Germans continued to resist, and the discovery

The Sherman tank was badly outgunned by its German opponents. The "Firefly" variant was equipped with a 17-pounder gun in an effort to close the gap.

Image source: United States Army Center of Military History

THE FALAISE GAP

The escape of a portion of the Germans in Normandy sparked a debate that still rumbles on.

Controversy has swirled over the failure to capture all of the German units trapped in the Falaise Pocket at the closing phase of the Normandy campaign. There is no doubt that the pocket could have been sealed with more effective and coordinated action from the Allies, but it is unclear exactly what that would have achieved.

Throughout the war, the Germans had shown themselves to be masters of escaping from encirclements. One of their greatest strengths was their calm acceptance of the situation and determined reaction. Given the desperation of their position following the Allied breakout, it is reasonable to suggest that any German units completely encircled would have fought with even more ruthlessness to break free. Casualties on the Allied side would have been inevitable.

Recent analysis of the situation has led some historians to believe the American commander, Omar Bradley, had deliberately avoided sealing the gap because he feared the consequences of putting the Germans into such a perilous position. (His official explanation was that he was mindful of the potential for friendly fire incidents if his men moved up from the south and met Canadian, British, and Polish units moving down from the north.) The Germans had been defeated, but they could still inflict losses, losses that were avoidable, and which would affect the outcome of the war not one iota.

Also worth noting is the fact that only a tiny fraction of the German army escaped. Something like 20,000 men plodded through the Falaise Gap, accompanied by an almost pitiful 24 tanks. As such, the failure to close the gap had negligible consequences on the overall war effort.

© Getty

of plans for Tractable helped, but the forces against them were becoming overwhelming. The Canadians were once more bombed by Allied planes, but the campaign was starting to draw to its conclusion.

The End of Overlord

The tattered remnants of Kluge's forces were now in imminent danger of encirclement as the Allies began to burst out. A pocket began to form around Falaise as Allied forces closed in. Kluge ordered a full retreat on August 16 and was relieved of command the next day. After being summoned to report directly to the Führer, he committed suicide.

> "ISOLATED POCKETS WERE BYPASSED AND THE AMERICAN ADVANCE GATHERED MOMENTUM . . . EVENTUALLY, A TIPPING POINT WAS REACHED AND THE DAM BROKE."

By August 20, the German army was slogging its way eastwards, harried by Allied artillery and air power. The so-called "Falaise Gap," a corridor of land separating the two sides, allowed some Germans to escape capture, but when that was closedon August 21 the campaign was over.

Upon entering the Falaise Pocket, Allied troops were met with a vision of hell. Dead and rotting men and animals dotted the landscape, among burnt-out vehicles, tanks, and buildings. Some soldiers resorted to wearing gas masks to cope with the dreadful stench.

The German defense of Normandy had been dogged and had resisted repeated offensives. The intolerable pressure, however, had finally told. More than 40 German divisions had been destroyed, with 450,000 men lost, along with 1,500 tanks and 3,500 guns.

Paris was liberated on August 25, while on September 1, Montgomery was promoted to field marshal, at the same time as being relieved of command of the Allied armies in France. Eisenhower would now pick up that mantle, perhaps inevitably, considering the growing imbalance in the makeup of the Allied forces, with new American units arriving all the time.

Brussels fell on September 3, and two weeks later the first American units set foot on German soil. Operation Overlord, though more challenging than anyone had anticipated, had finally succeeded.

American troops gaze at the Eiffel Tower after liberating Paris at the end of Operation Overlord.

FRIENDLY FIRE OFF NORMANDY

BY TOM GARNER

WWII naval veteran Claude Sealey reveals a deadly encounter with his own countrymen in a notorious but little-known incident off northern France.

Below: In this image, the shell splashes from the aircraft's four 20-mm cannon assist; the pilot in correcting his aim before unleashing a salvo of RPs.

Image source: photograph C 4641 from the collections of the Imperial War Museums.

Claude Sealey was wounded during the RAF attack on the 1st Minesweeping Flotilla on August 27, 1944.

Below: A salvo of 60-pound (27-kilogram) rocket projectiles fired from a Typhoon towards a German railway siding, March 30, 1945. Sealey would have been under attack aboard HMS Jason from the same aircraft and weapons.

Image source: photograph CL 2362 from the collections of the Imperial War Museums

It is a beautiful summer's day in August 1944 and six ships of the Royal Navy are sweeping the area near Le Havre for mines. Despite the dangerous task, the warm weather is a welcome relief for the recent veterans of the notoriously cold Arctic Convoys. Some are so relaxed that they sunbathe on deck, but a formation of aircraft appears out of the sun and suddenly dives towards the flotilla.

This would be an alarming situation if it were the enemy, but the sailors are more alarmed to see that these are Hawker Typhoons of the Royal Air Force and, without warning, the fighter-bombers attack their own ships. Explosions erupt everywhere and vessels begin to sink. Many men have to abandon ship, but to make matters worse, German shore batteries open fire and kill vulnerable sailors in the water. By the time the Typhoons leave, two ships have been sunk and hundreds of men are either dead or wounded.

One of the casualties is a young British stoker aboard HMS Jason named Claude Sealey. Although he became covered in shrapnel wounds, Sealey survived to recall his horrific experiences at the hands of his allies.

Powering a Minesweeper

Born in 1923, the teenage Sealey was eager to serve in the Royal Navy, "I joined in September 1940 when I was 17 years old. I got a shore job because I was underage, and I ran away from home to join up. My sister was at the barracks gate crying and I was given the choice to either go home or stay, but I decided to stay. Of course I wish I hadn't that day when I saw her crying."

When Sealey turned 18, he was transferred to general naval service and introduced to the ship that he would serve on until 1945. "I went in for a stokers course up at Skegness, and as soon as I came back down to Portsmouth I was drafted onto the minesweeper HMS Jason at Christmas 1942. The ship was at Leith docks near Edinburgh and I was a lone draft—I was on my own. I got the train from Portsmouth right up to Scotland and picked the ship up. HMS Jason was my only ship for the entire war."

As a stoker, Sealey worked in the bowels of the ship to keep it constantly on the move. He recalls that discipline was strict: "In the boiler room you had a petty officer and me as a stoker. There were six burners and if they signaled from the bridge or engine room that they wanted more speed, then you'd put more burners on to create steam. When the sirens alarmed that we were being attacked, I was always ordered to check the smoke glass. I had to go up a ladder and right across the back of the boiler to see if it was all clear because we weren't allowed to make smoke. The petty officer would wait at the bottom of the ladder so I couldn't get out—he wasn't a nice man."

Sealey's duties were split between the boiler and engine rooms. "There were two boiler rooms midship, and the engine room was in the stern where the turbines were stored that powered the propellers. There was a head and a stern turbine with a walkway towards port and starboard. At the end was a vat that was used for making fresh, clean water that was mainly for the boilers."

In the engine room, Sealey was responsible for an important part of the ship's capabilities. "I liked being in the engine room because an artificer and myself would take the throttles. This meant we were in charge of the ship's speed. The bridge used to signal down how many revs they wanted, and we'd open up the steam for the appropriate speed."

Conditions were hazardous in the lower parts of the ship and, if it were attacked, Sealey would have been in great danger, but he had little time to feel worried. "I felt vulnerable in the boiler room and not so much in the engine room, but most of the time I didn't think about it much because we were all busy. We just had to adapt and get on with it."

Clearing the Way on D-Day

Sealey's first active service was on an Arctic Convoy to Russia in August 1943 where he sailed to Polyarny, Murmansk and Archangel as part of the Allied attempt to supply the Soviet Union with arms and equipment. He experienced vicious storms, German U-boat and air attacks, as well as witnessing Russian brutality against their own people.

By the time Sealey returned to warmer waters, the journey had made him an experienced, if weary, seaman. "On the way down from Scapa Flow there was a U-boat off the Irish coast because

Poor communication caused the RAF bombers to attack Allied ships on that tragic day in August 1944.

"THE SAILORS ARE MORE ALARMED TO SEE THAT THESE ARE HAWKER TYPHOONS OF THE ROYAL AIR FORCE AND, WITHOUT WARNING, THE FIGHTER-BOMBERS ATTACK THEIR OWN SHIPS."

they used to hang about over there. We got the alarm and I remember there was an acting petty officer who went down on his knees and prayed, 'Please, we've got back this far, don't get us now!' Everybody was terrified. Luckily it didn't come to anything and we got back to Portsmouth. After that, we did a workout for D-Day."

Sealey was now a leading stoker on HMS Jason and, as a minesweeper, the ship would be one of the first vessels to sail on June 6, but Sealey almost missed his chance to take part in the event that changed the war: "Just before D-Day you couldn't see the Isle of Wight for ships, and we were anchored over there. The skipper gave us leave to be back the next day. There were three of us and we missed the liberty boat to take us back. I was terrified and I rang Portsmouth barracks, reported to the officer on the watch immediately, and he gave me a letter so we didn't miss the next day because that was the start of D-Day."

On June 6, 1944, HMS Jason sailed from England as part of 1st Minesweeping Flotilla (1st MSF). The minesweepers' responsibility was to lead the assault forces onto the Normandy beaches and clear the German minefield that protected the area. Officially code named Operation Neptune, the work of the minesweepers was an essential part of the beach landing process. German minefields were laid in depth within 10 miles (16 kilometers) of the French coastline, and the flotilla had to sweep ten "channels" to the beach assault areas for the troops to get through.

HMS Jason was one of 350 different vessels to participate in the mine-clearing operation, and her orders were to clear "Channel 9" of the approach route to Sword Beach for Allied troops to land. Consequently, the minesweeping flotillas led the way for the assault forces as Sealey recalls: "We took off on June 6, more or less as dawn was breaking, and we swept the mines. There were a lot of them and we had trawlers that went around shooting them up and exploding them."

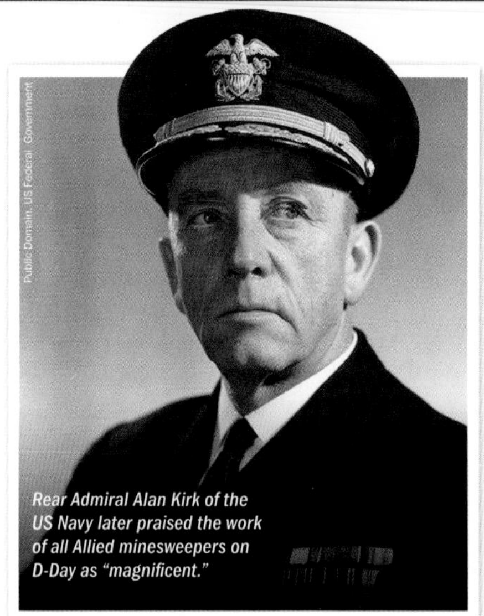

Public Domain, US Federal Government

Rear Admiral Alan Kirk of the US Navy later praised the work of all Allied minesweepers on D-Day as "magnificent."

France eventually came into view and HMS Jason got so close that Sealey could see individual landmarks. "As we got nearer to the French coast I could see this clock tower at Arromanches. I couldn't see the time on it, but I could see the tower. We went in as close as we dared and then turned to sweep mines again. Then all the big ships came in and started hammering the coast."

Sealey was aware that he was in the vanguard of the Allied invasion, but at the time he found it difficult to absorb the significance of the moment. "We were right in the forefront of the invasion, but we were so busy doing things that you didn't think about what was happening. The funny thing is when you're in with a lot of men together you've got that comradeship and you don't think about yourself."

The planning of Operation Neptune had been meticulous and, because of the courageous work of the minesweepers, relatively few warships, transport, or landing craft were seriously damaged or lost to the mines. All 350 vessels survived by the end of June 6, making Neptune the most well-executed minesweeping operation ever undertaken. The American naval commander of the Western Task Force Rear Admiral Alan Kirk praised all the Allied minesweepers: "It can be said without fear of contradiction that minesweeping was the keystone in the arch of this operation. All of the waters were suitable for mining, and plans of unprecedented complexity were required. The performance of the minesweepers can only be described as magnificent."

Nevertheless, HMS Jason's work was not over. Sword Beach was on the eastern flank of the Allied assault zone and therefore particularly vulnerable to attack from the Le Havre area. However, Sealey could not have foreseen that the most deadly problem would emerge from his own side.

Securing the Invasion Channels

After D-Day, Sealey continued performing minesweeping duties and almost had an unfortunate incident with part of the invasion force. "We kept sweeping mines in the English Channel for a long time and then we had a mishap with one of the landing craft, which was coming across with some tanks, and we went smack straight into her side!"

Shortly afterwards, HMS Jason was deployed to the area off Le Havre in late August 1944, 11 weeks after D-Day. By now, Allied armies had advanced well inland, but the Germans still held the important port of Le Havre, which had heavy shore batteries that continually threatened shipping. The Germans also had E-boats, midget

"THE PLANNING OF OPERATION NEPTUNE HAD BEEN METICULOUS AND, BECAUSE OF THE COURAGEOUS WORK OF THE MINESWEEPERS, RELATIVELY FEW WARSHIPS, TRANSPORT, OR LANDING CRAFT WERE SERIOUSLY DAMAGED OR LOST TO THE MINES."

Below: A rocket fired from a Typhoon of No. 181 Squadron, Royal Air Force, on its way towards buildings at Carpiquet airfield.

Image Source:photograph C 4460 from the collections of the Imperial War Museums

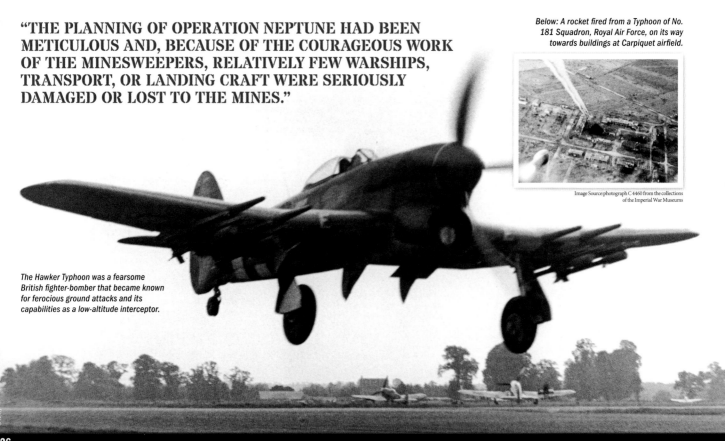

The Hawker Typhoon was a fearsome British fighter-bomber that became known for ferocious ground attacks and its capabilities as a low-altitude interceptor.

© Getty

"AMONG OTHER ACTIONS, HALCYONS RESCUED 14,000 SOLDIERS FROM DUNKIRK AND TOOK PART IN 78 CROSSINGS DURING THE ARCTIC CONVOYS."

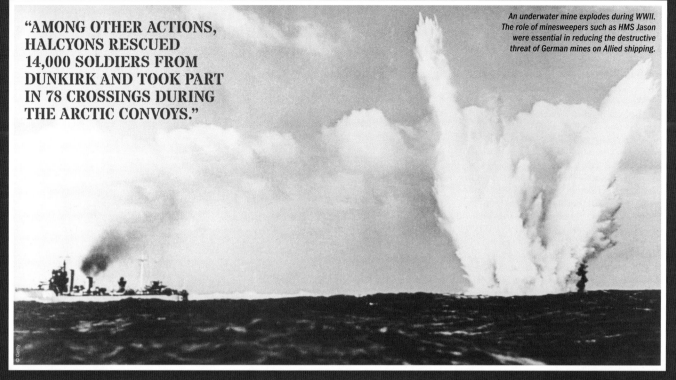

An underwater mine explodes during WWII. The role of minesweepers such as HMS Jason were essential in reducing the destructive threat of German mines on Allied shipping.

HALCYON-CLASS MINESWEEPERS

Claude Sealey's ship HMS Jason was part of an important but underappreciated group of naval vessels that cleared mines from the hostile waters of WWII.

Between 1934-39 the Royal Navy commissioned 21 oil-fired minesweepers that became designated as Halcyon-class ships. The navy had first deployed improvised minesweepers during the Crimean War, but the technology developed rapidly during WWI when Flower-class minesweeping sloops were introduced.

By the 1930s, the Halcyon-class minesweeper was being developed. These vessels had a weight displacement that was 175 tons less than their Grimsby-class sloop counterparts as well as being 20 feet (six meters) shorter. Because of the nature of their work, the minesweepers needed to be both small in size and have as shallow a draught as possible. Consequently, to save weight the ships were only provided with the most basic armament, including small numbers naval or anti-aircraft guns, machine guns, and depth charges.

To compensate for the relative lack of weapons, the minesweepers relied on cover from other warships or aircraft for protection. So long as there was adequate cover, Halcyon-class ships still had to continue sweeping for as long as possible even when under attack.

The minesweepers had various deployments during WWII including the Atlantic and Arctic Oceans, the North and Mediterranean seas, and home waters. Among other actions, Halcyons rescued 14,000 soldiers from Dunkirk and took part in 78 crossings during the Arctic Convoys. By May 1945, nine ships had been lost and 578 crew members were killed. At the end of the war, Winston Churchill recognized the minesweepers' service with an official statement: "The work you do is hard and dangerous. You rarely get and never seek publicity; your only concern is to do your job, and you have done it nobly. No work has been more vital than yours; no work has been better done. The ports have been kept open and Britain breathed. The nation is once again proud of you."

HMS Halcyon was the first in her class of minesweepers. Commissioned in 1934, the ship saw action at Dunkirk, the Arctic Convoys, and D-Day.

Image source: photograph FL 9841

HMS Jason in 1941. Sealey served on this Halcyon-class minesweeper from 1942-45.

Image source: photograph FL 14225 from the collections of the Imperial War Museums

Image source: photograph FL 9841

Image source: photograph FL 14225 from the collections of the Imperial War Museums

submarines, and explosive motorboats at their disposal that could inflict night attacks at Arromanches where Sealey had been sweeping weeks earlier. Despite the elapsed time, HMS Jason still operated out of Arromanches and anchored in the "Trout Line," which was a defensive perimeter of warships formed around merchant shipping.

1st MSF consisted of Halcyon-class minesweepers that included HMS Harrier, Britomart, Hussar, Salamander, Gleaner, and Jason. Their main task was to clear mines from the area between Portsmouth and Arromanches at night, but on August 22, 1944, their orders were changed. The flotilla was now required to clear a German field of magnetic mines off Le Havre, which would enable Royal Navy warships to bombard the port and assist the advancing Canadian Army.

Between August 22–25, the flotilla swept the minefield that was about five miles (eight kilometers) off the French coast between Fécamp and Cap d'Antifer before HMS Gleaner and HMS Harrier left for repairs. With a reduced number of ships, the flotilla was expected to stay in dock at Arromanches, but after 24 hours' rest the remaining vessels were ordered to return to minesweeping duties. One of Sealey's superiors aboard HMS Jason was the flotilla's navigating officer Lieutenant H.G.S. Brownbill, who later recalled that the redeployment order was not unusual. "We knew full well that the clearance and search of the area off Le Havre had not been completed, and we also knew that clearance was also needed to permit a heavy force to the area to bombard the Le Havre coastal region. I was promised that the orders would be amended to allow the 1st MSF to complete its unfinished search and clearance. Happy that all was at hand, I returned to Jason."

"THE SHIPS BURST INTO FLAMES WITH THE BRITOMART, LISTING, TO POR,T WHILE THE TYPHOONS SWEPT AROUND FOR ANOTHER ATTACK."

After these arrangements were made, signals of the amended order should have been circulated to other service commands. All services had to be given advance notice of movements at sea by Allied ships so that every activity could be accounted for. If all commands were well informed, then RAF aircraft based on landing strips in Normandy could intercept enemy vessels. Unfortunately, this normally smooth system of operations would not go to plan for the remaining ships of 1st MSF.

"Friendly" Fire

On August 27, 1944, HMS Jason set off with her fellow minesweepers HMS Britomart, Salamander, and Hussar along with the supporting trawlers HMS Lord Ashfield and Colsay. Sealey recalls that the weather was fine. "We got orders to go off the French coast at Le Havre because the Jerries still held that part of France on the Seine. We were out there sweeping in beautiful hot weather in August."

HMS Jason was guiding the flotilla and flanked by the Britomart and Salamander on either side. HMS Hussar was following behind while the two trawlers were laying buoy lines in the rear. At 1:30 p.m., Sealey recalled seeing RAF aircraft appear, but in unfavorable circumstances. "These airplanes came over and buzzed us a couple of times and we knew they were ours. However, before we knew what was happening they came back around and sunk two of our ships and blew one in half!"

The aircraft in question were 16 rocket-firing Hawker Typhoon fighter-bombers from 263 and

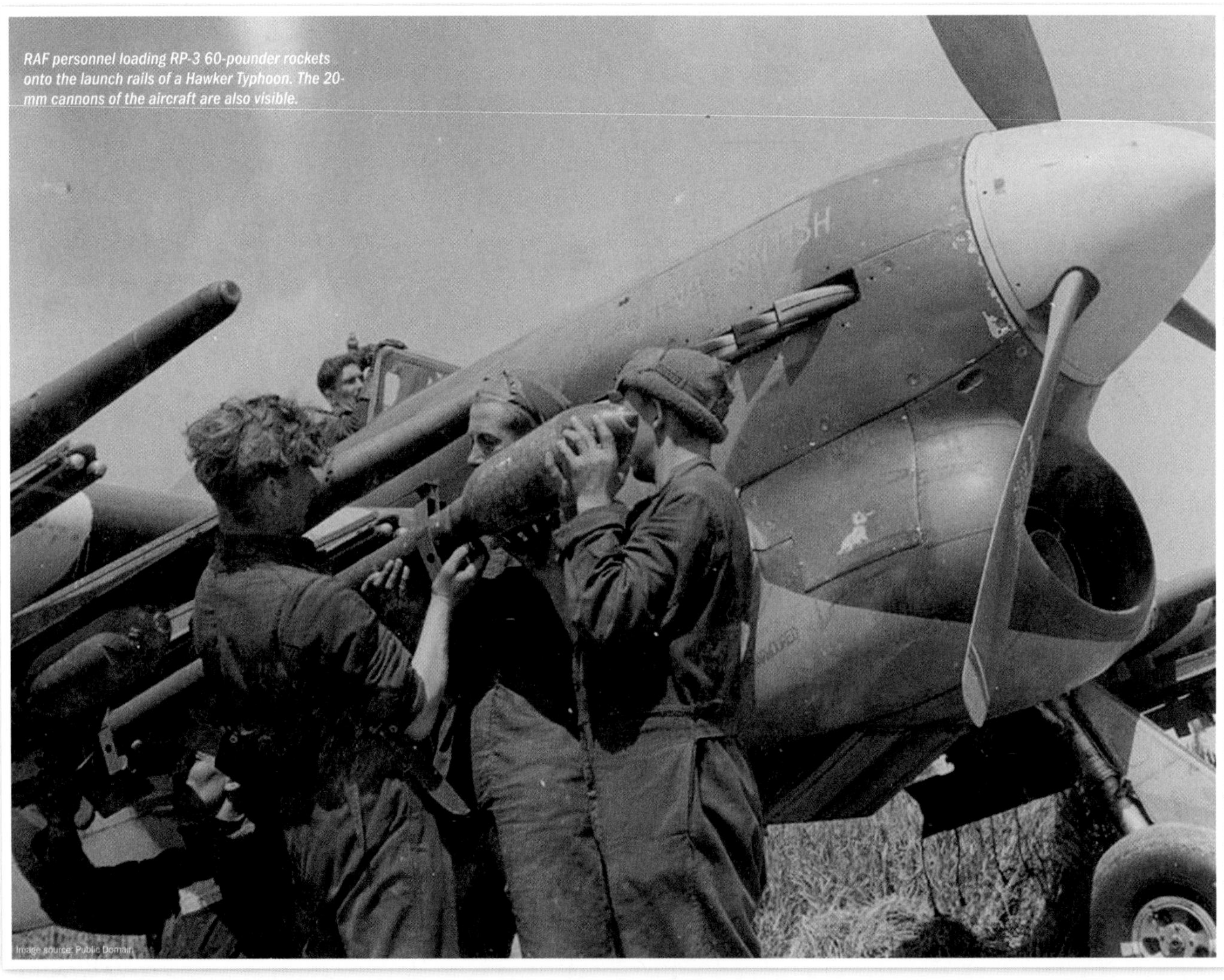

RAF personnel loading RP-3 60-pounder rockets onto the launch rails of a Hawker Typhoon. The 20-mm cannons of the aircraft are also visible.

Image source: Public Domain

Bombs hit the tail plane of an American B-17 Flying Fortress by the bomber flying above it during a raid over a German city.

ALLIED "BLUE-ON-BLUE" INCIDENTS OF WWII

The destructive power of the weapons used between 1939-45 increased the chances of devastating friendly fire attacks.

The friendly fire attack on 1st Minesweeping Flotilla off Le Havre was sadly not a unique case during WWII, and blue-on-blue incidents occurred everywhere on land, sea, and in the air.

Despite the meticulous planning, accidents were strikingly prevalent around the time of the D-Day landings. During a simulated exercise on April 28, 1944, eight LSTs (Landing Ship, Tank) were practicing landing troops into Lyme Bay, England, when nine German E-boats attacked the transports, leaving more than 600 Americans dead. To make matters worse, in the confusion a British cruiser then shelled the landing troops with live ammunition that resulted in another 308 Americans being killed.

As part of the Normandy breakout in July 1944, Allied aircraft accidentally bombed American positions. The incident was due to miscommunications over poor weather conditions, but the result was 136 American soldiers killed.

However, worse was to come on May 3, 1945 (five days before VE Day), when RAF Hawker Typhoons attacked German transport ships SS Cap Arcona, Deutschland, and Thielbek in the Bay of Lübeck. The three ships were filled with thousands of Allied POWs and prisoners from Nazi concentration camps, but the RAF did not know this and attacked with bombs, rockets, and cannon fire. The Cap Arcona and Thielbek were both sunk and at least 7,000 people were killed with only around 400 survivors. The incident has since become known as the deadliest case of friendly fire during the war and possibly in history.

"THE THREE SHIPS WERE FILLED WITH THOUSANDS OF ALLIED POWS AND PRISONERS FROM NAZI CONCENTRATION CAMPS, BUT THE RAF DID NOT KNOW THIS AND ATTACKED WITH BOMBS, ROCKETS, AND CANNON FIRE."

Image source: All images on this page from collections of the Imperial War Museums.

The artificial "Mulberry" harbor at Arromanches, June 1944. The construction of this harbor would not have been possible without the efforts of the 1st Minesweeping Flotilla on D-Day.

Image source: Photograph A 24675

Out of the two ships that were sunk on August 27, 1944, HMS Hussar suffered the most losses with around 55 men killed.

Image source: Photograph FL 22918

"WE WEREN'T ANGRY WITH THE RAF, BUT WE DID BLAME THE ADMIRAL."

266 (Rhodesia) Squadrons and 12 supporting Supermarine Spitfires from a Polish squadron. HMS Jason immediately fired her anti-aircraft guns before signaling at 1:32 p.m. and 1:34 p.m., "Am being attacked by friendly aircraft." At the same time, the other ships were also under attack, particularly the Britomart, Salamander, and Hussar. The ships burst into flames with the Britomart listing to port while the Typhoons swept around for another attack.

HMS Jason was raked by aircraft cannon fire that disabled the anti-aircraft guns and cut the steam pipe that made a loud shrieking noise. At 1:37 p.m., the Jason signaled, "Three ships hit and in danger of sinking," while the Britomart continued to sink, and HMS Hussar and Salamander burned heavily.

Sealey became one of the many casualties during the attack. "I got wounded. We were attacked by RAF Typhoons firing rockets, but what hit me was ordinary cannon fire. I was part of a watch party that was aft of starboard. It was just outside the wardroom where there was a ladder that went up to the boat deck. During the bombing, the area where we were suddenly became full of blue sparks flashing and I was bowled over on the boat deck. I ended up lying on the deck and when I got up there was blood everywhere and that was it. I wasn't wounded badly, but I was put in the wardroom with the other wounded. I had bits of shrapnel in my right foot, back, and three or four pieces in my hip. I had those pieces for ages."

After a final attack at 1:40 p.m., the airplanes flew away. The attack had only lasted around ten minutes, but the RAF left behind burning, sinking ships, and a sea that was strewn with debris and struggling survivors. Tragically, the ordeal was not over as Sealey explains: "HMS Britomart copped it and she went straight down, and then HMS Hussar also went down. HMS Salamander was blown in half, and my ship HMS Jason also got hit. At the same time the Jerries fired from their shore batteries, and there were all these survivors in the water and their heads were being blown off. It was so terrible."

Despite her own considerable damage, HMS Jason had taken the lead in rescuing survivors from the stricken Salamander and Hussar. During the evacuation from the Hussar, Jason's crew put down scrambling nets and rescued over a dozen survivors when the German shore batteries opened fire. One shell landed 295 feet (90 meters) from the Jason and forced her to retire with sailors still in the water. The ship then laid smoke screens to provide cover while it towed the Salamander back to Arromanches.

After returning to Arromanches, the Jason moved on to evacuate the wounded, including Sealey, in what turned out to be a personal blessing in disguise. "HMS Jason had quite a few holes in her, but our skipper steamed us into Cherbourg and there was a hospital ship ready for us for the wounded, including myself. We came back over to Portsmouth but instead of being sent to the local naval hospital, I was put on an army train to Basingstoke initially and then on to Sedgefield, County Durham, where I met my wife who was a nurse."

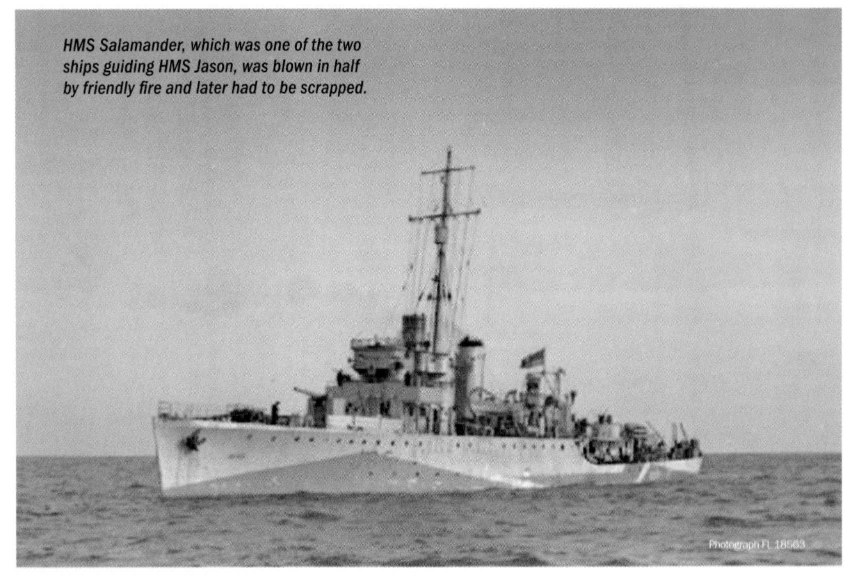

HMS Salamander, which was one of the two ships guiding HMS Jason, was blown in half by friendly fire and later had to be scrapped.

Photograph FL 18663

HMS Britomart's crew had been praised for their work on Arctic Convoys, but she was later sunk on August 27, 1944, with the loss of over 20 men.

Image source: Photograph FL 2980

The Cover-Up

The RAF attack on the 1st MSF had caused enormous damage. HMS Britomart and Hussar had been sunk while HMS Salamander was so badly damaged that she had to be scrapped. There was also heavy damage and casualties on other ships, and in total 117 sailors were killed with a further 147-153 wounded. It was the largest single naval loss of Operation Overlord that was not the result of German action.

Sealey contends that his attackers knew the ships' identity, but had to proceed because of pressure from the admiralty. "The planes knew who we were after flying around two or three times but whoever was ashore in France—an admiral apparently—said that shipping should not be in that area, and that they had to get on and do it. In those days you'd sometimes get a ship with a British flag up and it would turn out to be German, so the planes were given strict orders to sink whatever was there, but they knew we were British."

The tragic incident had occurred because of poor communication. Naval officers had signaled orders for the sweep on August 27, but a routine copy had not been sent. The officer responsible was new in his post and his supervisor had not noticed the error. Additionally, the naval shore radar was disabled that day, and consequently the flotilla was not spotted moving into the area.

Despite these errors, the RAF had themselves expressed doubt about German ships operating off Le Havre in broad daylight. The operations record book of 263 Squadron stated, "Six ships were located at the given pinpoint sailing southwest. Four were probably destroyers and two motor vessels. Owing to doubt as to the identity, the controller was asked four times whether to attack. The controller said there were no friendly ships in the area and ordered an attack."

Such miscommunication cost many lives, and there was an immediate cover-up of the incident. Sealey recalls, "We didn't know if there was an inquiry, it was all hushed up."

There had actually been an inquiry at Arromanches two days after the incident, which concluded that Rear Admiral James Rivett-Carnac had ordered the RAF attack because he had not been informed of the flotilla's work in the area. Three subordinate officers were subsequently court-martialled with one—Acting Commander D.N. Venables—receiving a severe reprimand for not thoroughly checking the amended order on August 27.

None of this complicated set of badly relayed orders was fully explained to victims like Sealey and his crew members, who were left in the dark over the details. "It was quite some afterwards when we knew what had actually happened. We weren't angry with the RAF, but we did blame the admiral. Somebody should have picked up a phone and said, 'We've sent these minesweepers around there because there were still Germans in the area.'"

The admiralty's embarrassment was so acute that recommended bravery awards for personnel caught up in the incident were almost denied until one outraged senior admiral intervened. Nevertheless, the cover-up was strictly imposed as Sealey remembers. "Afterwards we were told, 'Do not repeat what happened here and by whom.' We were given strict orders not to mention it."

It was an ignoble end to an avoidable incident that had been created by simple errors and inexcusable negligence. Men like Sealey from the 1st Minesweeping Flotilla had been a crucial factor in making the Allied invasion of Europe possible, and they were ultimately ill-rewarded for their hard work and success.

THE IMPORTANCE OF D-DAY

Victory may have been almost inevitable by the time the D-Day landings started, but the future of Europe was hanging in the balance.

BY DAVID SMITH

The statement scribbled down by Supreme Allied Commander Dwight D. Eisenhower was simple: "Our landings in the Cherbourg-Havre area have failed to gain a satisfactory foothold and I have withdrawn the troops. My decision to attack at this time and place was based upon the best information available. The troops, the air, and the navy did all that bravery and devotion to duty could do. If any blame or fault attaches to the attempt, it is mine alone."

The statement was written on the evening of June 5 (although Eisenhower was so preoccupied that he mistakenly noted the date as July 5), and it was kept to hand throughout the fraught days that followed, as the landing forces struggled to develop their toeholds on the beaches of Normandy.

Fortunately, Eisenhower did not need to deliver his statement. If he had, it would have been recognized as a brave acceptance of responsibility and a calm recognition of events having gone awry. It would not have hinted, however, at the dire consequences of such a failure. Defeat on the beaches and the recalling of the invasion force would not merely have been a military setback, it would have been a catastrophe, with ramifications that the world would still be dealing with today.

The Need for Hope

The importance of D-Day went beyond the tumultuous events of June 6, 1944. Its effect was inevitably felt in the days, weeks, and months following the landings, but it had already exerted an influence in the years of warfare leading up to it. In the dark days following the evacuation from Dunkirk—as France fell, as the Germans advanced deep into Russia, and as the defeats mounted

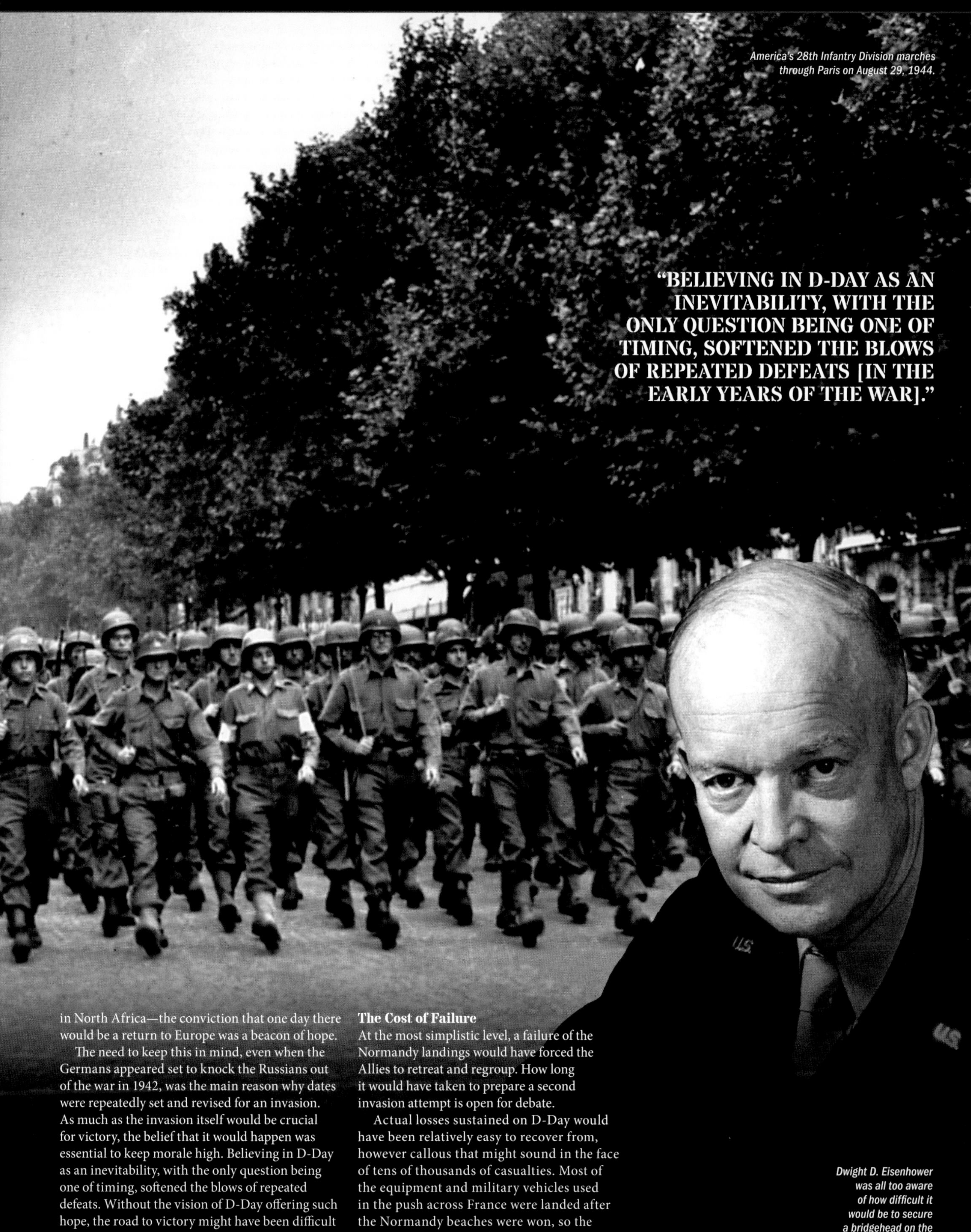

America's 28th Infantry Division marches through Paris on August 29, 1944.

"BELIEVING IN D-DAY AS AN INEVITABILITY, WITH THE ONLY QUESTION BEING ONE OF TIMING, SOFTENED THE BLOWS OF REPEATED DEFEATS [IN THE EARLY YEARS OF THE WAR]."

in North Africa—the conviction that one day there would be a return to Europe was a beacon of hope.

The need to keep this in mind, even when the Germans appeared set to knock the Russians out of the war in 1942, was the main reason why dates were repeatedly set and revised for an invasion. As much as the invasion itself would be crucial for victory, the belief that it would happen was essential to keep morale high. Believing in D-Day as an inevitability, with the only question being one of timing, softened the blows of repeated defeats. Without the vision of D-Day offering such hope, the road to victory might have been difficult to believe in.

The Cost of Failure

At the most simplistic level, a failure of the Normandy landings would have forced the Allies to retreat and regroup. How long it would have taken to prepare a second invasion attempt is open for debate.

Actual losses sustained on D-Day would have been relatively easy to recover from, however callous that might sound in the face of tens of thousands of casualties. Most of the equipment and military vehicles used in the push across France were landed after the Normandy beaches were won, so the Allies would not have been greatly weakened

Dwight D. Eisenhower was all too aware of how difficult it would be to secure a bridgehead on the

in terms of materiel, by a failure to secure an initial bridgehead.

More of a concern would have been the fact that D-Day would have tipped the Allies' hand. The Germans would have been given a warning, as well as insight into the tactics and strategies employed during the invasion. The Allies may have been forced to devise a completely new plan for a second attempt, or risk a rerun of the disaster.

The time needed to regroup and rethink might have allowed Germany to make further use of its new range of weapons. The V-1 bombing campaign commenced just days after D-Day, focusing on London, while V-2 rockets started to fly in September.

The V-2 was rushed into service before it had been perfected, and might have been turned into a more effective weapon in the months following a failed invasion attempt. Eisenhower himself commented that if V-2 rockets had been available to the Germans six months earlier, it would have been almost impossible for D-Day to succeed. A delay might have given the Germans enough time to improve their design and make Eisenhower's nightmare come true.

How close the Germans were to developing an atomic bomb is a contentious subject, but this devastating weapon made its debut just over a year later. A desperate Germany just might have been able to bring such a weapon to readiness, in some form, if given a respite following a failed invasion.

Even if such an apocalyptic scenario was infeasible, the V-1 and V-2 campaigns would have been given longer to run without the Allied presence in Europe following D-Day. London was spared when V-1 launch sites within range were captured by advancing Allied troops in October 1944. It is impossible to know how many lives in Britain would have been lost had the bombardment continued.

Industrial Might

D-Day had little impact on the fundamental outcome of the war, but victory would have looked very different had it failed. By the time Eisenhower made his fateful decision to authorize the Normandy landings, the direction of the great conflict was in little doubt. Nazi Germany remained a formidable opponent, but it was being steadily ground down, mostly by the actions of the Red Army on the Eastern Front.

The question of imposing an unconditional surrender upon the Germans had been a controversial topic, hotly debated at the many conferences held between the Allied powers. By 1944, however, there was no longer any doubt that it was the only way to satisfactorily end the war. The crucial issue had become deciding what the respective roles of the three major allies would be. It was therefore vital that the Western democracies played their part in the final victory.

Operation Overlord had taken years to come to fruition. It drew on the greatest strength of the Western powers—their massive superiority in terms of materiel. The fighting men of Britain, America, and Canada could not compete on level terms with their battle-hardened German opponents, but their huge advantage in terms of armaments and equipment proved decisive.

This was the main reason for the delays in launching an invasion of France. Although the Americans tended towards impatience, the British recognized the need to build up an overwhelming force.

This advantage in war-making equipment allowed the British, American, and Canadian forces to make progress, painful and slow at first (none of the first day's goals, aside from actually getting men onto the beaches, were met), but with increasing momentum. By the end of June, the

A failure on D-Day would also have delayed the American victory over Japan in the Pacific.

Image source: U.S. Federal Government, Public Domain

"HOW CLOSE THE GERMANS WERE TO DEVELOPING AN ATOMIC BOMB IS A CONTENTIOUS SUBJECT, BUT THIS DEVASTATING WEAPON MADE ITS DEBUT JUST OVER A YEAR LATER."

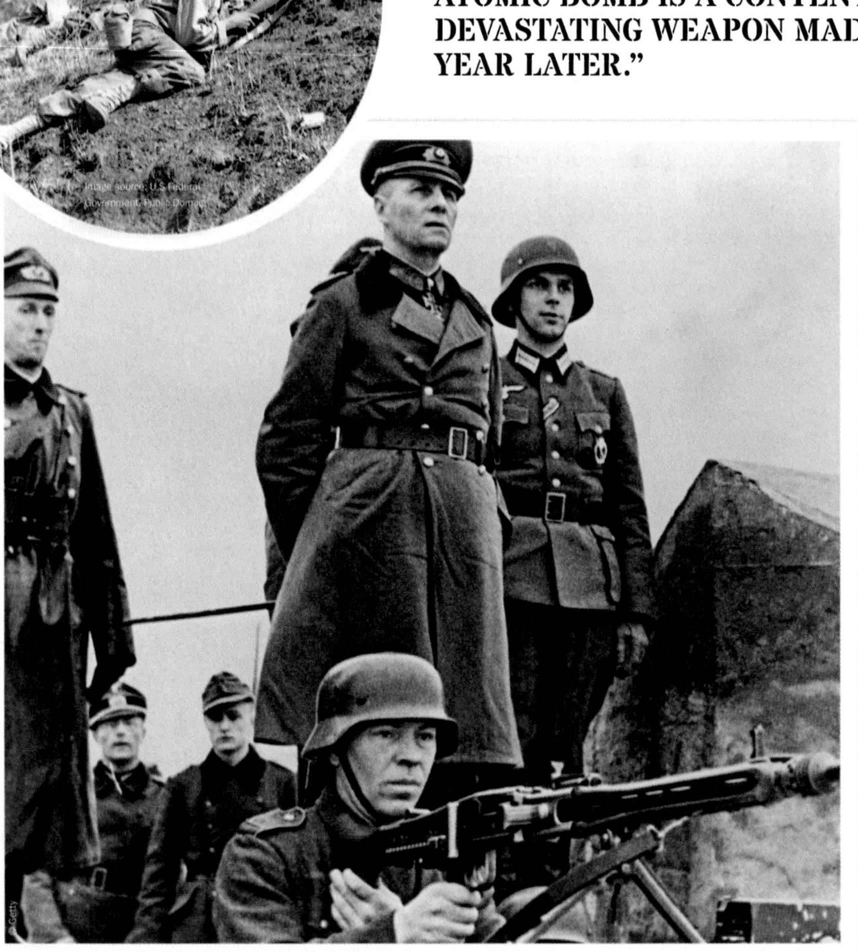

Above: A German propaganda poster revels in the destruction and fear spread by the new V-1 flying bomb attacks on London.

Left: Erwin Rommel was famously absent during the Normandy landings. The Allies might not have been so lucky if forced to launch a second invasion.

Above: The capture of Caen, following the Normandy landings, helped open the way to Paris.

Above: Had D-Day failed, American tanks would not have been able to stand against the Russians at the dividing line between East and West Berlin.

Above: The Allied strategic bombing campaign had already led to widespread destruction in German cities such as Hamburg.

Americans had control of Cherbourg. On July 10, the British occupied Caen. Paris was liberated on August 25, then Brussels on September 3. None of these dominoes could have fallen without the first one being pushed over on the beaches of Normandy.

Shaping the Future

Aside from the obvious fact that without the success of D-Day, the Allies could not have got to grips with their opponent, there were other factors at play. The result of the war may have been beyond doubt, but the shape of the post-war world was very much in the balance.

The British, American, and Canadian forces that landed on D-Day numbered five divisions, with three more airborne divisions providing cover on the flanks. It was a substantial invasion force, and one that Bernard Montgomery had been insistent on strengthening while planning the landings.

In contrast, just over two weeks later the Russians launched their summer offensive on the Eastern Front with 146 infantry divisions. The bulk of Germany's experienced units were fighting the Red Army, inflicting staggering casualties while being gradually pushed back.

The need for a second front had long been touted as essential to relieve pressure on the Russians. Now the urgency to get troops into France had a different imperative. Two years previously, the Russians had seemed on the verge of collapse, but by the summer of 1944 they were closing in on a complete victory. A failure on D-Day would have left the way open for the Russians to sweep across Western Europe. The "iron curtain" that Churchill so memorably described as descending across the continent, in March 1946, may have fallen much closer to the English Channel.

In an ideological sense, then, the war was being fought to spare as much of Europe as possible from the prospect of subjugation under a totalitarian regime. Failure to occupy territory before the Russians did would have forced many more people in Europe to simply swap one such regime for another.

The psychological implications of success on D-Day were also immense. Among the Western democracies there was a feeling that the "good guys" would, or at least should, prevail. It may have taken years of fighting for this to be borne out, but the success of D-Day proved, finally, that such faith had been justified.

PRODUCING THE GOODS

The combined industrial might of the Allies eventually proved too much for the Nazis to overcome.

The American war machine gathers strength: mass production of 28-ton tanks in Detroit, 1942.

The massive industrial advantage enjoyed by the Allies was hugely significant in the outcome of the war, and D-Day allowed them to put that advantage to dramatic use.

Prior to opening a new front in France, American and British heavy bombers had been taking the war to the Nazis, and as German production was hampered by the targeted raids, so the capabilities of Britain and America increased. The Germans were still able to produce around 40,000 new combat aircraft in 1944, but Britain countered that with 47,000 and the Americans produced a staggering 114,000.

There was a similar superiority in tanks and other war materiel. Germany managed to roll out around 6,000 new tanks a year, a number matched by Britain and her Empire, while the Soviets produced three times as many and the Americans churned out 50,000 Sherman tanks between 1942 and 1945. In 1943, the Allies produced a combined one million machine guns, while the Germans could manage only 165,000.

Without setting foot on French soil, however, these advantages could not have been driven home. More than 54,000 military vehicles were landed in the first five days of the invasion. By the end of June, that number had swelled to 148,000.

An officer in 2nd Panzer Division voiced the frustrations of German soldiers when he noted that, "Our soldiers enter the battle in low spirits at the thought of the enemy's enormous superiority of materiel."

The pessimism was justified. As soon as massive amounts of armaments began to be unloaded on the secured beaches of Normandy, in the days following the successful landings, the Third Reich's days were numbered.

WHAT IF D-DAY HAD FAILED?

The consequences of a failure on D-Day would have been felt for decades to come.

Despite the daunting prospect of landing troops on the beaches of Normandy, Allied planning and logistics were so impressive that the operation never really looked like failing. Even amid the carnage of Omaha Beach, a foothold was established.

Had certain events gone differently, however, things might have played out in a whole new direction. For all the planning and training, there were potential weak spots. It would probably have taken a combination of mishaps for D-Day to have completely failed, but they are not far-fetched events, and had the Allies been turned back from the beaches, the consequences would have been dire.

Here, military historian David Smith considers how D-Day might have failed, and what the fallout from such a failure might have looked like.

What if D-Day had failed?
It's a fascinating question, and even though it was unlikely to have been a complete failure, there were things that could have gone wrong. From various directions—security breaches, mistakes in planning, and a more concerted response from the Germans—there were threats.

Don't forget also that the weather might have played a decisive role. The Germans were already well along the road to defeat, but if the Normandy landings had failed, it is debatable how much of a part the Western democracies would have played in that defeat, and that could have had truly frightening repercussions.

What was the biggest threat to D-Day?
A security breach of some kind might have been disastrous, but German intelligence had been comprehensively wrong-footed by the Allies (most notably in the acceptance of the Operation Fortitude deception that kept so many German units tied up around Calais). The Germans knew an invasion was coming. If they'd been given a little warning as to where it was actually going to take place, reinforcements could have been shifted to the Normandy area.

Might that really have made a decisive difference?
That would depend entirely on how many reinforcements were sent to Normandy, and of what type. Panzer divisions would have made an impact, but remember that the Allies had air superiority and naval gun support as well, so it would not have been a simple matter for German tanks to dominate the landing area.

Could the weather have made a difference?
Absolutely, and especially if it had deteriorated throughout June 6. The landings had already been postponed due to bad weather. If they had started and then the weather had taken a turn for the worse, that would have been a dangerous combination. The "Great Storm" that blew up a couple of weeks later was unexpected and showed how destructive the elements could be. Of course, weather forecasts were a key part of Allied planning, but we all know that forecasters can get things wrong.

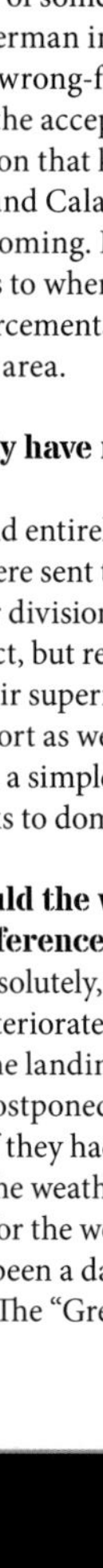

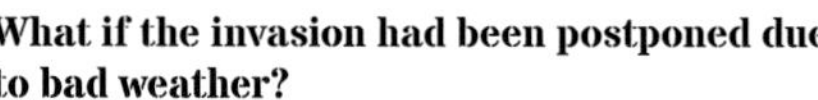

What if the invasion had been postponed due to bad weather?
Eisenhower made a brave decision to postpone the landings when the outlook was uncertain. If he had felt it was too risky to commit to June 6, and postponed the operation again, there would have been risks. The men would have started to suffer from stress and the risk of a security leak might have increased. It would have been two weeks before tides and the moon were next acceptable, and the Great Storm blew up around then.

Bad weather might have made it extremely difficult to feed more men and materiel onto the beaches after the initial landings.

DAVID SMITH

David Smith has had a lifelong fascination with military history and earned a PhD in the subject in 2013. He has lectured on the University of Chester's Military History MA program and now works as a freelance writer, contributing articles to *History Of War* magazine and writing books for Osprey. He has written on subjects as diverse as the Battle of Britain, Mongol warriors, Dunkirk, German stormtroopers of World War I, and the American War of Independence. His latest book, *Whispers Across The Atlantick*, was named Book of the Year by the American Revolution Round Table of Philadelphia.

If the Normandy landings had failed, the Red Army may have pushed into Western Europe after Nazi Germany had fallen.

What about the question of supplying the army after the invasion?

Thanks to superiority in the air and at sea, it is difficult to see how the Allies could have run into serious difficulties on the supply front. Even the destruction of one of the Mulberry harbors didn't hinder the Americans much (one admiral claimed the harbor was unnecessary anyway, preferring to land supplies directly onto the beach). The Pipeline Under the Ocean didn't work flawlessly either, and yet the Allies persevered and built up an overwhelming advantage in terms of materiel.

If the landings had been repulsed, what might have happened next?

That all depends on how quickly the Allies would have felt able to try again. The scale of the failure would have been important in this regard. Aborted landings due to bad weather might have been shrugged off, but massive loss of life, due to multiple factors going wrong after substantial forces had been landed, would have been a huge blow. How quickly could the Allies have regathered their strength and nerve? It seems reasonable to suggest it would have taken a long time. A timescale in terms of months is unrealistic. It would probably have taken at least a year.

How might the Allies have responded?

There is no possibility that an invasion would have been shelved indefinitely, but by this stage of the war the Allies were already hammering German cities with strategic bombing raids. This might have been considered an easier way to maintain pressure on the Third Reich while a second invasion attempt was planned.

Would there have also been consequences elsewhere?

Some experts have suggested that the Americans might have lost faith in the European strategy and shifted their focus to the Japanese in the Pacific. Others believe that Europe would have remained their priority and that fighting the Japanese would have taken a back seat for a while. Politically, a defeat might have dealt a serious blow to the reelection campaign of Roosevelt in 1944, and a new president might have signaled a new direction for the Americans. A further option would have been a shifting of emphasis to the Mediterranean. It had been considered something of a sideshow, but at least the Allies already had a grip on territory there. It might suddenly have seemed a much more palatable option.

The Russian flag flies over Berlin. Might Paris have seen similar scenes?

Image source: Ministry of Defense of the Russian Federation CC Attribution 4.0 Licence. Attribution: Mil.ru

© Getty

What about the Russians?

The Russians in the east were making steady progress against the Germans. If D-Day had been repulsed, the Germans might have felt safe to withdraw some of their Atlantic Wall defenders to stiffen resistance on the other front. It is difficult to see how this could have materially changed the outcome of the war, but the Russians might have been held up for longer.

Were the German Vengeance weapons likely to make a difference?

They had great propaganda value, but strategic bombing on a truly terrifying scale by the Allies was not bringing Germany to its knees, so it is difficult to see how even a more effective V-2 rocket campaign could have achieved much. The Germans were researching atomic technology, but people underestimate just what a massive undertaking it was to create the first weapons, and Germany just did not have the resources available. Just maybe, if the war had been dragged out for a year or more longer, the Germans might have produced a viable tactical weapon, but they would have needed many of them to stop the Russians in the east. Forcing a negotiated surrender might have been an option, especially if they developed strategic applications for an atomic bomb and either threatened or destroyed a major Allied city. We know the effect that sort of action can have.

How might the war have played out?

That would all depend on how quickly the Allies tried a second invasion. Eventually, the Germans were going to crack in the east, and Russian forces were going to spill into Germany. Without Anglo-American armies coming in the opposite direction, might the Russians have continued to push westwards? The war may have lasted longer, maybe by a matter of months, maybe by more than a year, but Germany was going to lose. The price of failure

Left: Russian military might grew steadily after the war and might have been enhanced with the addition of more territory in Western Europe.

Comparing real and alternative scenario timelines.

The Turning Point

THE NORMANDY LANDINGS BEGIN
June 6, 1944
As predicted, the weather on June 6 is acceptable and the landings proceed. Everything hung on whether or not the landings went smoothly. If any one of the multiple potential problems had arisen, the invasion may still have succeeded. If more than one thing had gone wrong, it might have been impossible to grab the necessary beachheads on "the longest day." Most importantly, if the meteorologists had got their forecast wrong, and the weather did not clear up on June 6, then D-Day may have failed outright. At the least, it would have been postponed again, maybe for two weeks, maybe for longer.

GAMBLING ON THE WEATHER
June 5, 1944
Eisenhower makes one of the boldest decisions of the war, postponing the invasion by a day in the hope that the weather will improve on June 6. He trusts his meteorologists, but he knows the risks if they have got it wrong.

REAL TIMELINE

ALLIES GAIN A FOOTHOLD
June 6
Although terrible casualties are taken on Omaha Beach, the necessary bridgeheads are secured and the Allies gain a foothold on the Normandy beaches.

BATTLE OF VILLERS-BOCAGE
June 13
The Allies struggle to break out from their bridgeheads, with the British butting heads with the strongest German units in Normandy and making much slower progress than anticipated.

THE GREAT STORM
June 18
Mother Nature shows what she is capable of by unleashing a serious storm that destroys the American Mulberry harbor and gives a chilling indication of how the landings might have gone badly if postponed.

ALTERNATE TIMELINE

THE WEATHER WORSENS
June 6
Almost as soon as the landings start, the weather turns, disrupting subsequent waves of landing craft and putting more pressure on the first men to reach the shore.

THE GERMANS RESIST
June 6
Having recently moved more units into the region, the Germans are able to hit the invasion force with considerably more firepower than anticipated. The invasion begins to stutter.

INVASION FORCES RECALLED
June 7
With his men floundering, Eisenhower makes the agonizing decision to call off the landings, issuing the statement of failure kept in his pocket and tendering his resignation shortly afterwards.

Source: IWMCollection IWM Photo No: B 5091

THE RUSSIAN SUMMER OFFENSIVE BEGINS
June 22
Oblivious to events in the west, the Russians begin their huge offensive against the bulk of the German army, pushing their way steadily towards the heart of the Third Reich.

would have been paid by the people of Western Europe.

What shape might post-war Europe have taken?

The iron curtain would probably have fallen much further to the west. How much further? Perhaps France would have been divided in the same way that Germany was as events actually played out. Some have even speculated that the Russians might have pushed on all the way to the coast. The Soviet Union would have been bigger and stronger in the post-war world and that would have had huge repercussions on the course of history. Would Britain and America have seen a need to embark upon a war against the Soviets immediately after they had taken over much or even all of Europe? As events actually unfolded, war with Russia was recognized as the next great threat as soon as the Germans were defeated, and it might have been unavoidable in this hypothetical scenario. It seems safe to say that we should all be extremely grateful that D-Day did not fail.

Could the Yalta Conference have taken place in 1945 if Anglo-American forces were not yet on the continent?

Source: U.S. National Archives and Records Administration

THE AMERICANS TAKE CHERBOURG
June 22
Progress at last in Normandy, as the Americans break out and take the strategic port of Cherbourg, only to find that it has been demolished by the Germans.

Source: U.S. federal government.

THE RUSSIAN SUMMER OFFENSIVE OPENS
June 22
Massive Russian forces swing into action in the east, putting the Germans under intolerable pressure as they struggle to hold their ground on two fronts.

THE BRITISH OCCUPY CAEN
July 10
The British continue to slog their way forwards, as Montgomery comes under increasing scrutiny for his failure to break through the German defensive line, but the Germans are about to crack.

Source: German Federal Archive

GERMANS ORDER THE RETREAT
August 17
As the Allies amass overwhelming forces in Normandy, the Germans have no alternative but to signal a full retreat. Almost half a million men have been lost in the defense of Normandy.

Source: U.S. federal government.

PARIS IS LIBERATED
August 25
The Allies move swiftly after breaking out from Normandy. Occupied territory is liberated and the end of the war appears to be in sight as German resistance crumbles.

Source: IWMCollection IWM Photo http://media.iwm.org.uk/iwm/mediaLib//49/media-49758/large.jpg

AMERICAN TROOPS CROSS GERMAN BORDER
September 16
With the entry into Germany, the Anglo-American forces have played their part in the downfall of the Nazis. Although the war will drag on for many more months, the outcome is in no doubt.

THE GERMANS REINFORCE THE EASTERN FRONT
July
Having seen off the threat of invasion in the west, Hitler orders his best divisions to the east, stiffening resistance against the Russians. The rate of progress for the Soviets slows.

Source: German Federal Archive

V-2 CAMPAIGN INTENSIFIES
April 1945
Having improved the V-2 rocket, Germany is able to employ it against London in response to the continuing bombing raids on German cities. A second "Blitz" claims thousands of lives.

Source: German Federal Archive

RUSSIANS ADVANCE INTO BERLIN
April 1946
Finally cornering their foe, the Russians are on the brink of ending the war, as only the most fanatical German units continue to resist.

BERLIN FALLS
June 1946
Hitler commits suicide as all resistance in Berlin ends. The Russians quickly move on into western Germany and beyond as the Allies prepare to attempt a new invasion.

Source: German Federal Archive

THE ALLIES INVADE NORMANDY
June 1946
Almost exactly two years after their failure on June 6, 1944, American, British, and Canadian forces land once more in Normandy. German units put up weak resistance, disheartened following the fall of Berlin.

ALLIES AND RUSSIANS MEET IN PARIS
August 1946
The borders of post-war Europe are set as the Americans, British, and French occupy western France, while the Russians occupy the east. Paris is divided. In 1961, a wall is erected dividing east and west Paris. It stands for nearly 40 years.

DESTINATION NORMANDY

From the D-Day beach assaults to the devastating final shots in the Falaise Pocket, this region is home to some of the most important battlefields and landmarks in European history.

BY **TIM WILLIAMSON**

Normandy is a region steeped in history, from the staging ground of the conquest of England in the 11th century, to the liberation of Europe in 1944. For anyone passionate about the history of WWII in particular, there are a huge number of commemorative sites, museums, and battlefields to explore, from the well-known to the more obscure.

To coincide with the 73rd anniversary of the D-Day landings, we were invited on a short tour of Normandy to experience what the region has to offer those in search of reflection, exploration, and remembrance. Here are just a few incredible locations to add to any itinerary, each of which has its own unique part in the story of D-Day.

BACK TO THE BEACHES

In June 2017, The Taxi Charity for Military Veterans mounted an incredible campaign to transport British veterans back to Normandy one last time.

On June 4, 2017, a convoy of 90 black cabs, all driven by volunteer London cabbies, set off from the Royal Hospital Chelsea with over 200 veterans and carers—their destination: Normandy. In an astonishing triumph of logistics, the convoy stopped off at Pegasus Bridge, Ranville war cemetery, and Bayeux Cathedral for a Royal British Legion service during its four-day tour of the region. The charity says this will be the final trip of its scale, as the number of veterans diminishes and those remaining are unable to make the journey.

Founded in 1948, the charity originally supported injured and disabled cabbies returning from the front line, but later expanded its remit to all the armed forces, organizing recreational trips to seaside spots, such as Worthing and Brighton. It now arranges annual trips, entertainment, and support for British military veterans of all conflicts.

To learn more about the charity and how you can donate, visit: ***www.taxicharity.org***

Right: The Taxi Charity for Military Veterans was founded in 1948 and continues to support those who served during WWII.

© Getty

UTAH

A late addition to Operation Overlord, this site saw the beginning of the march to Cherbourg, and has a curious connection with Texas.

First opened in 1962, the Utah Beach *Musée de Debarquement* is located on the exact site where the first soldiers of the US 4th Infantry Division landed at 6:30 a.m. on June 6, 1944. 600 men arrived in 20 LCPVs over a mile south of their planned point of attack due to unexpectedly strong currents in the Channel. "We'll start the war right here!" Brigadier General Theodore Roosevelt, Jr. famously declared.

Part of the main building of the museum itself is in fact built within an original German bunker, a strongpoint along the Atlantic Wall with the designation WN5. On June 6, there were just 75 Germans defending the position.

German resistance was relatively light at Utah, and the defenders quickly became overwhelmed with paratroopers of the 82nd and 101st Airborne, which had dropped in behind their lines during the early hours of the morning. In the event, the beach was taken in just 45 minutes, but it would be three weeks before the objective of the port city of Cherbourg would be liberated. However, the retreating Germans left the port in ruins, putting it out of action for months.

One critical element of the victory at Utah was the accurate bombing runs made by the US Air Force, which weakened the German defenses before the main assault began. Major David Dewhurst, squadron commander of the 386th Bomb Group, made the very last of these runs at 6:25 a.m., just five minutes before the infantry were due to arrive. Over 60 years later, his two sons David and Gene, visited the museum and recognized a photograph of their father with his B-26 Marauder, the "Dinah Might." This began a long relationship between the siblings and the museum, which they helped fund and expand.

> "ONE CRITICAL ELEMENT OF THE VICTORY AT UTAH WAS THE ACCURATE BOMBING RUNS MADE BY THE US AIR FORCE."

Today it is home to an original B-26 in the same D-Day stripes and markings of Dewhurst's "Dinah Might," in honor of his part in the operation. Elsewhere is an original and restored LCPV, or Higgins Boat, as well as an amphibious landing vehicle that was abandoned on the beach after the landing. One of the more obscure objects on display is an original remote-controlled tracked mine, or Goliath, discovered by the Americans on the beach. These small, explosive machines were designed to be remotely driven towards enemy vehicles, infantry formations, or buildings, before detonating.

For more information on the Utah Beach Museum, visit: *www.utah-beach.com*

On June 4, 2017, 197 lanterns were released over Utah Beach—one for each of the US soldiers killed during the landings there.

The museum is at the center of annual commemorative ceremonies as well as festivities celebrating the liberation.

© Alamy

"ATOP THE PLATEAU AT COLLEVILLE-SUR-MER NOW LIE OVER 9,300 AMERICAN SERVICEMEN WHO MADE THE ULTIMATE SACRIFICE DURING THE NORMANDY CAMPAIGN."

View from the Garden of the Missing, through to the sculpture, The Spirit of the American Youth Rising from the Waves.

OMAHA

Over 3,000 US soldiers were killed storming this stronghold, today the location of the Normandy American Cemetery & Memorial.

THE JUNO BEACH CENTER

Often overlooked in the history of D-Day are the 14,000 Canadians who fought on June 6 itself, as well as the thousands more who took part in the Battle of Normandy and beyond. The Juno Beach Center is a not-for-profit museum and memorial to all Canadians who fought and died during WWII. The center's permanent exhibition tells the story not only of Canadian involvement in the war, but also in the impact of the conflict on this young nation.

For more information visit ***www.junobeach.org***

Unquestionably the most infamous of the D-Day beaches, on June 6 Omaha was heavily defended by the 352 Infanterie-Division, which included many veterans returned from the Russian front. Ahead of the Americans was approximately 547 yards (500 meters) of open beach, littered with large obstacles—wooden stakes and metal "Czech hedgehogs"—intended to obstruct amphibious landings and vehicles.

The Germans occupied over a dozen main defensive positions along the beach, commanding the high ground of a plateau south of Omaha, parallel to the villages of Vierville-sur-Mer, Colleville-sur-Mer, and Saint-Laurent-sur-Mer. From here they were able to bring down highly effective sniper and mortar fire, as well as withering machine-gun fire, which proved devastating for the initial waves of American troops.

Atop the plateau at Colleville-sur-Mer now lie over 9,300 American servicemen who made the ultimate sacrifice during the Normandy campaign. Among them lies Theodore Roosevelt, Jr., who succumbed to a heart attack not more than a month after leading his men onto Utah beach—he is buried next to his brother Quentin, a fighter pilot who was killed in combat in 1918.

Overlooking the cemetery is *The Spirit of the American Youth Rising from the Waves*—a 22-foot- (6.7-meter-) tall bronze statue—behind which is the Garden of the Missing, where those soldiers whose bodies were never found or identified are commemorated—over 1,557 names line the walls of the garden.

For more information, visit: *www.abmc.gov*

Right: Lieutenant Colonel James Earl Rudder led the Rangers up the cliffs of Pointe du Hoc on June 6.

Image source: US Federal Government, Public Domain

POINTE DU HOC RANGER MONUMENT

One of the most daring missions in the assault on Fortress Europe saw US Rangers pushed to the edge of human endurance.

At 7:08 a.m. on June 6, 1944, 190 men of the 2nd Rangers Battalion, led by Lt. Col. James Earl Rudder, fired grappling hooks to the top of the 100-foot cliffs of Pointe du Hoc, and began their dangerous ascent towards the German positions above. Their objective was six 155-mm cannons, each with a range of 12 miles (19 kilometers) that could have brought down devastating fire upon both Utah (eight miles [13 kilometers] to the northwest) and Omaha (four miles [six kilometers] to the east). Ironically, these guns had been transported cross-country from the Maginot Line after the fall of France.

Today, the Ranger Monument commemorates the competence, courage, and sacrifice of the Rangers who fought that day, of which only 90 survived the vicious fighting. Much of the original fortifications and gun positions are still in place, and the surroundings are peppered with the same shell craters that Rudder and his men would have fought across. Visiting Pointe Du Hoc not only provides a strong insight into the importance of the position but also an appreciation of the enormous and perilous task the Rangers faced.

For more information, visit: *www.abmc.gov*

The "lunar landscape" of Pointe Du Hoc is still visible today, giving visitors a real sense of the devastation caused during the battle.

Image source © LimoWreck licenceCC BY-SA 3.0 /GFD

One of the gun emplacements at the Pointe. The guns themselves had already been moved inland before the arrival of the Rangers.

Image source: Public Domain

The sculpture of Lord Lovat, commander of No. 4 Commando at Sword Beach on June 6.

OUISTREHAM & COMMANDO KIEFFER

The easternmost Overlord sector is to be the home of a new memorial museum dedicated to the British troops.

From 7:25 a.m. on June 6, 1944, the first elements of the 3rd Infantry Division began landing at Sword Beach, along with the 47th Armored Brigade and the 1st Special Service Brigade led by Brigadier the Lord Lovat. It was the first step of what would be a long and bloody struggle to liberate Caen.

Although Sword is known as a British landing site, the first to reach the beach were in fact Frenchmen. Landing at the head of Lovat's commandos were 177 Free French soldiers, the 1st Battalion Fusiliers Marins Commando, led by Lieutenant Commander Philippe Kieffer. Arriving in the UK after the fall of France, Kieffer became impressed by the newly created British commando units, and was granted permission to form his own unit comprising all Free French soldiers. Commando Kieffer, as the unit subsequently became known, successfully assaulted German-fortified positions on the beachhead, before moving to Pegasus Bridge in the afternoon–the unit suffered 41 casualties during the day.

Today, over a million passengers pass through Ouistreham's ferry terminal each year, making it one of the most popular routes for visitors to Normandy. In 2014, the port town welcomed Queen Elizabeth II and other dignitaries, to commemorate the 70th anniversary of D-Day. It was at this time that plans began for a new memorial museum, honoring the British troops who fought on Sword Beach, while also exploring the centuries of Anglo-Franco relations. The 15-million-Euro project took six years to complete, and opened on June 6, 2021.

For more information visit: **ouistreham-rivabella.fr** and **www.brittany-ferries.co.uk**

Below: The Free French Monument, known as La Flamme, is dedicated to the men of Commando Kieffer who took part in the landings at Sword.

CLOSING THE POCKET

In August 1944, men of the 1st Polish Armored Division mounted a valiant defense at Mont Ormel.

By August 13, 1944, roughly 150,000 troops of the 7th German Army were encircled in what was later known as the Falaise Pocket, in southern Normandy. With the American 90th Division moving up from the south, and British and Canadian forces arriving from the north and northwest, the 1st Polish Armored Division (part of the 1st Canadian Army) was tasked with closing the German lines of retreat to the east in the area between Falaise in the northwest and Chambois to the southeast.

During the retreat, thousands of German troops, armor, artillery, and horses became caught in the narrowing route leading northeast towards Vimoutiers, which became known as the Corridor of Death. By the end of the fighting, some 200 tanks and 1,000 artillery pieces were destroyed by Allied fire.

Also standing in the way of this retreat was the high ground of Mont Ormel ridge, comprising Hill 262 North and South. Between August 18–22, German forces fell upon the Polish positions, forcing them back to the very summit of Mont Ormel, where, low on ammunition, they eventually were forced to engage in vicious hand-to-hand fighting, defending themselves day and night.

Over 50,000 Germans managed to escape during the Battle of the Falaise Pocket, many of them slipping past the besieged Poles on Mont Ormel. These men would go on to hamper the Allied advance east, however some 10,000 of their comrades lay dead in the field and many more had surrendered. The Poles dubbed the Battle of Hill 262 as Maczuga or "The Mace," and it is considered to be the last pitched battle of the Normandy campaign.

The site is now home to the Montormel Memorial Museum, which provides the same commanding view of the valley and the plains below that the Polish defenders would have seen. The surrounding countryside visitors look down on today is in fact the site of several large unmarked graves, the final resting place of German soldiers who lost their lives.

For more information visit: *www.normandy-tourism.org*

"SOME 200 TANKS AND 1,000 ARTILLERY PIECES WERE DESTROYED BY ALLIED FIRE."

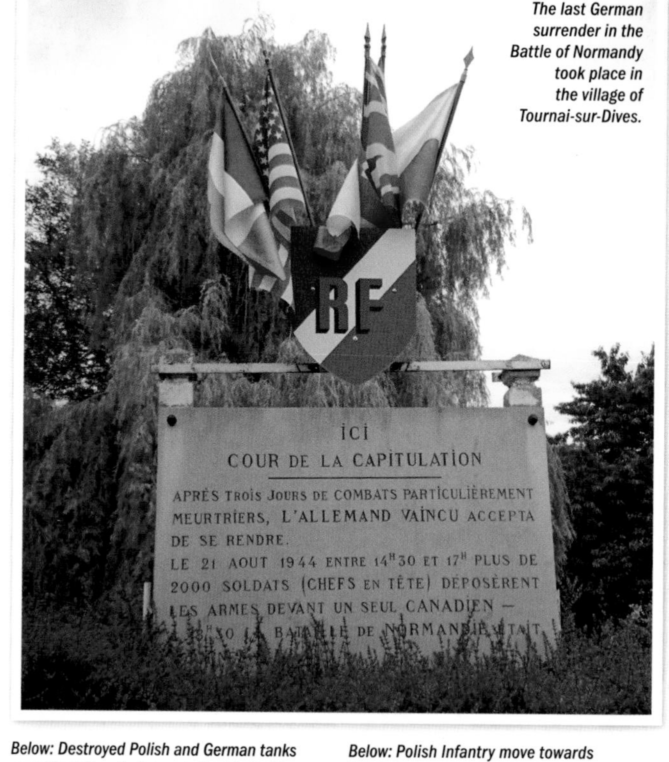

The last German surrender in the Battle of Normandy took place in the village of Tournai-sur-Dives.

Below: Destroyed Polish and German tanks near Mont Ormel, pictured after the battle.

Image source: Public Domain

Below: Polish Infantry move towards Hill 262, August 20, 1944.

Image source: Public Domain

The memorial at Montormel is dedicated primarily to the 1st Polish Armored Division, but also all the Allied liberators.

Americans read the news in Times Square, NY and vicinity on D-Day.

WORLD WAR II ALLIED STATISTICS

Two million Allied soldiers, medics, pilots, and sailors from **12** countries contributed to the planning and executing operations of Operation Overlord.

On June 6, 1944, D-Day, **160,000** Allied troops landed at Normandy on Utah and Omaha beaches:
73,000 were American
83,000 were British or Canadian
4,000 were from other Allied countries.

4,414 Allied troops were killed on D-Day
2,501 were American
5,000 American troops were wounded

There were **11,000** Allied aircraft, **7,000** ships and boats, and thousands of other vehicles involved on D-Day. Overall, in the Battle of Normandy **73,000** Allied forces were killed, **153,000** were wounded, and **20,000** French civilians were killed.

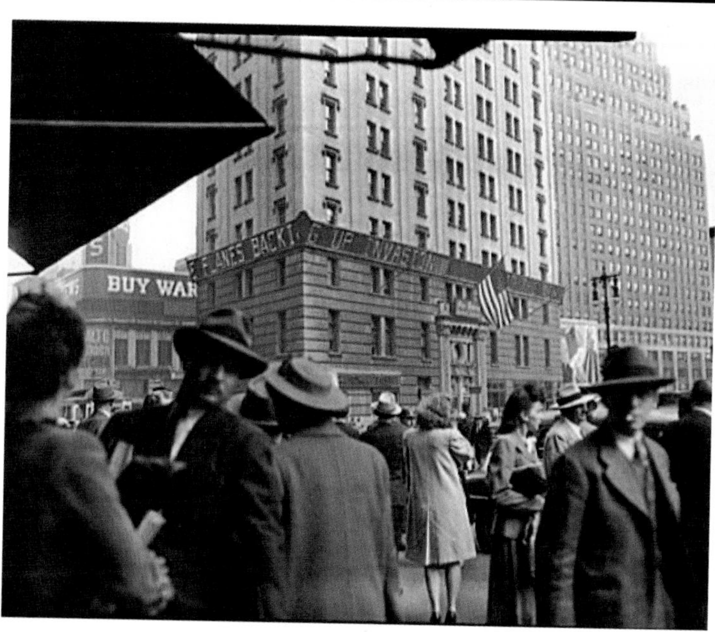

People stopped in the street to watch an electrical news sign on the Times Building in Times Square, New York, New York on June 6, 1944.

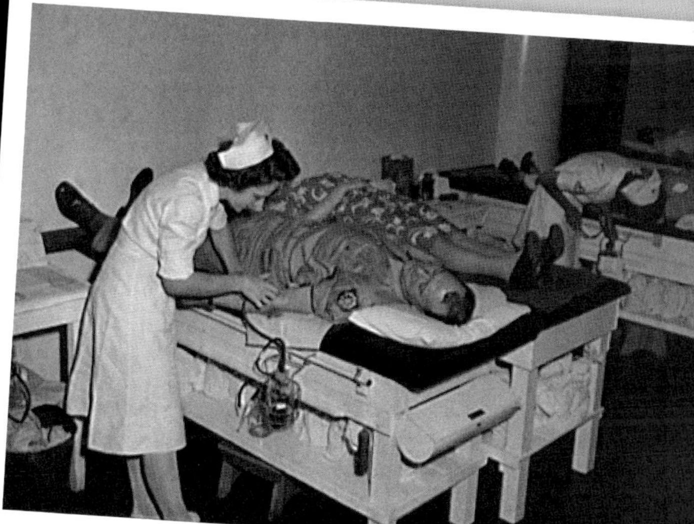

Americans give blood to honor the soldiers on the front on D-Day in New York City.

People in New York stop to hear the latest news about the D-Day invasion.

Sailors wait for news about the invasion of Normandy on June 6, 1944.

A woman finds a quiet corner to say her prayers during noon mass at St. Vincent de Paul's Church on D-Day.

The people of New York pray for their soldiers on D-Day.

Two women and a man leave the D-Day Services at the synagogue on West 23rd Street, NY.

A pencil drawing of "Epps" by Victor Alfred Lundy during a quiet moment on D-Day.

A pencil drawing of "Shep" by Victor Alfred Lundy while he was passing the time on D-Day.

Waiting for D-Day: A drawing by Tracy Sugarman (1912-2013) from March 1944. It shows a group of soldiers sitting at rest on a tank landing ship (LST) during what they would later learn were preparations for D-Day.

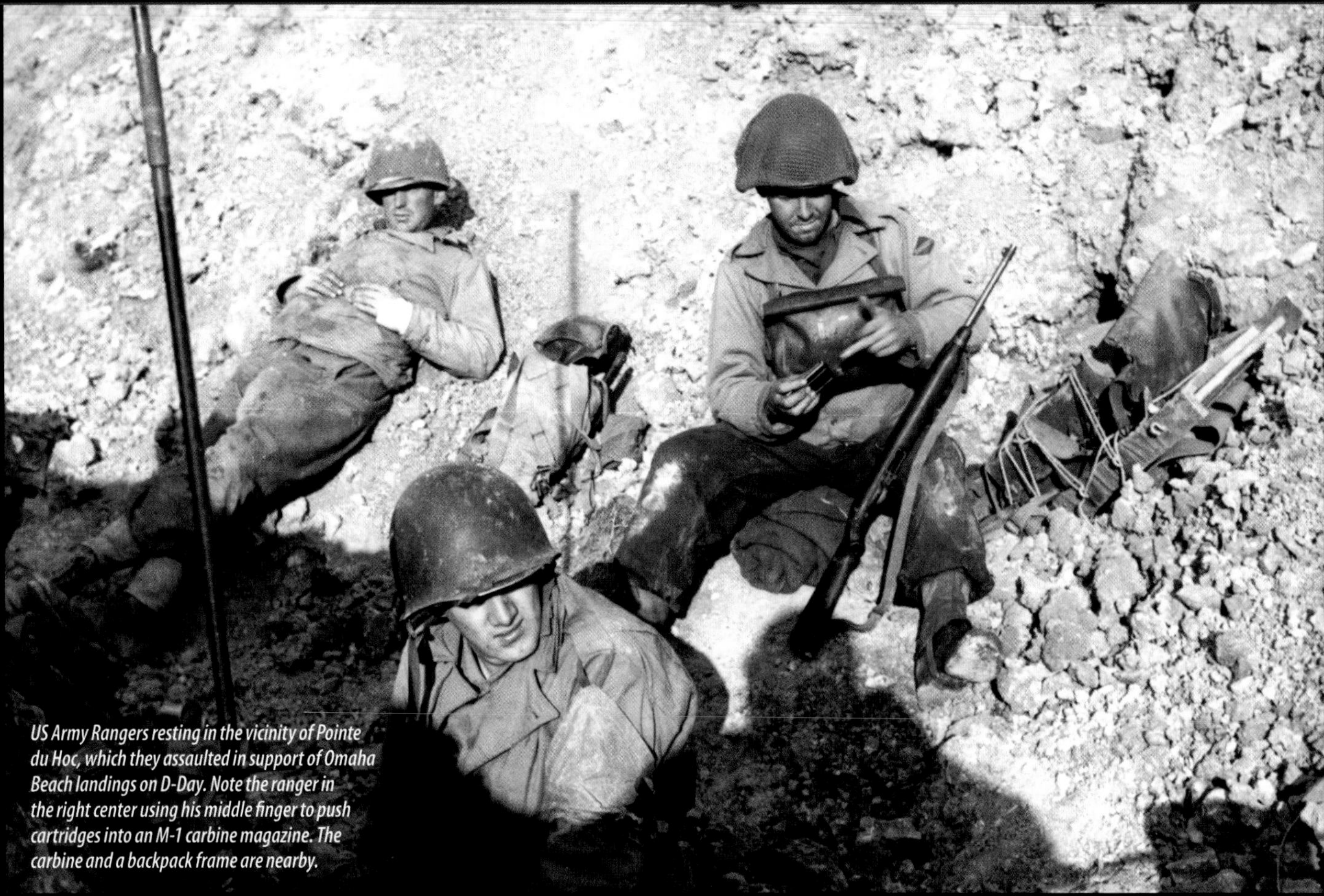

US Army Rangers resting in the vicinity of Pointe du Hoc, which they assaulted in support of Omaha Beach landings on D-Day. Note the ranger in the right center using his middle finger to push cartridges into an M-1 carbine magazine. The carbine and a backpack frame are nearby.

Scene on Omaha Beach on the afternoon of D-Day showing casualties on the beach, a bogged-down Sherman tank, several wrecked trucks, and German anti-landing obstructions. An LST is beached in the left distance and invasion shipping is offshore.

D-Day beach traffic, photographed from a Ninth Air Force bomber on June 6, 1944. Note vehicle lanes leading away from landing areas, and landing craft left aground by the tide.

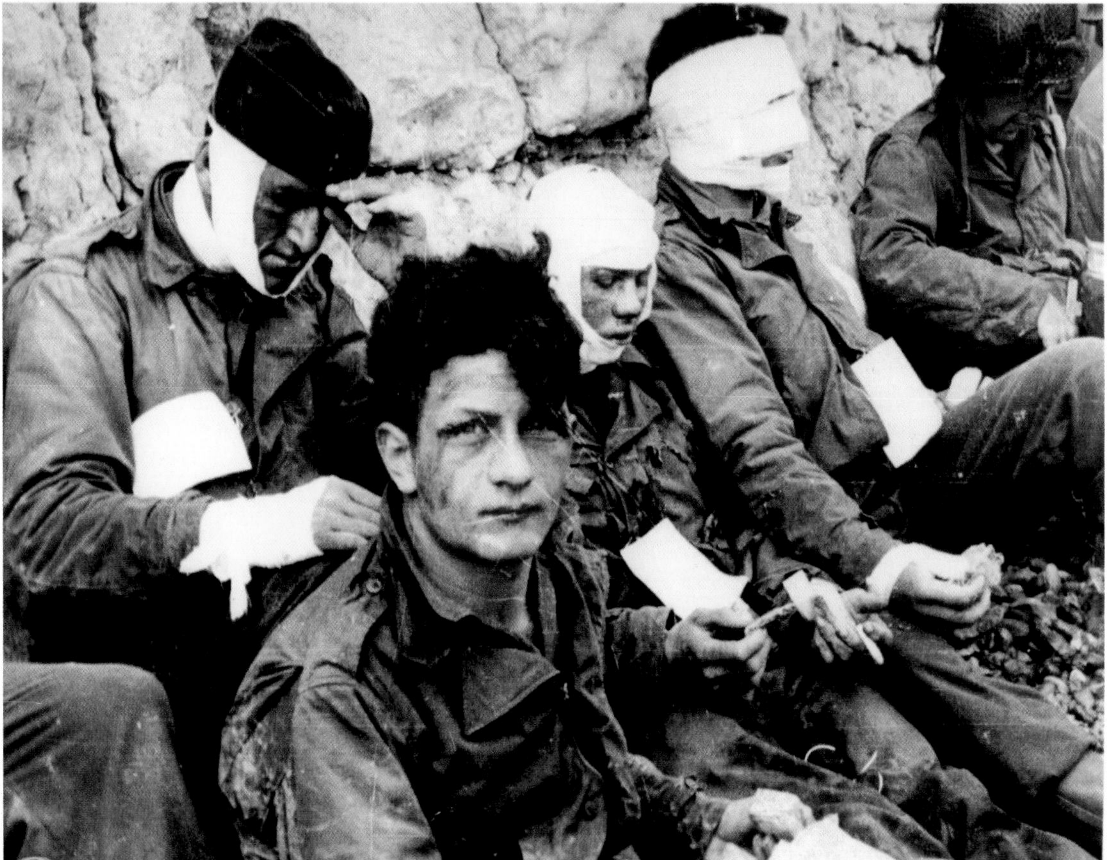

LEFT

Wounded men of the 3rd Battalion, 16th Infantry Regiment, 1st Infantry Division receive cigarettes and food after they stormed Omaha Beach on D-Day.

LEFT

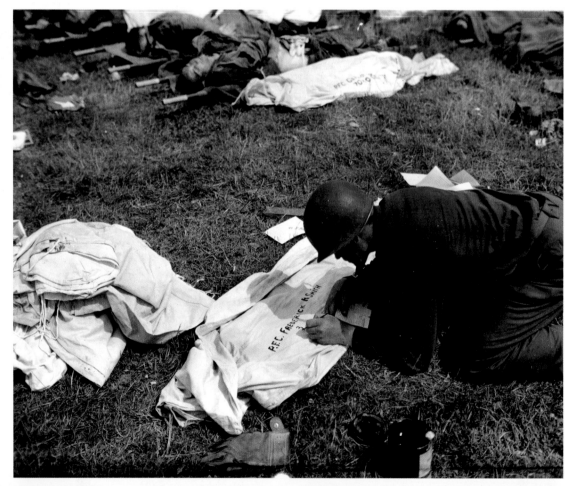

A U.S. soldier inscribes a name on a burial bag for an American who died on D-Day at a temporary cemetery near an Allied beachhead in France. Note the sad presence of fallen soldiers on stretchers lined up behind the soldier.

RIGHT

US Army Rangers show off the ladders they made and used to storm the cliffs at Pointe du Hoc, which they assaulted in support of Omaha Beach landings on D-Day.

Vintage photo of Second Lieutenant Arch Lewis from Indiana circa 1939, 337th Parachute Field Artillery Battalion, 101st Airborne Division.

WWII photo of Arch J. Lewis, 337th Parachute Field Artillery Battalion, 101st Airborne Division at the 50th anniversary of D-Day with his wife, Alice, at Normandy Beach.

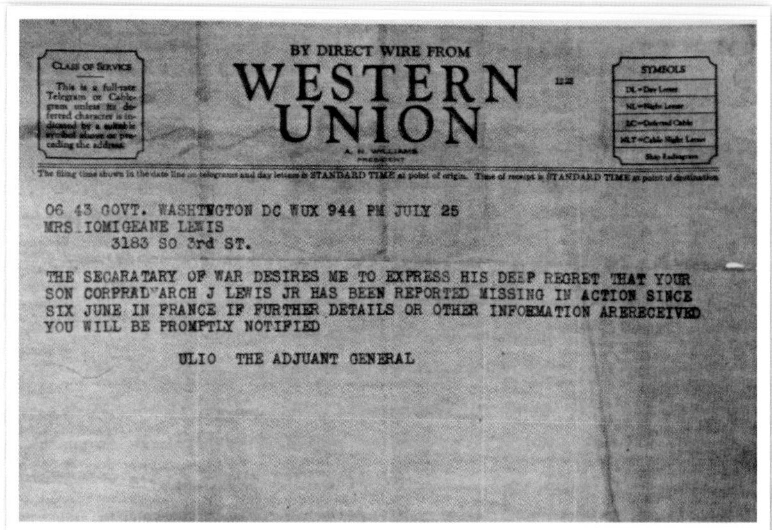

BY DIRECT WIRE FROM
WESTERN UNION
A. N. WILLIAMS PRESIDENT

06 43 GOVT. WASHTNGTON DC WUX 944 PM JULY 25
MRS. IOMIGEANE LEWIS
3183 SO 3rd ST.

THE SECARATARY OF WAR DESIRES ME TO EXPRESS HIS DEEP REGRET THAT YOUR SON CORPRAD ARCH J LEWIS JR HAS BEEN REPORTED MISSING IN ACTION SINCE SIX JUNE IN FRANCE IF FURTHER DETAILS OR OTHER INFOEMATION ARERECEIVED YOU WILL BE PROMPTLY NOTIFIED

ULIO THE ADJUANT GENERAL

This is a photo of the first Western Union telegram that Arch Lewis' mother received from the military stating that her son was missing in action.

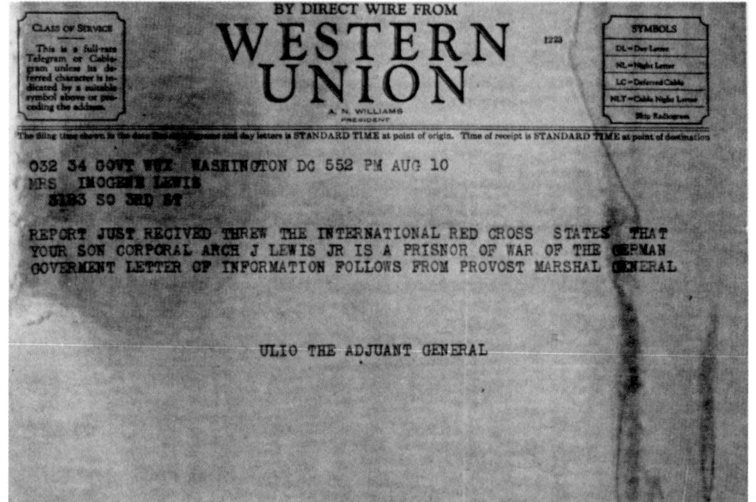

BY DIRECT WIRE FROM
WESTERN UNION
A. N. WILLIAMS PRESIDENT

032 34 GOVT WUX WASHINGTON DC 552 PM AUG 10
MRS IMOGENE LEWIS
3183 SO 3RD ST

REPORT JUST RECIVED THREW THE INTERNATIONAL RED CROSS STATES THAT YOUR SON CORPORAL ARCH J LEWIS JR IS A PRISNOR OF WAR OF THE GERMAN GOVERMENT LETTER OF INFORMATION FOLLOWS FROM PROVOST MARSHAL GENERAL

ULIO THE ADJUANT GENERAL

About two weeks later, Arch Lewis' mother received a second Western Union telegram informing her that he was alive, but a prisoner of war.

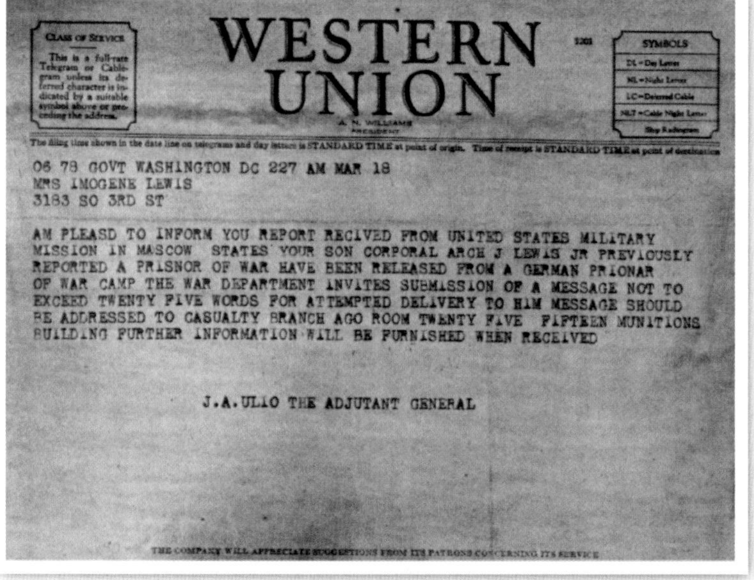

WESTERN UNION
A. N. WILLIAMS PRESIDENT

06 78 GOVT WASHINGTON DC 227 AM MAR 18
MRS IMOGENE LEWIS
3183 SO 3RD ST

AM PLEASD TO INFORM YOU REPORT RECIVED FROM UNITED STATES MILITARY MISSION IN MASCOW STATES YOUR SON CORPORAL ARCH J LEWIS JR PREVIOUSLY REPORTED A PRISNOR OF WAR HAVE BEEN RELEASED FROM A GERMAN PRIONAR OF WAR CAMP THE WAR DEPARTMENT INVITES SUBMISSION OF A MESSAGE NOT TO EXCEED TWENTY FIVE WORDS FOR ATTEMPTED DELIVERY TO HIM MESSAGE SHOULD BE ADDRESSED TO CASUALTY BRANCH AGO ROOM TWENTY FIVE FIFTEEN MUNITIONS BUILDING FURTHER INFORMATION WILL BE FURNISHED WHEN RECEIVED

J.A.ULIO THE ADJUTANT GENERAL

THE COMPANY WILL APPRECIATE SUGGESTIONS FROM ITS PATRONS CONCERNING ITS SERVICE

It wasn't until seven months later that Arch Lewis' mother received the third and final telegram from Western Union. Her son was released as a prisoner of war. Mrs. Lewis was lucky—not all mothers would receive such good news.

Plumes of black smoke emerge from the cannon fire aboard a ship on D-Day.

LCM landing craft, evacuating casualties from the invasion beaches, brings them to a transport for treatment on D-Day, June 6, 1944.

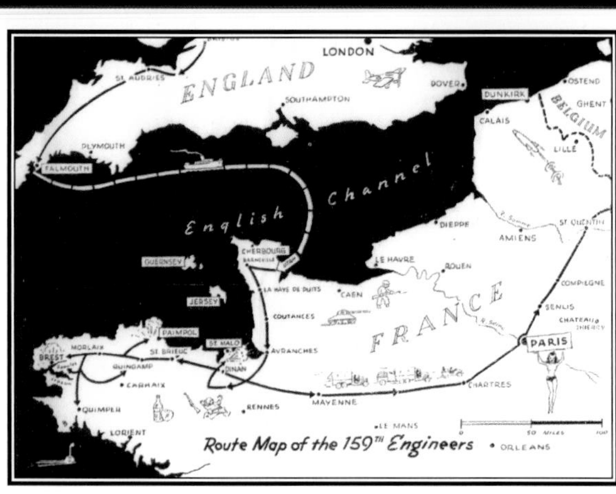

The Route Map of the 159th Engineers on D-Day.

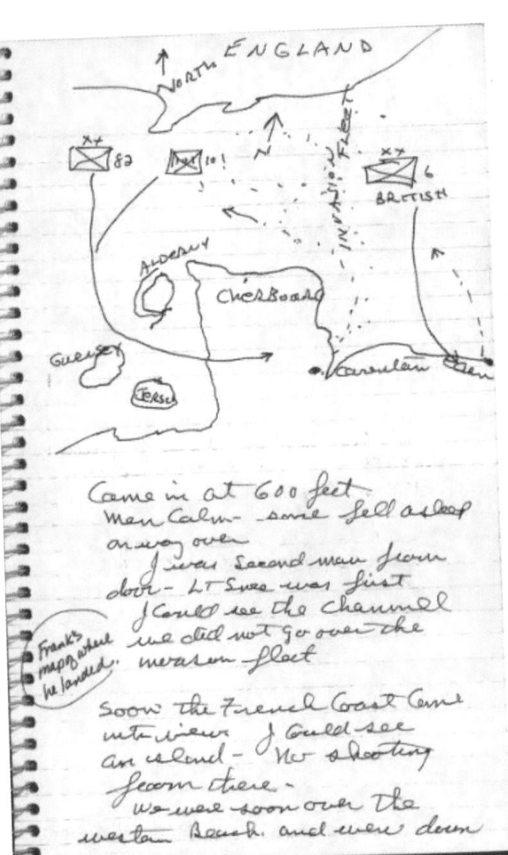

A hand-drawn map of the D-Day drop zone by Sergeant Frank E. McKee from New York, 2nd Battalion, 508th Paratroop Infantry Regiment, 82nd Airborne Division.

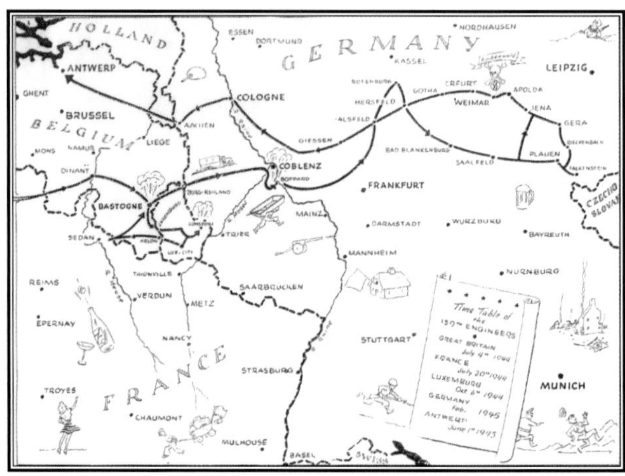

The timetable of the 159th Engineers on D-Day.

In preparation for the invasion, artillery equipment is loaded aboard LCTs at an English port in Brixham, England.

The D-Day assault was rigorous and required soldiers to be prepared for an attack that started at sea and ended on land. This drawing by combat historian Lt. Jack Shea, who was attached to the 29th Infantry Division illustrates that soldiers were well-equipped for an amphibious attack.

A painting of recollections of D-Day on Utah Beach, Normandy, France by Joseph Gary Sheahan, 1944.

AFRICAN AMERICANS IN WWII

Seaman First Class Henderson Biven working on an aircraft, April 26, 1944.

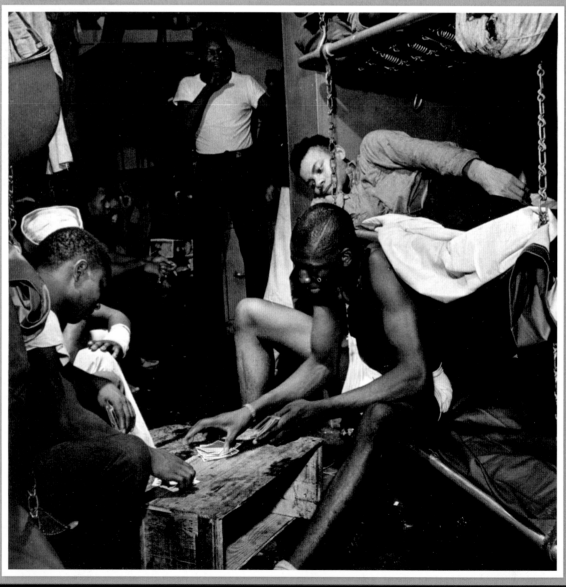

Passing the time with a card game in their berthing space on board an aircraft carrier.

Although they weren't on the beaches on D-Day, 1,700 African Americans participated in the form of air support, including a section of the 327th Quartermaster Service Company and the 320th Anti-Aircraft Barrage Balloon Battalion, which protected troops on the beach from aerial attack. After D-Day, the all-Black 761st Tank Battalion, the Black Panthers, fought its way through France with Patton's Third Army. They spent 183 days in combat and were credited with capturing 30 major towns in France, Belgium, and Germany. The most famous member of the 761st Battalion was First Lieutenant Jack Roosevelt "Jackie" Robinson. To think that if Jackie hadn't survived their 183-day siege, baseball might not be the game it is today.

From 1941-1946, around 1,000 Black pilots were trained at Tuskegee Institute (now Tuskegee University) in Alabama. The airmen's major success was in escorting Allied bombers during World War II. They have one of the lowest loss records of all the escort fighter groups and were in constant demand for the service.

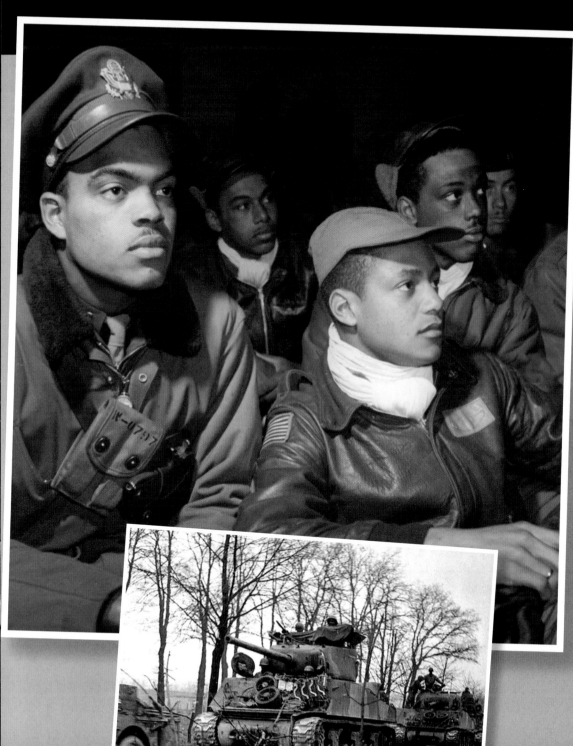

Members of the elite Tuskegee Airmen listen and take notes during a briefing before the D-Day attack. The Tuskegee Airmen gained notoriety through the movies The Tuskegee Airman starring Laurence Fishburn, and Red Tails starring Terrance Howard and Cuba Gooding, Jr.

The official Black Panther logo of the 761st Tank Battalion.

The 761st Tank Battalion rolls through the streets on their way to battle, winter 1944.

THE WOMAN'S ROLE IN WWII

During World War II, American women held more than six million wartime jobs in manufacturing factories and in agricultural positions. On the home front, three million volunteered for the Red Cross, and over 200,000 served in the military as part of the Women's Army Corps (WAC), Women Accepted for Volunteer Emergency Service (WAVES), and Women Airforce Service Pilots (WASP).

However, in 1944, women were not eligible for combat roles, so no women landed on the beaches on D-Day ready to fight. However, the U.S. Women's Army Corps followed close behind the soldiers after D-Day. Their main jobs included baking, clerical, driving, and medical services. Many became nurses to help the men who were injured in combat.

In the Allied countries, according to National Public Radio journalist Eleanor Beardsley, women also participated in WW2 as spies and resistance fighters. Author Sarah Rose also discusses the important role of five women in her book, ***D-Day Girls: The Spies Who Armed the Resistance, Sabotaged the Nazis, and Helped Win World War II***, which describes the efforts and sacrifices of Odette Sansom, Andrée Borrell, Lise de Baissac, Yvonne Rudellat, and Mary Herbert, five ordinary women who answered Churchill's call to arms to defeat Hitler's Germany by parachuting into occupied France, sabotaging bridges, derailing trains, shutting down utilities, delivering weapons, collecting intelligence, distributing propaganda, and supporting the French Resistance.

Dorothy Cutts, nee Walters, was a member of the Women's Army Auxiliary Corps, Administrative Specialist School in Fort Des Moines, IA, the Medical Corps at Fort Oglethorpe, GA and the Cadet Nurse Corp. Here she models her uniform.

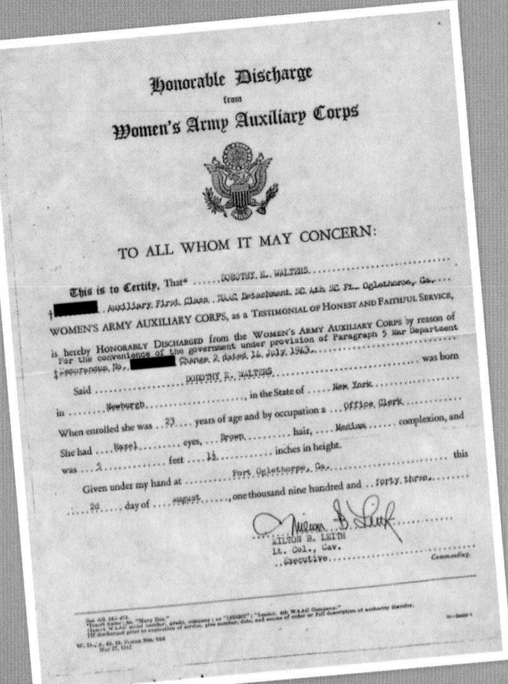

Honorable Discharge
from
Women's Army Auxiliary Corps

TO ALL WHOM IT MAY CONCERN:

This is to Certify, That* DOROTHY E. WALTERS
† [redacted] Auxiliary First Class WAAC Detachment SC 4th SC Ft. Oglethorpe, Ga.
WOMEN'S ARMY AUXILIARY CORPS, as a TESTIMONIAL OF HONEST AND FAITHFUL SERVICE, is hereby HONORABLY DISCHARGED from the WOMEN'S ARMY AUXILIARY CORPS by reason of ‡ For the convenience of the government under provision of Paragraph 5 War Department Memorandum No. [redacted] Change 2 dated 14 July 1943.

Said DOROTHY E. WALTERS was born in Newburgh, in the State of New York.
When enrolled she was 23 years of age and by occupation a Office Clerk.
She had Hazel eyes, Brown hair, Medium complexion, and was 5 feet 11 inches in height.

Given under my hand at Fort Oglethorpe, Ga. this 20 day of August, one thousand nine hundred and forty three.

MILTON B. LEITH
Lt. Col., Cav.
Executive
Commanding

The honorable discharge paper of Dorothy Cutts, nee Walters.

RIGHT

Two women perform clip and bolt assembly on the Frankford Arsenal in Philadelphia during World War II.

An American woman helps on the Baltimore and Ohio Railroad during World War II.

the only woman who witnessed D-Day firsthand.

Landing ships load cargo ashore on one of the invasion beaches, at low tide, June 1944. Among the identifiable ships are USS LST-532 (center); USS LST-262 (3rd LST from right); USS LST-310 (2nd LST from right); USS LST-533 (partially visible at far right); and USS LST-524. Note the barrage balloons overhead and the Army half-track convoy forming on the beach